OUT OF THE
BOTTOMLESS
PIT

website : www.outofthebottomlesspit
.co.uk

YOUTUBE CHANNEL: INSIGHTS'
@stephenstrutt

E-mail : stephenstrutt@btinternet.com

S.N. Strutt

Published by SN Strutt

Publishing partner: Paragon Publishing, Rothersthorpe

First published 2022

© SN Strutt 2022

ISBN 978-1-78222-975-9

Book design, layout and production management by Into Print

www.intoprint.net

01604 832149

Credits & Acknowledgements

To my daughter Suzanna, who inspired me with her amazing artwork, for the front cover of this book, and my dear wife who assisted in the making of this book. Also to the many friends and readers, who have asked for a sequel to my first book **'OUT OF THE BOTTOMLESS PIT' BOOK I**

Artwork work for the front cover Suzanne Strutt

www.suzannestruttartist/instagram.com
www.suzannestruttartist/facebook.com

CONTENTS

CREDITS & ACKNOWLEDGEMENTS.. 3

PREFACE 7

INTRODUCTION.. 8

CHAPTERS

1 'SUMMARY' OF 'OUT OF THE BOTTOMLESS PIT I' 9

2: THE FRONT COVER SETTING: .. .. .23

3: PRE-HISTORIC BUILDINGS FOUND IN SCOTLAND 28

4: CYCLOPEAN STRUCTURES' .. .. .32

5: THE ANCIENT WORLD .. .. .38

6: TIAHUANACO .. .. .40

7: TOWER OF BABEL. .. .. .43

8: GARDEN OF EDEN .. .. .46

9: GIANTS. .. .. .50

10: VITRIFIED ROCKS.. .. .. .53

11: ANCIENT ATOMIC WAR? .. .. .55

12: IS SCIENCE WRONG?.. .. .. .57

13: THE PYRAMIDS .. .. .58

14: LEY-LINES.. .. .. .60

15: 'ANTI-GRAVITY' .. .. .62

16: 'BERMUDA' TRIANGLES.. .. .. .64

17: THE PHILADELPHIA EXPERIMENT .. .. .65

18: TIME CONTROL .. .. .67

19: SONIC LEVITATION. .. .. .68

20: 10 TOES OF DANIEL 2 TURNING FROM CLAY TO IRON .. .. .70

21: THE 4 HORSEMEN .. .. .79

22: THE HOLLOW EARTH.. .. .. .82

23: THE SPHINX .. .. .83

24: THE GREAT WHORE .. .. .86

25: CERN & PORTALS 102

26: MARK OF THE BEAST. 105

27: THE BRIDE OF CHRIST. 107

28: ANTARCTIC SECRETS 111

29: SUPERNATURAL ENCOUNTERS 112

30: THE 3RD TEMPLE. 114

31: THE GODS OF EGYPT. 128

32: DWARFS 130

33: ALIEN ABDUCTIONS.. 134

34: THE 'CANOPY' 135

35: DRAGON & PHOENIX 146

36: THE ANTI-CHRIST 152

37: 'CHANGES' 1999-2022.. 158

38: VAMPIRES 165

39: UNDERGROUND BASES 168

40: ALIEN TECHNOLOGY 181

41: HEAVEN IS REAL 182

42: SERAPHIM 188

43: HALLOWEEN. 195

44: HELL, GEHENNA, & SHEOL 198

45: THE HAUNTED CASTLE. 202

46: CHIMERAS. 205

47: ALIEN DISCLOSURE. 209

48: MULTI-DIMENSIONS 212

49: UFO'S 218

50: 'WHEN HEAVEN CALLS'. 221

51: FAIRIES.. 233

52: PLAGUE?.. 235

53: GMO'S 244

54: OXYGEN DEPLETION. 263

55: PRE-FLOOD CONDITIONS. 268

56: A HEAVENLY GIFT 273

57: BRAIN DECAY. *278*

58: THE MESSIAH *280*

59: 'LIFE AFTER DEATH'. *293*

60: 'LIGHT' AT BIRTH. *299*

APPENDIX: 110+ EXTRAS. **303**

PREFACE

OUT OF THE BOTTOMLESS PIT II is a sequel to my 1ˢᵗ book **OUT OF THE BOTTOMLESS PIT I** about the paranormal and the supernatural. This book has many personal testimonies of strange experiences both good and bad and some terrible, some beautiful. Do angels exist? What about demons and other strange creatures? The aim of this book is to inform the readers that we are not alone, and that God exists, and that other dimensions must exist all around us, which even modern science is now recognizing. Why do some people see beautiful & odd things and yet others hardly notice anything? Millions have experienced 'Life after Death'. What is really going on above and beneath our feet? What goes on in other dimensions? Why is this world in such 'organized chaos'? Where is all the confusion of the past years leading to? There is a lot of scientific evidence presented in this book that evil is very present in this world, but that also wonderful things exist and that the 'miraculous' does happen. Are we headed for a transhuman world in the near future? What are the ramifications for us all? Is technology taking over and going to be a danger like the Terminators or I-Robot? Each chapter stands on its own and yet many of the chapters do connect. -S N Strutt – Author

INTRODUCTION

SOME OF THE chapters in this book are quite shocking as in regard to advanced technology and what is really happening on this planet. I have deliberately also put some very beautiful experiences in this book for balance. Life is after all both good and evil. For some, you can choose which chapters you particularly like, and others I know will enjoy reading all the chapters. The intent of this book is to inform. I hope that you find it exciting, interesting, very informative but also liberating.

CHAPTER 1

'OUT OF THE BOTTOMLESS PIT I'
(From my first book, which was published in 2014')

AUTHOR: SINCE MY new book **'Out of the Bottomless Pit II'** is a sequel to my first book **Out of the Bottomless Pit I**, I am giving a summary of the topics and conclusions of my Ist book here:

'We have discussed many topics including the following important amazing subjects:

1) Bermuda Triangles and their dangerous powers.
2) The Hollow Earth Theory
3) Admiral Byrd and Olaf Jensen's visits to the centre of the earth
4) Adolf Hitler, Occult NAZIS, the "Hollow Earth" and the "Alien Connection".
5) The Philadelphia Experiment, with Tesla and Einstein's involvement.
6) The Montauk Experiments in Time and Brain-Washing. Creating material objects using the minds of psychics together with advanced alien technology.
7) The Occult societies.
8) Subterranean tunnels & underground races.
9) The Illuminati & Serpent cults and races
10) Fallen angels, Giants/Nephilim
11) UFOs based in the centre of the earth
12) Abductions of humans for experimentation.
13) Reptilian races and "Blond" races
14) Bottomless Pits and tunnels honey-combing the entire planet.
15) A soon-coming Disclosure Event and a possible big UFO Invasion.
16) The Rise of the Anti-Christ to power and his One World Government. The Last 7 Year Peace Pact.
17) The Final Nuclear War
18) 14 Points of the End-time occurring before the 2nd Coming of Christ.
19) 4 Blood Moons & 2 Solar Eclipses during 2014-2015 occurring on sacred Jewish holidays.
20) The Mark of the Beast
21) Life after Death
22) Current Events in Ukraine and build-up to a regional War.

Conclusions To Some of The Topics of This Book

In studying and researching all of the topics of this book, I have found it quite staggering reading the little-known-to-most-people books of Enoch and

2 Ezdras, both of which seem to allude to a hollow earth, as do parts of the Bible and many other books. It is truly mind-boggling to discover!

In the description given by Enoch in chapters 17-34 he is shown many strange lands, and among many specific details he is also shown the garden of Eden, the tree of life & the tree of the knowledge of good & evil.

It is very interesting to note that before Enoch is shown these strange lands, that in chapter 20 it specifically mentions the names of the angels who take him on a tour. The one in charge of Tartarus is called Uriel.

In the next chapters it is Uriel who shows Enoch all of these strange lands and together with the angel Raphael who is listed as "being in charge of the souls of men" flies over the garden of Eden in chapter 32.

As pointed out in one of the earlier chapters, it would seem that my Jewish friend*(chapter 3) is correct about the earth being hollow according their ancient sages & that the garden of Eden was there at one time.

It would also appear that the same is true as far as the book of Enoch is concerned. In Enoch's vision from chapters 17-32 he does not mention seeing any normal people, except the following type of people: (Enoch 17.1 "and they took and brought me to a place in which those who were there were like flaming fire, and when they wished, they appeared as men").

Were these creatures perhaps fallen angels? Enoch does however mention many types of exotic colourful birds and plants and tall trees, flowers and very strong aromas, some of which he says he is unfamiliar with as well as volcanic mountains and deep abysses and fallen angels imprisoned in such fiery places. (Tartarus) He also mentions seeing different varieties of very large creatures such as mammoths & different types of dinosaurs/dragons.

Enoch very accurately describes the topography of inner earth in a very similar way to other earthly famous explorers who have managed to somehow travel inside the earth in fairly modern times, such as Olaf Jansen in 1829, and admiral Richard Byrd in 1927 & 1947. Olaf mentioned a town called Eden inside the earth and the 4 rivers mentioned in the bible as flowing out of Eden. The same topography is mentioned in great detail in "Flying saucers from the centre of the earth" by Dr Raymond Bernard.

All of these writers mentioned large creatures such as mammoths. All of the above writers talk about volcanoes, lots of mountain ranges & an inner world where it is mostly land, estimated at 80% by those who know about the hollow earth in detail.

I want to re-iterate here for the record, that many explorers to the North Pole have seen many different coloured snows, which when scientifically analysed were found to contain pollen of flowers not found on the outer surface of the planet. (Red, green, yellow, blue, orange & black) The black snow was found by scientific analysis to contain iron and ash from volcanoes when there are no volcanoes in the Arctic, so the black ash originated from the inner earth and came out of the northern opening (so-called North Pole).

Enoch describes the lands that he is shown as volcanic with vapour clouds and a northern entrance. He also mentions 12 portals through which the stars pass. It is very interesting to note that there are 12 constellations which pass above the earth every year.

There are also 12 Bermuda Triangles which I believe Enoch could actually be referring to in the book of Enoch. Here is a list of distinct probabilities:

1) The earth, the moon, the sun & comets were all created hollow. A simple illustration concerning these astral bodies would be the old-fashioned child's spinning top toy. One had a spiral plunger of metal going through the centre of the top. One plunged downwards and the top would spin beautifully for a long time. Observation: the top was hollow. If we take the child's spinning top and fill it with concrete, we find that it will no longer spin! Hollow spheres have the property of being able to spin indefinitely in a vacuum like outer space. Solid spheres would slow down because of inner friction of opposing inner fluids supposedly liquids and solids and because of the great mass inside. Calculations have been made that the whole mass of the earth could be accounted for by even in that case of a hollow earth. It has also been calculated that if the earth was solid that the gravity would be so great as to crush all living beings on the surface of the planet! These are just a few examples of what honest scientists have discovered about the properties of our planet and in fact other planets, moons and suns as well.

2) Inner Earth was probably the original location of the Garden of Eden
Some questions that need answering: If we can conclude that 1 & 2 are indeed correct then:

3) When was man forced to leave the inner earth? There are some who say that mankind left the inner earth when Adam and Eve were kicked out of the garden of Eden. Others hypothesise that it happened after the Great Flood?

4) When we consider Enoch was shown the Garden of Eden by the angels: he was also shown the tree of life and the tree of the knowledge of good & evil (Book of Enoch chapter 25 & 32). It is very apparent that although he mentions the garden of Eden, plants, trees and animals he does not mention people! Does this perhaps mean that no humans and giants were living inside the earth at the time of Enoch around 500-800 years after creation?

5) When we consider that of all the people on earth at the time, (500 years after creation or around 5500 years ago), Enoch had a thorough knowledge of both the fallen angels and the giants. He had direct conversations with the fallen angels. So, it seems quite odd that he does not mention people or giants in the aerial view he had of the strange lands that he passed over in the vision that God gave him.

6) Enoch does talk about Tartarus and hell and mentions the judgement of wicked souls. The book of Enoch also mentions paradise known in the time of Jesus as "the bosom of Abraham" which Jesus also alluded to as being inside the earth; although up until recently, I had thought he was only talking of a spiritual place & not an actual hollow earth. My conclusion is that the inner earth has both a physical domain and a spiritual domain.

7) In this book you have read how that Cain's line is only listed in the Bible for 6 generations and then seemingly disappears. Could Cain's descendants have descended into the inner earth sometime after creation or close to the time of the flood to start the so-called Aryan race? Did Cain's descendants get inside information from the fallen angels about God's coming judgements in the form of the Great Flood of Noah?

8) Pre-flood Atlantean rulers (demi-gods) have been said to have known about the coming great flood in their time. How did they know in advance? They allegedly also escaped to the inner earth and took their "alien technology" with them whilst Atlantis sank beneath the waves.

9) What was originally an inner paradise of God for mankind has been turned into a hell's hornet's nest as clearly predicted in revelations chapter 9 with the bottomless pit being opened some time in the not-too-distant future!

10) We have shown in this book how that inside the earth it is:

A) Hell -a prison for the souls being punished.

B) Paradise is there also as a wayfaring station for the good souls being prepared for heaven in a higher dimension.

C) The lake of fire for the very worst souls such as Satan etc

D) A spiritual location of spirits, demons, sirens etc

E) Physical location which is inhabited by millions of human inhabitants living in many underground crystal cities, with very advanced technology, giants and the serpent race in many forms as well as so-called pre-historic large creatures such as dragons, mammoths and dinosaurs.

A very interesting verse showing that the earth is actually hollow is found in:

2 Ezdras 4.41 "And he said unto me, "In Hades the chambers of the souls are like a womb! a perfect description of a hollow earth!

11) In the early chapters of the book of Enoch we find that the angels of God are commanded to provoke the giants (Nephilim), sons of the Annunaki (fallen angels), to fight against and destroy each other! As brought out so well in Greek and Roman mythology in the many wars of the demigods. In ancient times the giants ended up wiping each other out!

12) Certain eastern religions believe in the inner earth as well. Some monks apparently guard the tunnels which honeycomb our planet and lead from the outer surface to the inner surface in the Tibetan regions. It is interesting that these oriental religions believe in pacifism and vegetarianism and in the most dedicated cases being celibate. The most dedicated also believe in supernatural powers and some of their gurus can perform amazing stunts such as walking on hot coals of fire; lying on a bed of nails and even throwing a rope 20 metres straight up in the air and it just hangs there, whilst the guru's son climbs up the rope! How to explain that other than it being supernatural?

13) According to Dr Raymond Bernard's book "Flying saucers from the centre of the earth", the inhabitants of the inner earth are pacifists & vegetarian. They no longer fight wars against each other, at least the humans no longer do. The Serpent race are apparently much more dangerous and beguiling!

14) In Olaf Jansen's book "Voyage to Inner Earth" he stated that in 1829 he and his father stayed with several "12-15" foot giants for two years & that they were treated well by the giants.

15) Those in the inner earth according to Dr Raymond Bernard do not believe in Jesus & actually vehemently deny his existence! Those of middle earth worship the god Ra, or better known as god of the inner sun (black sun).

16) This god of theirs apparently puts on a show once in a while to keep all of the inner world physical humans and giants in line with certain Satanic teachings, especially of non-belief in Jesus! Enoch mentions that when he was inside the earth, he saw people who looked like beings of fire, but that when they wished to, they could appear as ordinary men!

17) What if Satan as this inner master of the underworld wisely decided a long time ago to stop the giants and humans inside the earth from fighting against each other? "The book the "Coming Race" which came out in the late 19th century, was talking about a race of giants! Satan wants to create an army of physical people and giants to eventually be trained as his army to invade the outer surface of the earth when the time is ripe!

I think it very likely that Satan inspired people to create a pacifistic religion and vegetarianism to keep his inhabitants calmer and more pacified. It also stops the giants from eating meat and becoming blood-thirsty & going back to cannibalism. He has also promised them that one day he will lead them to victory against the humans on the outer surface of the earth as suggested in the book, "The Coming Race".

18) There will come an invasion of the outer earth. Some terrible things will happen as described in this book at the beginning of the tribulation or when Satan finally fully possesses the coming antichrist. The very worst things however will only happen after the rapture and all of the true believers in Jesus have gone home to heaven.

19) The Mark of the Beast and the Image of the Beast happen during the 2nd part of the Antichrist's 7- year reign. Many writers have talked about the coming "Mark of the Beast" under the coming Antichrist regime as shown in Revelations Chapter 13. An unfortunate number for many of us; however, have you ever wondered why? Why the Mark of the Beast, and in particular, why now at the end of time?

Why not under a past empire of man? To understand this, we again need to go behind the scenes of this physical realm or matrix! Satan has ruled this physical realm for the past 6000 years, mostly from the invisible realm or from what some call the next dimension around the earth and in fact within it as well. apparently, Satan and his fallen angels, who in the past have had access to other dimensions, (Job 1.7) and perhaps both our solar system and even other galaxies, with time they have been restricted more and more; and eventually they will be totally locked up inside hell and then Tartarus. (Revelations 20.1-3)

One day soon Satan and all his angels are going to be involved in a very big war against Michael the archangel and the forces of light. Satan is going to lose and actually get kicked out of the spirit world (Revelations 12.7). Since Satan has had control over so many people on earth both through demon possession and oppression from the spirit world, how can he continue to maintain control over them once he is thrown out of the spiritual realm?

Satan knows that this will happen to him, so he inspires man to make microchips which initially have started off as something helpful, and benign such are implants in the brain to help those with impaired vision or hearing; or an electronic cyborg arm to replace an amputated one. However, Satan's aim is to eventually bring on total control of every human being's mind on the planet & to make them into willing slaves and mindless zombies, a collective consciousness or a type of Borg.

Obviously, he will have to time the "Mark of the Beast", in such a way that it happens just before he gets kicked out of the higher dimensions or he is going to lose the control over millions of people! By the same logic and reasoning, those who are truly saved & refuse the Mark will no longer be constantly bombarded and pestered by the negative influences of the negative spirit world or hell, and all static will disappear. Then their link to heaven will become much stronger and cause them to become very bold witnesses of the truth. (Daniel 12.3) Inspired writers

20) I believe that the famous writers C S Lewis and J R R Tolkien with their famous inspiring books of the Chronicles of Narnia & Lord of the Rings were talking about future spiritual and physical battles which are to come on this planet as the war of the worlds begins in earnest when the key to the bottomless pit is finally opened and all hell literally breaks loose! H G Wells also wrote about war of the worlds or an invasion of planet earth by giant robots. His invasion comes from mars. He could not have known when he wrote "War of the Worlds" that NASA has photographed many mysterious giant pyramids and a sphinx on mars as well as other strange phenomena. What were they used for? Some say that the pyramids are actually Star-gates to other worlds. Is Mars perhaps one of the bases of the fallen angels masquerading as "advanced aliens, from which they will launch an invasion of earth?" H G Wells also wrote the famous book, Time Machine. Were his writings also both inspired & predicting future happenings?

Lewis Carol with his books about Alice in Wonderland & especially in the description of going down the rabbit hole to another world far underground where things were very different in size/time and behaviour. A world where the size of things could be changed at will! The books about Alice, I think were also giving us a little insight into the inner world, either the physical or the spiritual or a bit of both. The writer of the book "the Green Door" describes the inner world of Hell and Tartarus as "dimensions where things are inside out, upside down as well as a backwards & shrinking diminishing world". Then you have the other very famous book which is more obvious in its content as the very title tells all:

"**Journey to the Centre of the Earth**" by Jules Verne. This book is both fascinating and very interesting, as it shows that there are tunnels and large underground caverns on the way down to the inner earth, whole lands and seas and so-called pre-historic large dinosaurs. Jules Verne was clearly prophetic in his writings as he also wrote about "Rocket to the Moon" in the 19th century. These are just a few examples of many books written about Middle Earth or Inner Earth and other strange subjects.

21) Many of those who study Creation Science with tell you that before the great flood that the earth was surrounded by a protective layer of water around 100 miles above the earth. This scientific theory is based on genesis 1.6-8 "Let there be a firmament in the midst of the waters, and let it divide the waters from the waters.") This layer of water supposedly protected those on earth from dangerous radiation from the sun and from space. It would cause the earth to have a greenhouse effect and as a result to have a uniform temperature.

22) This canopy of protective water could also apparently have acted as a giant lens and enabled those on earth to see the moon and the stars as if they were close up. (I have a theory about this.) The people lived much longer than today and up to 960 years as in the case of Methuselah. The vegetation grew much bigger and the people were much taller. There is a very interesting verse in the book of 2 Ezdras where the angel tells Ezra that before his time mankind used to be taller and that in the future as the world degenerated that people would get smaller. (II Ezdras 5.52) (written around 450 BCE)

23) Bang goes the theory of Evolution which is also denied by the simple Second Law of Thermodynamics, which states, "That any object left to itself, & given time will disintegrate, and tend to a greater state of disorder" and not integrate and bring complex order as evolution erroneously teaches with the very silly improvable "big bang" theory, which does not make any sense at all! There are many examples in the bible & other scriptural books where clouds were used to deliberately conceal from the view of mankind certain things that were happening. There is a long list of scriptures in the index about this matter.

24) In Ezekiel chapters 1 & 10, God's UFO and throne show up initially concealed by clouds, I suppose so that most people would not notice this amazing event. In the case of Bermuda Triangle happenings many of the accounts by witnesses of these strange occurrences state seeing odd, coloured clouds enveloping a ship that is in the process of disappearing. In the case of the man-made Philadelphia Experiment they also reported a strange green mist covering the ship.

25) The Philadelphia Experiment This experiment in 1943 was pivotal to understanding that the time continuum can be messed around with & actually altered! The ship vanished from sight for 9 hours. 1. It was transported, (dimensionally shifted), to a very similar port 100 miles further north on the same coast. 2. It re-appeared 9 hours later at the port in Philadelphia. 3. The sailors on the ship were never the same again, and many eventually died early.

4. Some of the sailors kept disappearing and re-appearing for the rest of their often-short lives. 5. When the ship did reappear after 9 hours of vanishing, some of the sailors to the horror of the on-lookers re-materialized half embedded in the metal hull of the ship. 6. Putting these facts together we can clearly see that time and space can be altered to some extent. The big question is by how much has it already been altered? 7. Back in 1896 Nicholi Tesla was one day utilizing his giant coil cage with him sitting inside of it. Millions of volts were involved in this experiment. Something went wrong and Tesla says that suddenly he saw his own entire future life as well as his entire past and present as if they were just a moment in time. (Tesla Man Out of Time- Margaret Cheney) (This was a very similar experience to those mentioned in the cases of Life after Death.) 8. According to Al Bielek and others like Nichols Prestman they tried doing this Time Continuum Experiment again in 1983. (Something to do with 20-year magnetic field cycles of the earth.)

26) The Montauk Project & Armageddon "Man does not do anything or invent anything but that it is given by inspiration from either the forces of light or forces of darkness" – unknown. When it comes to Time Travel as mentioned as possible by Nikola Tesla in 1896 and brought to fruition by both Tesla and Einstein in first the Philadelphia Experiment in 1943. Later their theories were used with the Montauk Project in the late 70's and 80's; such a possibility would seem to put us in the realm of science fiction or even science fantasy to most people. But is it perhaps possible? According to Revelations 10.6-7 the days are soon coming when Time shall be no more! This would infer that we live in a sort of Time Matrix which shall soon come to an end, at least in its limited present form. According to one of the wisest men who ever lived, Solomon 3000 years ago "There is nothing new under the sun that which has been is that which shall yet be done." (Ecclesiastes 1.9; 3.15)

When it comes to time travel and mind-control as well as mass mind-control, how could the spiritual forces of darkness operating in the shady realms behind the scenes of this world or let's say in a slightly lower dimension than the physical existence, benefit by inspiring man to dabble in time travel as in the Montauk project? What is the ultimate purpose?

27) Zombie army

Earlier on in this book I briefly mentioned about the tower of Babel and how the people building it acted not only like slaves but more like drones of a beehive! (Chapter 7) Mass Mind Control! Let's imagine for a moment that Satan, lord of darkness and ruler of this present physical domain as according to (Matthew 4) knows that very shortly his time will be up after he gets a

7-year fling of being the antichrist for the last 7 years of human history. The lord of darkness or "Satan's goal" has always been three-fold:

1) To be worshipped as God

2) Control the world

3) Eventually destroy all of God's creation So far through history Satan has been prevented time and time again from totally taking over and totally destroying god's creation. Now in these modern times he finally has the possibility in his grip, as only in the past 60 years, since the advent of the atomic age, has man the capability of totally destroying the planet. (2 Thessalonians 2.7-12)

God's protection of this planet because of its continued extreme wickedness will eventually be withdrawn. If you wanted to create a physical army which was the most vicious, violent and totally insane destructive army with absolutely no conscience how could it be done?

When Satan & the fallen angels are finally permanently kicked out of heaven (Revelations 12.7), we can assume that also means "out of the higher dimensions", so that Satan and his hoards will in fact be stuck in the physical realm, or lower dimensions.

What have many emperors and dictators done throughout history in the past in order to get rid of some "undesirables"? In order to take the blame away from themselves directly, they normally let some of the worst criminals and dangerous psychos out of prison with the promise of a legal pardon if they will do some specific "dirty work" of getting rid of certain "undesirables".

Later the authorities could have these same criminals assassinated by their own special forces using the excuse that they were only escaped convicts! Is it possible that the antichrist will use the exact same tactics, and even more so Satan who is the one behind it all?

Satan has been king of empires since the world began as clearly shown in the 7-headed red dragon in Revelations 12. In the negative spirit world Satan has hordes of very dangerous criminals locked up. Satan also trains many in his army in the spirit world. What if, and this is only an idea, Satan wanted to re-use some of the worst criminals or villains of the entire history of mankind or the past 6000 years because they were excellent generals of armies and totally ruthless?

Down in the earth in the negative spiritual plane in hell there are characters like Genghis khan and Adolf Hitler, as well as many diabolical former Greek and Roman emperors. One day after all of the truly saved have been resurrected and raptured to heaven with Jesus (at the very end of the 3 and a half years of tribulation), and thus all light has left the planet for a while until Armageddon, his would then be the perfect time for the rising of total darkness from the bottomless pits and tunnels all around the earth. There would be no restraining force! Satan has a problem however, in that most of his forces are currently in the spiritual realm.

28) The ultimate purpose of the Montauk Project? Secret and very wealthy organizations financed this project for years according to Nichols Prestman in his book "The Montauk Project" in fact he tells us that they spent hundreds of billions on this one project. Why? In the future Satan is going to be in a fix as he knows that he has but a short time before he will be defeated at the battle of Armageddon, and finally locked up in the bottomless pit.

I believe he has inspired man to do the time project and the mass mind control experiments using hapless and countless victims, who have been sacrificed and who mostly eventually died & who were mostly children (10.000 children) from off the street. Why is it that often-scientific so-called progress often involves sacrificing either people or animals such as in the case of the atom bomb tests?

It is almost as if they are sacrificing to Satan, Lord of darkness without even realizing it? He has inspired man to do these awful experiments in order to be able to create a zombie army in the 'not too distant future'.

I know that the following is possibly only a quantum leap of imagination ...but? Satan could attempt to re-unite the very wicked spirits in hell such as Genghis Khan and Adolf Hitler with their young physical bodies by going back in time using some sort of futuristic scientific witchcraft to put their spirits back into a younger body.

This could also be another reason why very soon after this happens that the 7th angel will sound, and time shall be no more. In that case there will be no more messing around with time itself! Of course, no one knows the ramifications of messing around with time and possibly causing a time paradox!

Note that according to Revelations chapter 13 the Antichrist was wounded unto death and yet he did live, and then became Satan incarnate. (a voodoo zombie?) He will be resuscitated by scientific witchcraft and trying to imitate the resurrection of Christ.

29) What if? Scientifically speaking we know of 12 major Bermuda Triangles, which it is maybe possible, are also mentioned in the book of Enoch, except he calls them 12 portals. I am certainly only theorizing here that God originally installed the 12 Bermuda Triangles as multi-dimensional doors from the outer earth to the inner earth.

We know that at the beginning on creation in the Garden of Eden, Adam and Eve had many powers both mentally, physically and spiritually that are not apparent to us today. It is also a valid argument that God would not create all the wonderful universe full of galaxies and stars, moons, and planets where mankind could not both see and appreciate them as in the case if the garden of Eden was created inside a hollow earth!

If my theory is correct, then it could explain how that even if the Garden of Eden was inside the earth that Adam and Eve could still have seen the stars and sun and moon on the outside of the outer earth. Once mankind fell, he could no longer "see through the crust of the earth" and also lost many of his ESP powers.

I propose that somewhere much later after creation the former multidimensional doors (Bermuda Triangles) were re-opened by the fallen angels but for an entirely different purpose, and that was to ensnare souls on the outer surface and kidnap them and bring down to the inner surface to probably make slaves of them.

Is it a possibility that the fallen angels in the guise of Atlantean Rulers placed the many pyramids around the earth and indeed under the Saragossa Sea right in the middle of the Bermuda triangle? It is also interesting to note that the Bermuda Triangles being dimensional doors could enable the earth's surface to appear "see-through" in certain places, if one was attuned to that frequency as I believe Adam and Eve originally were as it states in the "Lost book of Adam and Eve" that they could see into heaven and see the angels and I am just figuring that they could also see right through the crust of the earth to see the beautiful marvellous stars and planets as though they were very close-up.

No wonder Adam and Eve were very sad and depressed & devastated when kicked out of the Garden of Eden as you can read about in the "Lost books of Adam and Eve".

30) Edmund Halley's Theory of concentric circles inside the globe. There is a lot more on this topic which I will not go into in this book concerning the thoughts of the great discoverer of Halley's Comet, but would like to write about it at a later date, but as briefly mentioned on page 30 in chapter 3 of this book, here again is what was stated about Edmund Halley:- Edmund Halley's theory of the concentric circles or globes inside the earth (pg. 30) Chapter 3. "Halley believed that the earth was a hollow shell about 500 miles thick, with two inner concentric shells and an innermost core about the diameter of the planets Venus, Mars and Mercury.

The shells were separated by atmospheres, and each one had its own magnetic poles. The spheres rotated at different speeds.

He suggested that each sphere was capable of supporting life, because each sphere was bathed with light from the atmosphere that filled each of the inner spaces. He suggested the possibility of a "more ample creation" within the earth.

His hollow earth theory came about from the examination of the gradual motion of the lines of magnetic declination. It was based on the value of lunar relative density given by Sir Isaac Newton.

His hollow earth theory appeared as the first significant deduction to be drawn from Isaac Newton's Principia."

I won't go into the details just yet, but I think that Halley was probably right. Considering that both Sir Isaac Newton who discovered gravity and Edmund Halley who discovered Halley's comet were obviously brilliant scientists why has the hollow earth concentric theory been so ignored in the past 100 years? I do think it possible that God made the creation rather like concentric globes, one within another.

i) The original outer protective layer of water all the way around the earth

ii) The shell of the earth

iii) Other worlds within the hollow earth including hell and Tartarus which are both in lower dimensions, although occupying the physical space of the inner earth are in fact in a lower dimension and therefore invisible to the human eye.

iv) I have several theories about these ideas by Halley and hope to write about them at a later date.

31) In the case of so-called alien abductions where people are allegedly taken far underground, they are also abused in different ways by these inner earth beings.

32) UFOs

Many of the UFO sightings cause scientists to conclude from their behaviour that they are from another dimension. Scientists are becoming more and more aware that there are many other dimensions. They tell us that they can only detect 5% of the known mass in the universe and that there have to be other dimensions working "behind the scenes" of this physical universe to account for the mass discrepancy! That sounds very spiritual to me!

33) God banished the fallen angels from heaven, and they made their abode in the dimensions around the earth, as well as inside the earth. They sometimes put on dramatic appearances to scare mankind as in the case of the demi-gods of the past. I think we will see them put on amazing appearances in the time of the end, they are finally totally kicked out of the entire spirit world (Revelations 12.7)

Then they will have to look very impressive to mankind in order to deceive then into believing that they are aliens form a faraway galaxy come to rescue mankind whom they will say that they seeded on this planet millions of years ago and have come to help mankind fully evolve into a higher consciousness.

34) Transhumanism Some crazy scientists actually think that man can evolve with a little technological help! These trans-humanists should read the article listed in the website index at the back of this book by a top geneticist, who categorically states that after 30 years of studying population genetics that mankind is actually getting smaller, weaker and dumber and not as evolution falsely claims taller, stronger and smarter.

The famous geneticist goes on to say that the doctrine of eugenics of the survival of the fittest simply is not true and not borne out by experimentation. He warns that even if the elite do wipe out 95% of the world's population of "useless eaters" as called by members of the hellish Illuminati, it would not result in a better and more manageable world! Why? Because each one of us produces around 100 mutational gene defects which are passed onto our kids, and this applies to all of us, and the elite included. This famous geneticist concludes by stating that mankind is going to die out anyway not evolve through transhumanism, but actually die out because of degraded genetics.

He also concludes that the Bible is 100% true in stating that since mankind brought sin into the world mankind has started dying and that only the saviour Jesus Christ can reverse our defective genome, before we all cease to exist in this physical world. Please tell others whom you think could handle this information.

CHAPTER 2

'OUT OF THE BOTTOMLESS PIT II'

THE FRONT COVER of this book shows a Red Dragon coming out of the Bottomless Pit & its expression is ferocious as it breathes a swarm of flying hybrid locust/scorpions out of its mouth.

Revelation 12:3,9 – And there appeared another wonder in heaven; and behold a great red dragon, having seven heads and ten horns, and seven crowns upon his heads.

And the great dragon was cast out (of heaven or better said, 'the spirit world.'), that old serpent, called the Devil, and Satan, which deceives the whole world: he was cast out into the earth, and his angels were cast out with him.

Revelation 11.7 And when they shall have finished their testimony, the Beast that ascends out of the Bottomless Pit shall make war against them, and shall overcome them, and kill them.

Giants are also coming out of the Pit. In the distance there are small buildings of a city.

In the front you see a man with a locust with a scorpion-tail attacking him.

The hybrid scorpion/locusts coming out of the Bottomless Pit are attacking people that have 'implants' in their hands or foreheads is as described in the Bible very clearly and graphically in Revelation Chapter 13 which is infamous for 666.

THE BOTTOMLESS PIT

Revelation 9.1-3 And the fifth angel sounded, and I saw a star fall from heaven unto the earth: and to him was given the key of the Bottomless Pit. And he opened the Bottomless Pit; and there arose a smoke out of the pit, as the smoke of a great furnace; and the sun and the air were darkened by reason of the smoke of the pit.

HYBRID LOCUSTS WITH SCORPION'S TAILS

Revelation 9.3-6,10-11 And there came out of the smoke locusts upon the earth: and unto them was given power, as the scorpions of the earth have power.

And it was commanded them that they should not hurt the grass of the earth, neither any green thing, neither any tree; but only those men which have not the seal of God in their foreheads.

And to them it was given that they should not kill them, but that they should be tormented five months: and their torment was as the torment of a scorpion, when he strikes a man. [6] And in those days shall men seek death and shall not find it; and shall desire to die, and death shall flee from them. And they had tails like unto scorpions, and there were stings in their tails: and their power was to hurt men five months.

And they had a king over them, which is the angel of the Bottomless Pit, whose name in the Hebrew tongue is Abaddon, but in the Greek tongue hath his name Apollyon.

GIANTS

In the Septuagint version of the Old Testament we find a very interesting verse in the Book of Isaiah.

Isaiah 13.3 (God) 'I give command, and I bring them: Giants are coming to fulfil my wrath, rejoicing at the same time, and insulting.

The giants mentioned before the Great Flood and the smaller giants mentioned in the Bible after the Great Flood were all very dangerous and extremely violent bent with a lot of attitude.

The Book of Enoch states that when the Giants first came into existence that it was not long before they started devouring mankind. Not a nice prospect indeed. The giants were cannibals.

Genesis 6 explains well how the giants came into existence because the Fallen angels came down to the earth and co-habited with the women and that the women agave birth to monstrous giants.

The Fallen angels did not expect that their sons would turn out as giants and monsters and cannibals, but they did.

See my books Enoch Insights, Jasher Insights, Jubilees Insights and Eden Insights to know much more about the Giants and the Fallen Angels.

Here is link to my AUDIO/VIDEO channel on YOUTUBE: (306) THE NIGHTLIGHT PODCAST ("Enoch Insights – The Book of the Watchers" – with Stephen Strutt) – YouTube

I was seeing some of the following in vision last night and it seemed to be in the future as there were people with the implants in their heads and hands but more than that there were some people with transhuman hybrid arms or legs and the Mark of the Beast implants actually glowed and it was easy to see them. It was as though there had been some catastrophe and this city was now a new city in the New World Order and millions had already died in some catastrophe real or manmade and the Anti-Christ was building a new world for its citizens. That is the impression I had last night in vision after talking to you about the possible front cover. It seemed to be in the future like in 'Back to the Future' – so much advanced technology and transhumanism

Here are some background verses about the dragon and a full description of Satan from the Bible.

DRAGONS ALSO MENTIONED IN THE BIBLE KJV:

Isaiah 27:1 – In that day the LORD with his sore and great and strong sword shall punish leviathan the piercing serpent, even leviathan that crooked serpent; and he shall slay the dragon that is in the sea.

Revelation 12:9 – And the great dragon was cast out, that old serpent, called the Devil, and Satan, which deceives the whole world: he was cast out into the earth, and his angels were cast out with him.

Ezekiel 29:3 – Speak, and say, Thus saith the Lord GOD; Behold, I am against thee, Pharaoh king of Egypt, the great dragon that lieth in the midst of his rivers, which hath said, My river is mine own, and I have made it for myself.

Jeremiah 51:34 – Nebuchadnezzar the king of Babylon hath devoured me, he hath crushed me, he hath made me an empty vessel, he hath swallowed me up like a dragon, he hath filled his belly with my delicates, he hath cast me out.

Malachi 1:3 – And I hated Esau, and laid his mountains and his heritage waste for the dragons of the wilderness.

Isaiah 34:13 – And thorns shall come up in her palaces, nettles and brambles in the fortresses thereof: and it shall be an habitation of dragons, and a court for owls.

Psalms 74:13 – Thou didst divide the sea by thy strength: thou brake the heads of the dragons in the waters.

Isaiah 43:20 – The beast of the field shall honour me, the dragons and the owls: because I give waters in the wilderness, and rivers in the desert, to give drink to my people, my chosen.

The picture on the front of the book shows a ferocious Red Dragon that is in a rage. Why is he in such a rage? It is because he knows that his time is up and his game of trying to rule the world and dominate mankind is almost over! Does Satan in the form of the Red Dragon and his Fallen angels that have just been kicked out of heaven in the picture repent of all their evil committed over 6 millennia or more? No, there are cast into the earth, and they are determined to stamp out mankind in their twisted sense of vengeance for being kicked out of heaven or the spirit world onto the physical earth.

Revelation 12.12 Woe to the inhabitants of the earth and of the sea! for the Devil is come down unto you, having great wrath, because he knows that he hath but a short time.

Revelation 12.9 And the great dragon was cast out, that old serpent, called the Devil, and Satan, which deceives the whole world: he was cast out into the earth, and his angels were cast out with him."

Revelation 12.13 And when the dragon saw that he was cast unto the earth, he persecuted the woman (the church of all true believers) which brought forth the man child.

Satan will finally be cast into the Bottomless Pit himself but not before he has wreaked havoc on the earth for three and half years according to the Book of Daniel and the Book of Revelation. An infamous period known as the Great Tribulation, which is also mentioned by Jesus in Matthew 24.15

Revelation 20:2 – And he laid hold on the dragon, that old serpent, which is the Devil, and Satan, and bound him a thousand years,

More Bible Verses on dragons

Isaiah 13:22 – And the wild beasts of the islands shall cry in their desolate houses, and dragons in their pleasant palaces: and her time is near to come, and her days shall not be prolonged.

Isaiah 51:9 – Awake, awake, put on strength, O arm of the LORD; awake, as in the ancient days, in the generations of old. Art thou not it that hath cut Rahab, and wounded the dragon?

Psalms 148:7 – Praise the LORD from the earth, ye dragons, and all deeps:

Micah 1:8 – Therefore I will wail and howl, I will go stripped and naked: I will make a wailing like the dragons, and mourning as the owls.

Psalms 91:13 – Thou shalt tread upon the lion and adder: the young lion and the dragon shalt thou trample under feet.

Deuteronomy 32:33 – Their wine is the poison of dragons, and the cruel venom of asps.

Job 41:1-34 – Canst thou draw out leviathan with an hook? or his tongue with a cord which thou let down?

Jeremiah 14:6 – And the wild asses did stand in the high places, they snuffed up the wind like dragons; their eyes did fail, because there was no grass.

HORRORS AWAITING THOSE WITH THE MARK OF THE BEAST

ANTICHRIST BEAST WORLD RULER:

Revelation 13.16-18 And he causes all, both small and great, rich and poor, free and bond, to receive a mark in their right hand, or in their foreheads:

[17] And that no man might buy or sell, save he that had the mark, or the

name of the beast, or the number of his name.

[18] Here is wisdom. Let him that hath understanding count the number of the beast: for it is the number of a man; and his number is Six hundred three-score and six.

Revelation Chapter 9.6-11

[6] And in those days shall men seek death and shall not find it; and shall desire to die, and death shall flee from them.

[7] And the shapes of the locusts were like unto horses prepared unto battle; and on their heads were as it were crowns like gold, and their faces were as the faces of men.

[8] And they had hair as the hair of women, and their teeth were as the teeth of lions.

[9] And they had breastplates, as it were breastplates of iron; and the sound of their wings was as the sound of chariots of many horses running to battle.

[10] And they had tails like unto scorpions, and there were stings in their tails: and their power was to hurt men five months.

[11] And they had a king over them, which is the angel of the Bottomless pit, whose name in the Hebrew tongue is Abaddon, but in the Greek tongue hath his name Apollyon.

Revelation 11.7 [7] And when they shall have finished their testimony, the Beast that ascended out of the Bottomless pit shall make war against them, and shall overcome them, and kill them.

Revelation 17.8 And the Beast that was, and is not, even he is the eighth, and is of the seven, and goes into perdition. (The Bottomless Pit)

Revelation 20.1-3 20 And I saw an angel come down from heaven, having the key of the Bottomless Pit and a great chain in his hand. And he laid hold on the dragon, that old serpent, which is the Devil, and Satan, and bound him a thousand years, And cast him into the Bottomless pit, and shut him up, and set a seal upon him, that he should deceive the nations no more, till the thousand years should be fulfilled: and after that he must be loosed a little season. [**See Chapter 25 for more on 'THE MARK OF THE BEAST'**]

See My Audio Series On This Topic: Monsters From The Bottomless Pit On YouTube Part 1-3:

(250) 'MONSTERS' FROM THE BOTTOMLESS PIT: REVELATION 9 – YouTube

(250) MONSTERS FROM THE BOTTOMLESS PIT PT 2 – YouTube

(250) MONSTERS FROM THE BOTTOMLESS PIT 3 by author S N Strutt – YouTube

CHAPTER 3

AMAZING PRE-HISTORIC BUILDINGS FOUND IN SCOTLAND'

INTRODUCTION

WHAT HAVE WE discovered? Back in august 2019 I made a series of videos on **YouTube** showing:

'Our Discoveries of Cyclopean Structures here in Scotland' I have since contacted some experts, and without telling them exactly where this location is as of yet: See all my videos of these megalithic structures here in Scotland: ANCIENT RUINS -VIDEO – www.outofthebottomlesspit.co.uk

See The Comments from Others: ANC. RUINS COMMENTS – www.outofthebottomlesspit.co.uk

Why am I not revealing where the location is, as of yet? The reason for that, is because we are not sure if we want lots of people digging up the beautiful landscape, just for the authorities to come up with some evolutionary timeframe and thus a dismissive explanation instead of telling the truth.

What *is* the truth about these megalithic structures all around the world?

We can see them all over the world, and yet modern man does not want to believe in anything that does not fit into his 'Evolutionary false paradigm'. In other words, man is supposed to be evolving and going forwards and that we are bigger and smarter and stronger than those who came before us – but that simply does not add up to the facts. There is lots of evidence that the races in the past were taller than us and stronger and, in some cases, more advanced in technology than we are today!

You are entitled to believe what you want as God has given all mankind – choice. I choose to believe in the Creation story is told in the King James version of the Bible, and that the earth is a young earth of around only 6000 years old – which can be proven in many ways for those with their eyes open.

If we go according to the Bible, we find some very strange events including massive giants roaming the earth in the Pre-Flood times and other monsters due to the escapades of the Fallen angels as mentioned in Genesis 6. I have tried to cover the Pre-Flood times of around 1560 years in my books: ' INSIGHTS' BOOKS' – www.outofthebottomlesspit.co.uk

Modern man dismisses things like 'Atlantis' as mere myth when there is so much evidence that what Plato said in ancient times about the ancient continent of Atlantis was true of which the structures we found, could be related.

I was recently fascinated reading a chapter from Charles Berlitz' Book of

'Atlantis' – I will quote it as it mentions the kind of structures that we have found and relates them to Atlantis!

Investigation

When I asked those who understand about ancient structures and rocks including scientists and archaeologists, I was told that when they saw my videos, that the structures looked like 'dolmens'.

Here is the definition of the word dolmen: 'A megalithic tomb with a large flat stone laid on upright ones, found chiefly in Britain and France.'

However, we seem to have discovered something far more interesting than a dolmen or menhir.

Here is a quote from the famous book 'Atlantis' by Charles Berlitz – the author of the Best seller: The Bermuda Triangle, which I covered in my first book 'Out of The Bottomless Pit'

I picked up his book Atlantis a couple of days ago, or to be precise on the 29/08/21, and felt that I should read the last chapter for some reason, and lo and behold, I had actually never read that chapter before and the whole chapter shed some light on our 'Archaeological findings' here in Scotland 2 years ago.

Here is a quote from Charles Berlitz famous book Atlantis from the 14th chapter called 'The Bridge Through Time':

'Legends of lost lands and cities of various coasts form a great circle around the shores of the North Atlantic. And as we fly or sometimes sail across the Atlantic, we often wonder whether there really does exist a sunken continent miles below us, inaccessible and lost in time but one that we seem to instinctively remember.

But on a more realistic plane, more than memories suggest and point to lost lands under the sea, since vestiges of sunken civilizations have been found offshore at different places along the Atlantic coast and adjacent seas.

The stone roads of Yucatan and the avenues of stone Dolmens and Menhirs of Brittany, both which lead to the edge of the sea and then continue down under it, and the underwater stone roads of walls of Bimini, cut stone flights of steps and roads on undersea plateaus in the Caribbean and on the Atlantic sea-mounts all seem to point to the more extensive ruins farther out in the ocean.'

More on Dolmens: Dolmens and Menhirs: 'In the mind of the general reader Brittany is unalterably associated with the prehistoric stone monuments which are so closely identified with its folklore and national life. In other parts of the world similar monuments are encountered in Great Britain and Ireland, Scandinavia, the Crimea, Algeria, and India, but nowhere are they found in such abundance as in Brittany, nor are these rivalled in other lands, either as regards their character or the space they occupy.'

Source: Legends and Romances of Brittany: Chapter II: Menhirs and Dolmens (sacred-texts.com)

Editor: What is now becoming apparent is that what we have found appears to be unique! Why? All other so-called dolmens that I have looked at so far, seem to be of only one or two or just a few heavy rocks.

What we discovered is many rocks piled one on top of the other at least 10 to 20 rocks in ways that seem impossible, like a giant totem pole made of rocks some of which must be many tons in weight – as I related on the videos two years ago. We in fact don't know how many rocks there are as they seem to go deep into the ground and up high on the mountain as well.

The rocks defy gravity it would seem! Why do I say that the rocks appear to defy gravity? Well, in school we were taught that as a rule in building a castle or house or any structure that one puts the big slabs for the foundation and the smaller rocks and bricks on top. Why do many of the strange structures around the world have small stones first and then much larger ones on top? Did those who built them in ancient times know about anti-gravity?

Normally these structures are found at sea-level but in the case of what we discovered they are at around 1500 feet up the mountainside.

The mountains were volcanic in the distant past. These structures have apparently been buried for thousands of years by both soil and in places lava – thus preserving the ancient structures in an unusual way. Could these mountains have been thrust up in a big hurry many thousands of years ago even pushing the original giant megaliths high up the mountain? That would seem unlikely. Amazingly, I have heard of exactly that happening before. I cover this below.

SUMMARY

11/08/19 – These rock formations are truly amazing. I hope that archaeologists will dig up this 'top of the mountain' here in Scotland – to reveal the splendour of a massive 'ancient fortress' full of interesting artefacts and perhaps even some 'giant' skeletons. I think that this fortification was probably built by a 'race of giants' in the days before the 'Great Flood' around 5000 years ago – using ancient and advanced technology – We certainly could not build these structures today! If we tried, they would simply fall over! What did the ancients know about 'balancing' rocks that we simply have forgotten about how to do? Was 'levitation' or some sort of 'ant-gravity' used? If the ancients could levitate rocks, then temporarily it wouldn't matter whether the big rocks were at the top of the pile or in the middle or at the bottom of the structure. Once the rocks were in place it wouldn't matter. In modern times we have to put the large rocks into the foundation and then build with smaller rocks – Why? because we are limited by – gravity – but if the ancients before the 'Great Flood' had access to anti-gravity technology and levitation then it would have made it 'child's play' for them to build both 'large and heavy structures' very quickly – like a giant playing with kids blocks levitating them and quickly putting them together. Why were the builders in such an obvious hurry to build these roughly formed cyclopean structures – which were probably fortifications – what were they afraid of? Was there something more dangerous than the giants themselves – even if some races of giants were 35 feet tall? Could it have been giant dinosaurs, dragons, and pterodactyls much bigger than the smaller giants of 15 to 20 feet tall? ANCIENT RUINS -VIDEO – www.outofthebottomlesspit.co.uk

CHAPTER 4

CYCLOPEAN STRUCTURES' – FROM PRE-HISTORIC TIMES

Staggering Cyclopean 'Archaeological Discovery'

THIS SECTION WAS originally written on August 10th - 2019 by the author of this book – S N Strutt

Today I went on an adventure to film a very strange rock formation here in Scotland (UK).

I have been shocked to find what look like large *cyclopean structures* in the mountains or tall hills.

No one else seems to have even noticed these rocks. Many of these rocks are 6 feet x 7 feet x 5 feet or 2 x 2 x 2 meters = 8 cubic metres each. As far as I know, these structures are normally more typical for Tiahuanaco in Peru and Baalbek in Lebanon or Easter Island or even Stonehenge in England.

It would appear that for whatever reason that these rocks have probably been hidden underground for a very long time, but because of erosion by the wind, rain and water over the millennia and past centuries these large, sculptured rocks are now jutting out of the ground high up on the mountain side.

These mountains apparently used to be volcanic as late as 3800 years ago. In filming the area, one had the impression that one is seeing just the tip of the iceberg of a massive ancient fortress which runs a long way underground with gigantic rocks piled the one upon the other.

In other words, most of the structures cannot be seen at present and it would be wonderful to have archaeologists dig it all up to find an ancient large fortress here in Scotland.

Many of these rocks are piled on top of each other in great precision. In some places it looks like there is some sort of covering mortar pasted around the edges.

We have also found some evidence of some of the rocks are seemingly 'fused together by very great heat'- but how was that done in very ancient times? ['Ancient fortifications in Europe had melted stone walls—but it wasn't battle damage. A mystery has puzzled historians since the 18th century, when a survey in the Scottish Highlands found an ancient fort with walls made from stones that had been melted together.'] *https://en.wikipedia.org/wiki/Vitrified_fort*

Strangely some of the rocks seem to have some sort of mortar at least on the outside of the joinings which is not normal for Cyclopean stone structures.

What is odd is that the mortar appears to be lava and crumbles to dust in one's hand. It is sort of layered in structure and looks like mineralized rock. It is also very heavy just like the rocks that it connects together. I suppose that it is possible that the structures were built first – and then the lava came afterwards.

We can see as high as 15 metres of these structures going straight up, of rocks placed on top of each other with great precision but they are mostly buried by forest and earth. They probably descent deep down into the earth. The rocks also appear to travel on for quite a distance laterally, but are mostly covered by the land at present, including forests.

What impressed the three of us the most was:

I) The size of the rocks

II) No mortar used to cement many of the stones together. Some of the rocks could have a strange type of mortar- lava? It looks very odd indeed!

III) Apparently Lava covering the rocks at the seams of the rocks in places.

IV Another feature was that there were long 1 -1 ½ cm round holes going right through a few of the rocks from one side to the other. These holes are very smooth inside. (When were the holes made and why?)

V) Another observation is that some of the very big stones are rounded and smooth but only some of them. How did that happen? For my understanding that is a sign of erosion by sea water.

I would suggest that these rocks were buried by the ocean at some time in the very far past. I myself have visited this area many times in the past. Every time I do go to the forests that cover these mountains – after it has rained what does one invariably see – but sand running down with the water. These mountains were indeed covered in both the ocean and some sand at one time.

VI There are also large sandstone rocks here further down the mountains due to water erosion, so big in fact that someone carved a cave inside one of them centuries ago.

VII There were also cut marks in the stones as though two stones were held tight close together by some sort of metal fastening large clamp pin of very odd design. The pins had long ago disappeared into the dusts of history- showing that these structures were indeed very old.

I have seen videos showing similar markings in the rocks in the location of India- with the massive stone buildings there also.

VIII One of the rocks which was around 4 feet long and 3 feet wide and 3 feet thick was – formed like a reptile and there were eyes and a mouth carved into it.

IX My daughter suggested that it probably had been a carved stone on top of the tower or ancient building and had fallen down to the ground.

X Someone just suggested to me when I asked why build these structures in such a strange unusual way? For example, why have some of the very big rocks been placed on top of very small stones that are shaped. Their answer I thought was very relevant. 'The ancients who built these structures were 'making a statement' to the generations that would inevitably come after them – and now it is thousands of years later – that they of the far past were much smarter than we are today and that they had much more advanced technology. How is it even possibly to explain what looks like liquid rock which has been solidified between the rocks in order to join them together? To melt rock takes very high temperatures. How was it done? We don't even have technology like that today which is known to the public?

XI There are many large stones scattered over the ground up there in the mountains.

XII It is hard to understand why no professional archaeologists have noticed this amazing find- why would the authorities not want to know about such finds – is it because it must show that their old theories of archaeology are simply wrong?

Conclusion: By the author: 24/07/19:

I) Since re-discovering these megalithic boulders on the 26th June 2019, I have done extensive research in fields of both science and ancient history as well as archaeology. (Read below). It is my conclusion that the location of the find is exactly where one would expect to find such cyclopean buildings. I have been studying many ancient sciences also, since discovering the cyclopean rocks such as ley-lines & energy lines which are also found close to the spot of the find.

II) I believe that these big cyclopean stones were built into a massive, long fortress probably around 5000 years ago. later there came a worldwide flood. The buildings became submerged under the sea. Soon after the Great Flood there was a lot of volcanic activity and parts of the structures were covered in lava which has somewhat crumbled away with time into dust as it has a layered rock structure. If I take a piece of the 'heavy lava' and try to crush it – it easily crumbles to dust in my hand showing that it is very old.

III) At first glance it would appear that the authorities know about the Cyclopean buildings, but they have deliberately ignored them and have tried to cover them up in the past by having planted many trees to sort of camouflage the area. they also minimize the find in the press. Wikipedia only gives these ancient buildings one sentence Iron-age forts in the hills.

IV Today I was reading the official Tourist board 'Interesting walks' in the area. This is a board up on the hills themselves. Some ancient archaeological sites are mentioned in the area from the Iron Age or as they say 500 BCE – 600 AD.

The above photos that I am mentioning in the video, I am convinced are from 5000 years ago – are not more than 150 yards from that Tourist Billboard.

V The Tourist board mentions nothing about these rocks that I clearly have shown do exist on my video, which incidentally are surrounded by woods (deliberate camouflage?).

All the current archaeological sites in these hills, and I have seen all of them up close (Around 5 small sites) do not compare in the scope to what I have covered in this video.

Why have the authorities covered it up? It is not even mentioned to tourists who come to the area. That I find very odd!

VI I am not yet certain whether the right authorities know about this particular exact area and this discovery or if they even realize how important this archaeological 'find' actually is?

VII I have not told the authorities about this find. Why? Because it is now obvious to me that they already know about it and just want to let it stay buried for whatever reason. To be on the safe side for the time being – I will not reveal the exact location of this rock formation at the present time – except to say that it is in Scotland. I think that the rocks speak for themselves to those who are listening. So perhaps the exact location is not really that important when obviously the authorities are trying to cover-up these rocks or hope that no-one notices their importance. I finally realized that it does not matter exactly where these rocks are situated, as long as we can show the rocks on film and in photographs.

VIII So far, no one has even bothered to excavate the massive structures to see how big and extensive the fortifications are – and why are they built of massive rocks that we humans could not possibly lift? Sad that the authorities have so far shown no interest in what could be a national treasure?

IX You probably wonder if I have lived in Scotland and already seen these structures years ago then why haven't I reported this seeming important find years ago? A very good question indeed! The truth is that most people can look at something like this structure even as I did for years, but because you don't have a clear reference point to understanding exactly what you are looking at one sort of switches off, simply because you can't understand what you are seeing.

In other words, you have no reference point. Well, that changed some months ago when I happened to be watching some videos by Timothy Alberino and Steve Quayle about rock formations and cyclopean structures around the world and in particular in Sardinia – and exactly where to find them and under what climatic conditions such as an ancient former volcanic area. (Timothy Alberino – ancient cyclopean structures: https://youtu.be/gt2r2vu574i?t=2178)

My hope in making these videos is to make as many people in Scotland & in fact the whole world aware of these national treasures – as it could be very good for tourism and for the UK – if this site is thoroughly dug up. Someone needs to wake up the authorities about the importance of this site. If enough people show an interest (Please 'like' the 'video' or even better make some constructive comments), *then* maybe we can change things – that eventually the whole site will get dug up to reveal an ancient large fortification?

I am convinced that many treasures will be found in these formerly volcanic high hills (1500 feet and 1800 feet high respectively). I would like to challenge the right authorities to 'do' something about what would appear to us as an incredible find'.

From a purely archaeological point of view alone – it is important for many people to get directly involved in this project. there are probably many more of these fortifications dotted around Scotland. They just remain to be found and dug up!

['Cyclopean' definition: Cyclopean masonry. 'Cyclopean masonry is a type of stonework found in Mycenaean architecture, built with massive limestone boulders, roughly fitted together with minimal clearance between adjacent stones and no use of mortar.']

'The term cyclopean comes from the belief of classical Greeks that only the mythical 'Cyclops' giants had the strength to move the enormous boulders that made up the walls of Mycenae and Tiryns.' strange rock buildings that defy explanation –

I have found out that here in Scotland one is not allowed to make any new archaeological discoveries, as it is against the law unless it conforms to the paradigm of what is taught i.e., evolution.

If one discovers things that defy the accepted scientific belief system, discoveries are simply ignored or buried – literally.

Strange Rock Buildings That Defy Explanation

(**Added June 2022**): **Author:** I have since contacted the Heritage Trust in Scotland and the Environment Scotland but they are not interested in what we have found buried in the ground even though it is a massive discovery, as they say all old buildings that are 'discovered' are normally kept buried underground for their own preservation rather than excavating them to show the public about the amazing finds.

It is simply the case that there must be 1000's of such amazing buildings buried under the ground all over the world, and most of them never see the daylight anymore, because the governments of this world are controlled by 'international controllers' that have a Satanic agenda and that is to 'hide the truth' in whatever way the truth shows up.

If what we have discovered in Scotland is proven to be ancient and built by an advanced race of very tall people or even giants who had levitation technology amongst other things, then modern science has a problem. Why? Well, we are taught by the paradigm of Evolution which has no proof whatsoever, by the way, that we are advancing and getting bigger and stronger and more intelligent all the time, and that life is both random and a big co-incidence. What if those assumptions are totally erroneous. What if much smarter beings once lived on this planet and built many of the massive structures around the planet, including the ones that we have personally discovered. I have told the authorities that there exist rock structures here in Scotland that simply defy explanation. Why do I say that? Because in modern times no one in their right mind would build structures like that which defy physics and logic. You have to see them to understand what I am taking about. I do have them on videos.(3) AMAZING ARCHAEOLOGICAL STRUCTURES – VIDEO 2 – YouTube

See my many other videos about these Pre-Flood structures built by a super-race of giants: ANCIENT RUINS -VIDEO – www.outofthebottomlesspit.co.uk

CHAPTER 5

THE ANCIENT WORLD
(PRE-FLOOD WORLD = MORE THAN 4500 YEARS OLD)

'CYCLOPEAN MASONRY IS a type of stonework found in Mycenaean architecture, built with massive limestone boulders, roughly fitted together with minimal clearance between adjacent stones and no use of mortar. The boulders typically seem unworked, but some may have been worked roughly with a hammer and the gaps between boulders filled in with smaller chunks of limestone'

[Cyclopean masonry. Cyclopean masonry is a type of stonework found in Mycenaean architecture, built with massive limestone boulders, roughly fitted together with minimal clearance between adjacent stones and no use of mortar. The term comes from the belief of classical Greeks that only the mythical Cyclopes had the strength to move the enormous boulders that made up the walls of Mycenae and Tiryns. Pliny's Natural History reported the tradition attributed to Aristotle, that the Cyclopes were the inventors of masonry towers, giving rise to the designation Cyclopean.]

https://redice.tv/news/
cyclopean-masonry-a-mystery-of-the-ancient-world

'Pliny the Elder, in his *Naturalis Historia* (AD 77-79), attributed the name Cyclopean Masonry to Aristotle, claiming that it was he who believed that only the mythical race of giant Cyclops was strong enough to have moved such huge boulders and set them in place. Most examples of this type of construction are today called Cyclopean, though the technique is found throughout the world in many different cultures.'

https://paranormalpeopleonline.com/
cyclopean-masonry-a-mystery-of-the-ancient-world/

Why limestone is such a good construction material? The construction industry uses limestone for walls and floors on buildings. From the ancient pyramids of Egypt to the contemporary architecture, this natural stone has a high strength, durability and resistance to corrosion. Their non-slip and heat-resistant properties are highly prized.

https://www.google.com/search?client=firefox-b-d&q=why+use+limestone+to+build+ancient+buildings

More useful qualities about limestone.

Lime is in its original state, calcium carbonate. It is anti-bacterial, resistant to ultra-violet light, and will allow moisture to release from surfaces from the inside out, rather than trapping moisture, as some other modern coatings can do. It allows the moisture in, but unlike other compounds, allows it out again. When worked into a plaster form, lime absorbs carbon dioxide from the atmosphere and then forms a strong yet permeable coat of limestone.

http://www.sustainablebuild.co.uk/usinglime.html

The Enigma of the Cyclopean Limestone Pre-Historic Blocks

1) Most of the cyclopean structures around the world were built in volcanic areas including high mountainous areas. these rocks are proven to be limestone.

2) Limestone is not a volcanic rock! the fact is that limestone is formed under water or under the sea or in mountain caves where water is dripping

3) How would an ancient culture have moved massive rocks from sea-level to high up in the mountains to build ancient fortifications many thousands of feet above sea level?

4) Why didn't the builders choose to simple use volcanic rocks that must have been strewn all around the mountainside? Or is there another missing factor? a) Could it be that when these ancient cyclopean structures were originally built that they were not yet volcanic areas.

5) Could it also be that what are today are mountainous areas were once at sea-level? Let's see what we can find about these possibilities.

Is it just possible that somewhere on the planet we could find evidence that a city of cyclopean structures which is now in the high mountains was once actually at sea level in mankind's timeframe on the planet of only 6000 years? A change which happened over only many thousands of years and not millions of years?

CHAPTER 6

TIAHUANACO, ANCIENT "SEAPORT" 2.5 MILES ABOVE SEA LEVEL, OLDEST CITY ON EARTH?

STRANGELY, TIAHUANACO IS a port, although the nearest body of water is Lake Titicaca, some 15 miles away. The theories about how this happens to be are several. On the rock cliffs near the piers and wharfs of the port area of the ruins are yellow-white calcareous deposits forming long, straight lines indicating pre-historic water levels. These ancient shorelines are strangely tilted, although once they must have been level. The surrounding area is covered with millions of fossilized seashells. It appears, from the tilting of the ancient shoreline striations and the abundant presence of fossilized oceanic flora and fauna, that a tremendous uplift of land has taken place sometime in the ancient past.

"There is evidence that the city was once a port, having extensive docks positioned right on the earlier shoreline of the now inland waterbed. One of these wharves is big enough to accommodate hundreds of ships." "According to Incan legends, Tiahuanaco was built by a race of giants whose fatherland had been destroyed in a great deluge that had lasted for two months.".

Many of Tiahuanaco's buildings were constructed of massive, finished stones, many tons in weight, which were placed in such a manner that only a people with advanced engineering methods could have designed and transported them. ... "The particular andesite used in much of the Tiahuanaco's construction can only be found in a quarry 50 miles away in the mountains."

Reference: https://www.physicsforums.com/threads/seaport-2-5-miles-above-sea-level.160584/

Author: Now here is the real problem. Scientists tell us that the mountains were thrown up in the Andes 100 million years ago – but we have evidence that in fact Tiahuanaco was once at sea level and a sea-level port. In other words, it was built by man in the 'recent past' like 4000-5000 years ago. apparently, the whole land mass was thrust upwards at around the time of the great flood of Noah some 4500 years ago. according to the bible the continents moved apart right after the Tower of Babel was destroyed or around 2300 BCE or around 200 years after the Great Flood. On the leading edges of the land masses that were forced outwards the land stopped moving as it came into the resistance of another continental shelf and the land buckled and was forced upwards into mountains. This is why one sees high mountain ranges all the way from Alaska down the coast to the USA and central America as well as south America. On the other leading edge, we have Russia's East coast going down to China and Japan on down. All those areas have high mountains, and many are volcanic. All the places mentioned above are in the area today known as the 'Ring of Fire'.

The following is an excellent video by walt brown called the hydro-plate theory which explains what I have just written about the continents having moved apart around the time of the great flood. https://youtu.be/sd9zgt9ua-u?t=15

The official position at present concerning ancient forts in the hills of Scotland: A little investigation reveals that the official position according to Wikipedia, is that there are some iron-age (500 BC- 600 AD) forts in this area (Somewhere in Scotland) – but the report is only one line long and is totally evasive. Furthermore, it does not explain how the ancient forts came into being – because obviously they don't know how they were built.

After all the official position is based upon what archaeologists and scientists tell them which is in itself based on the false science of Evolution.

Those people think in terms of millions & billions of years of evolution – but what if they are wrong, and that the world was created by God around 6000 years ago? What if there was a Great Flood circa 4500 years ago? I think it must be very difficult for most people if you actually believe in the false doctrine of Evolution which has absolutely no evidence to support the Theory. Why would that make it difficult for people? Well, when you are taught that things happened on our planet over 'millions of years' then thousands of years mean seemingly nothing compared to the geological record of time itself of billions of years. So, what difference could 500 years make in time itself you may well ask? well consider the following: if Noah's flood was real as documented in the Bible and by most cultures all around the world then the exact date of the great flood is very important to our study at the present time concerning ancient cyclopean buildings and structures. If the Great Flood of Noah happened around 4500 years ago then we probably do know who built the structures that I have filmed.

DISINFORMATION: Another point is that one finds in doing research into archaeology is that sometimes the 'powers that be' and in this case the governments of mankind many times don't like new discoveries and they often try to hide them such as the infamous Smithsonian Institute in the USA, which deliberately covers up and even takes away evidence of archaeological digs especially when it involves giants and giant skeletons. Why? Because such 'finds' prove that the 'crutch of science' i.e., Evolution to be simply wrong. Yesterday I was again filming the same area and apart from the area being hedged in with trees when there are no trees on the rest of the barren rock on the mountain, we also found something odd. A rock which seemed out of place with everything else that we were filming. The rock was only around a foot long. I turned it over as we noticed some plastic around the bottom of it. We thought that seemed odd. When we turned it over there was a big piece of plastic under it and it was clear that someone had made an imitation rock out of cement by putting wet cement and leaving it in the plastic bag. If that was done deliberately as some sort of 'disinformation' then it certainly didn't do the job but instead it made us suspicious that someone does not want anyone to believe that the big rocks, we have filmed were an ancient building built in pre-historic times but that it was built recently somehow. Sorry, but that fake stone shows us to what crazy lengths 'the powers that be' will go to hide amazing finds like these gargantuan rock buildings here in the mountains.

CHAPTER 7

TOWER OF BABEL & THE BOOK OF JASHER: ANCIENT TIMES

– www.outofthebottomlesspit.co.uk

I WAS RECENTLY asked a very important question by a gentleman in China concerning our recent archaeological 'find' in Scotland.

He asked me if I was sure that the cyclopean structures were built before the Great Flood or just right after the Great Flood at the time of the Tower of Babel? (250 years after the Great Flood or 2250 BCE)

Link to cyclopean archaeological discovery in Scotland by S.N.Strutt : http://www.outofthebottomlesspit.co.uk/443196894

Amazingly, I was just going through my new book '**Jasher Insights' Book I,** when I came to chapters 9-10 which were talking about the **Tower of Babel**.

(See my new book Jasher Insights Book I: http://www.outofthebottomlesspit.co.uk/443208580]

Why is this important to the argument you might ask?

The Cyclopean fortification which we have found would seem to have some sort of mortar holding the giant rocks together – although it is a very strange type of mortar that is both multi-layered and it crumbles to dust in ones hand, although it is very heavy and a substance that is just as heavy as the substance of the massive rocks around it.

We even thought that the mortar used – could have possibly been lava – but who knows – we need expert opinion on this one.

The following is a direct quote from my book '**JASHER INSIGHTS' BOOK I – Chapter 9.24**

JASHER 9.24 ‹And they began to make bricks and burn fires to build the city and the **tower** that they had imagined to complete›.

GEN.11:3 'And they said one to another, 'Go to, let us make brick, and burn them thoroughly'. And they had brick for stone, and slime had they for mortar'.

Book of Jubilees 10:20 ‹And they began to build, and in the fourth week they made brick with fire and the bricks served them for stone, and the clay with which they cemented them together was asphalt which comes out of the sea, and out of the fountains of water in the land of Shinar›.

JASHER 9.27 ‹And when they were building they built themselves a great city and a very high and strong tower; and on account of its height the mortar and bricks did not reach the builders in their ascent to it, until those who went up had completed a full year, and after that, they reached to the builders and gave them the mortar and the bricks; thus was it done daily>.

JASHER INSIGHTS BK I

Chapter 10:2 'And when the Lord had scattered the sons of men on account of their sin at the tower, behold they spread forth into many divisions, and all the sons of men were dispersed into the four corners of the earth'.

'*All the sons of men were dispersed into the four corners of the earth*'. God forcibly moved the continents with the peoples that were on them; so obviously it happened sometime *after* the collapse of the Tower of Babel. It is stated in the Bible that the earth was divided in the days of Peleg'.

At one time apparently, all the continents of the planet were joined together. – Pangaea

At the time after the destruction of the Tower of Babel by God Himself, the lands were separated from each other very suddenly, as they moved apart at around 50 miles/hour.

This is indeed an amazing concept, as if all the continents were moving apart relative to each other sometime immediately after the collapse of the Tower of Babel because of God's judgements, then how did the peoples of the earth survive the gargantuan movement of the earth's crust without being killed? A very good question. see the hydro-plate theory below.

Supposedly, the original mass of the earth was separated into 7 continents all joined together rather like the seams on a baseball which occurred at the Flood.

All it took, was for another major calamity some 250 years after the Great Flood, right in the centre of all the land masses and then all the continents started moving apart. Probably quite rapidly at first and eventually they slowed down drastically.

This also explains many of things and animals found common to all the continents [Walt Brown's Hydro-plate theory: https://youtu.be/sD9ZGt9UA-U?t=36]

In examining the evidence, it would appear that before the Great Flood there was an advanced race of Giants who were also known as the gods and demi-gods who were the sons of the Annunaki or the Fallen angels.

Before the Great Food they built empires such as Atlantis and Lemuria and the land of Mu.

These advanced civilizations were probably not the ones who built all the cyclopean structures all around the world such the pyramids and many other amazing structures.

Notice that the amazing structures built before the Great Flood were made of gigantic rocks piled the one on top of the other and without mortar'

On the other hand, the Tower of Babel was made with bricks and mortar – using lime and thus forming limestone.

From the above analysis it would seem much more likely that the fortifications in our Scottish mountains were probably made by races who were driven away by God himself at the time of the destruction of the tower of babel and where he forcibly dispersed the nation to the 4 corners of the earth.

They took their knowledge of building from having been part of the original team of people who helped to build the Tower of Babel with them and built the cyclopean structures here in the Scottish mountains.

Well, that is one possibility.

But there are other more challenging possibilities.

Once that had happened then the earth itself split apart at the seams of the continents in what is know as the continental drift.

However, this did not happen millions of years ago – but only around 4200 years ago. We can prove that from the Bible and from the Apocryphal books as well as other ancient texts.

It also happened suddenly and quickly in the days of Peleg 250 years after the Great Flood of Noah.

This also means that the inhabitants of Scotland originally came to live here around 4200 years ago.

See the video of Walt Brown's Hydro-plate theory as it explains the spreading out of the continents very well.

https://youtu.be/sD9ZGt9UA-U?t=36

CHAPTER 8

GARDEN OF EDEN

QUESTION: WAS IT built before or after the Great Flood of Noah?

IF YOU ARE familiar with both my website and my first five books then you will know that I believe that the 'earth is hollow', and not solid. With that in mind let's examine the following.

The Garden of Eden according to the Jewish mystic book of the Zohar was originally created inside a hollow earth so also says the books of Enoch, Jasher and Jubilees as well as the Bible itself also alluding to it for those who want to see. I have also read a book by an author called Alan Trenholm who claims to have visited hell itself in the inner earth in a vision mentioned in his excellent book 'Journey to Gragau' – which you can find at Amazon.com – where he was so surprised to see that the inner earth had an inner sun.

Everything that I have researched during the past 8 years has always lead me back to the 'earth' being 'hollow'.

Why is this important you might say concerning our discussion of our recent possible Cyclopean find here in Scotland? Well let's consider the following.

When you study all five of my books (Update: now 9 books – December 2022) – 4 of which are based on Apocryphal books and ancient Jewish books – it is like putting together the pieces of a big puzzle and the overall picture from these books together with the Bible would indeed indicate that the Garden of Eden was created inside an Inner Earth.

Also, in my books you will find the consistent story of Fallen Angels having come done to earth before the Great flood and having mated with the human women which created hybrid humans and giants known in old times as the gods and demi-gods.

As the perversion of the fallen angels increased in the post Enochian times or around 1000 AC = years after the Creation until the Great Flood in 1658 then the next lot of Fallen angels started mating with both animals and even fish and other creatures creating in essence chimeras of all sorts. Fortunately, most of these were destroyed at the time of the Great Flood.

This is a very big topic in itself, which I have covered in my books. It would seem that the only hybrids that survived the Great Flood were those who lived in the sea such as Mermaids or the daughters of the Sirens -which I covered in my books and on my website.

Here is what I personally think happened from the Creation until just after the Tower of Babel which resulted in the dispersion of mankind to the 4 quarters of the earth and subsequently was followed by the dividing of all the 7 continents on the planet around 4250 years ago or 250 years after the Great Flood.

1) God created the Garden of Eden inside the earth.

2) God kicked Adam and Eve out of the Garden – and they went to live somewhere outside of the Garden of Eden, but still inside the Inner Earth.

3) Cain was banished and went to live in in distant region from the original Garden of Eden but also inside the hollow earth

4) Noah came along – the Great Flood finally carried what was left of mankind to the outer earth with the 8 souls yet remaining.

5) I have many times wondered why if there were around 1 Billion people living before the Great Flood how come we don't have more records of that past and in particular about supposed advanced races that lived and reigned over mankind before the Great Flood?

Well, if Noah lived inside the earth until the Great Flood it is very possible that he didn't know about what was going on the outer surface with the depraved 'advanced giant civilizations' – who ended up destroying each other.

I think we only came to know about these advanced civilizations after the Great Flood – as mankind started finding the ancient ruins such as the Pyramids and Easter Island and perhaps these amazing cyclopean structures that we have just discovered here in Scotland.

The ancient knowledge was observed after the fact by their ruins and writings on ancient structures.

It was as though those Giants before the Great flood knew that judgement was coming upon them (See the Book of the Giants), and they built great structures – as they wanted to make a name for themselves that would be remembered throughout all time – even circumventing the Great Flood.

6) There used to be a Book of Noah that unfortunately has largely disappeared. Whether accidently or deliberately covered up I can't tell you, but why did the Catholic church hide the Book of Enoch for 1000 years on the threat of death?

7) I would love to see the original book of Noah. Today we can find around 5 chapters from the original book of Noah weaved into the Book of Enoch.

8) According to the book of Jubilees (which I am working on for my 6th book –'Jubilees Insights' which should be available in a few months' time) – Noah wrote a book about herbs & spices which was dictated to him by God's angels of the Presence telling him the secrets of all the herbs and spices on the earth and how to cast out bad spirits. Why do you suppose that that particular

book has disappeared?

9) There is so much evidence that there existed a super-race of giants or the sons of the Fallen angels who moved from the inner earth some 500 years before the Great Flood and came to set-up their kingdoms on the virgin outer-surface of the earth. Apparently, they established amazing kingdoms such as Atlantis and Lemuria and the Land of Mu and other such civilizations. They took peoples from the original INNER EARTH as their slaves. There are some amazing books in India that do talk about this time period of 5000 years ago mentioning advanced civilizations who used flying machines and also lasers and had deadly weapons. Apparently, some of these kingdoms wiped each other out in massive wars well before the Great Flood. All of that remained of those advanced kingdoms were destroyed by the Great Flood. But that is only a little bit about them. What about Portals and the Fallen angels travelling to other worlds and star systems and other dimensions? Why were the pyramids and Stonehenge and other cyclopean structures all aligned with the stars and in particular with Orion's Belt? Many tell us that the pyramids are Portals to other realms.

10) In the Pre-Flood world the earth was nowhere near as mountainous as today and probably no more than 6000 feet high mountains at least on the outer surface of the earth. The high mountain ranges were pushed up as the continents drifted apart sometime after the destruction of the tower of Babel by God Himself in 2250 BCE.

11) Why are there ancient Cyclopean structures such as in Machupicchu – in Peru at 13000 feet which used to be a Sea Port? What happened? (See my article: http://www.outofthebottomlesspit.co.uk/443253837

Were The Cyclopean Buildings That We Recently Found In Scotland Built Before The Great Flood Or After – How About The Possibility Of Both?

I think that it is still possible that the ancient Cyclopean structures that we have personally discovered in Scotland this June 26th 2019 were originally built before the Great Flood or around 5000 years ago – when the UK was still part of one large land mass (Pangaea) and was located pretty much in the centre of that massive land mass.

There were also seas and oceans inside Pangaea, but they were nowhere near as deep as the seas became after the Great flood.

Here is what I propose could be one possibility. The buildings that we found in Scotland were built before the Flood in an area that belonged to one of the super races.

At the time of the Great Flood everything was buried by sand and sea.

In the process the earth had become cracked where we find the continental plates today – except they all used to be joined together and not spread apart.

The judgement by God Himself of the Tower of Babel was so destructive that the weak point in Pangaea super-continent broke and the 7 continents started to drift apart (*See my article: http://www.outofthebottomlesspit.co.uk/443253837)

In some places on the earth mountain ranges were forced up just after the Tower of Babel's destruction by God Himself. I think that this is the case here in Scotland.

Even though we have found some kind of mortar between the massive rocks – the following is a possible scenario:

The Fortifications were originally built at Sea level – thus using Limestone (a rock found under water or created by water).

After the Great flood the mountains ranges were thrust up and so were the cyclopean buildings here in Scotland. This was also around the same time that God drove mankind away from the Tower of Babel and mankind was separated to the four winds.

CHAPTER 9

GIANTS: WERE THE THEY THE FIRST TO INHABIT THE UK?

Apparently, it was Japheth's son Gomer who pioneered the British Isles and his sons pioneered Scotland in around 2250 BCE. (Here is something someone just sent me: 'He traces the names of the kings of the 4 royal houses of the Anglo Saxons clear back to Japheth the son of Noah in their writings. Also the Welsh who still speak in native tongue what is called "Gomeraeg" after his son Gomer' -John Benjamin)

(See my new book **'JASHER INSIGHTS' BOOK 1** – Chapter 10.8) 'And the children of Gomer according to their cities were the Francum in the land of Franca – that is another name for France today which is right next to the UK over the British Channel – so the UK would have been the very next country to have been inhabited after France.

The new inhabitants of Scotland could have rebuilt the ancient cyclopean structures that they now found in the mountains and this time they used mortar to repair the ancient ruins as they had used mortar in the building of the Tower of Babel.

It is clear that after the Greet Flood that new Giants reappeared (not as monstrously big as before the Great flood) but without the same powers and technology that was afforded before the Great Flood.

God not only got rid of disobedient mankind, but he also put big restrictions on the Fallen angels and their sons the giants who when they died or were killed in battle became the disembodied spirits of the giants known today as demons.

Before the Great flood mankind could see both the fallen angels and their sons the Giants. After the Great Flood mankind could no longer see the Fallen angels and the original Pre-Flood giants as they were now invisible or in a different dimension.

So, there were many things that were very different after the Great Flood as compared with before the Great Flood.

What I have written above are two different possibilities as to when many of the cyclopean structures and buildings were actually built.

I would still like to see some archaeologists take a big interest in digging up the massive stone Fortifications that we have stumbled across here in Scotland.

(Update 2022. When phoning those in charge in Edinburgh, Scotland, I was told that it was 'in the best interests of the underground buildings that they be kept buried in order to preserve them'. – Imagine what utter lunacy! No, they

simply don't want to face the ramifications of such discoveries that will prove their so-called science of Evolution totally wrong, so keep the old buildings buried as much as possible as we the authorities don't want to hear about giants and their possible ramifications in our past history. – author S N Strutt 21/10/2022)

Giants Before the Great Flood

According to the Bible there were many races of Giants living in the 500 years leading up to the Great Flood who could have been 35 feet high or higher. Where did these giants originate from?

According to the Bible they were the offspring of Fallen Angels and human women. – See my books of 'Jasher Insights' book I & II which was published on August 6th, 2019 – As well as 'Enoch Insights' (which was published in April 2018). My latest book 'Jubilees Insights' will come out later this year of 2019.

We cannot build these structures today

We modern humans are not strong enough to build these ancient cyclopean structures at least not without advanced technology:

Let's do a little maths to prove the point: we just saw some cyclopean structures with rocks carefully piled the one on top of the other for around 15 meters high. Each stone could have weighed 13-20 tons. 1 ton is 1000 kilos. The average man lifting a 50-kilo rock today would struggle. 20 tons = 20,000 kilos Divide this by 50 = 400. This is stating that it would take 400 men to get under such a rock and lift it, but it is physically impossible to get 400 men under a rock that measures 2 x 2 x 21/2 metres.

Similarly at Baalbek where there are slabs of stone 90 feet long by 15 feet wide and 12 feet high with a weight of 3000 tons it would take 240,000 men to lift it assuming each man carried a weight of 50 kilos each. As massive as the slabs of stone are it would be physically impossible to get that many men under the rock to lift it up and move it. So how where these massive stones moved so easily in Pre-flood times? One thing is for certain: the old versions of thousands of slaves in Egypt helping to create the pyramids is simply impossible. They were created much earlier in Pre-flood times by a giant race which had advanced technology.

Evidence: There is concrete evidence that before the Great Flood there were massive giants of at least 35 feet high. These giants also had access to ancient, advanced technologies such as levitation and anti-gravity. With such technology it would have been child's play for the giants which would appear to us as giants playing with kids blocks and quickly forming them into a big structure of rock without even using mortar just as a child today with his kid's blocks. What is today impossible for modern man was in fact very easy for the giant culture of pre-flood times.

All over the world

From India to China to South America to North America to Scotland and Stonehenge in England in particular as well as parts of Europe and over to Sardinia in the Mediterranean we see these giant structures

CHAPTER 10

VITRIFIED ROCKS – IN SCOTLAND
https://youtu.be/S75GzpTbO0A?t=3

HERE IS THE write-up from this video: Scotland is a country which holds many mysterious tales of ancient beings who were said to once dwell within the astonishingly beautiful highlands. From fairies to ancient sea monsters many a legend is to be found here including the odd piece of compelling evidence to back up such claims. However, our next Scottish mystery of focus is abundant with evidence, in fact, the evidence left surrounding this mysterious ancient technology is actually the mystery itself, over 200 years ago archaeologists exploring the ancient ruins found to dot the rural countryside, began to notice a remarkable characteristic of about 60 mysterious structures found dotting the Scottish Highlands. Made using rocks with no mortar (Cyclopean), instead the rocks on the outer layer of these structures upon completion, went through an as yet, unknown process of vitrification (fused to glass by intense heat) , the builders of these extremely ancient forts, were somehow able to heat the stones to such a degree that the outer layer actually turned to glass, fixing the stones in place and making them virtually impenetrable to erosion, meaning that the true age of these miraculous structures maybe far, far older that we are lead to believe. Although for the first 250 years of study these forts were presumed to have been exclusive to Scotland, thanks to the results of the research, they have actually begun to turn up in other regions of the world most specifically western Europe. With such overwhelming evidence, in the face of adversity, academia it would seem have reluctantly been resigned to agreeing with the extremely controversial facts displayed within these ancient stone forts, quote. "No lime or cement has been found in any of these structures, all of them presenting the peculiarity of being more or less consolidated by the fusion of the rocks of which they are built. This fusion, which has been caused by the application of intense heat, is not equally complete in the various forts, or even in the walls of the same fort. In some cases the stones are only partially melted and calcined; in others their adjoining edges are fused so that they are firmly cemented together; in many instances pieces of rock are enveloped in a glassy enamel-like coating which binds them into a uniform whole; and at times, though rarely, the entire length of the wall presents one solid mass of vitreous substance. It is not clear why or how the walls were subjected to vitrification." End quote. Although the explanation put forward after examining these facts, could be seen as a desperate attempt to continue to deny the existence of a highly aware, highly capable, intercontinental ancient civilisation, which once flourished here on our planet. Who built these forts? What clearly advanced, yet ancient heat technology did they use to turn the outer casing stones to glass? With the pace of such discoveries being revealed to the world increasing, it is only a matter of time before we find out. http://www.worldheritageireland.ie/sk... https://en.wikipedia.org/wiki/Vitrifi...

CHAPTER 11

ANCIENT ATOMIC WAR

Was There A Pre-Historic Atomic War In Ancient India & Other Places On Earth?

WHAT IS NOW left of the ancient Rama empire in India west of Jodhpur – in what today is called the That desert also has buildings fused together as if hit by an atomic blast 5000+ years ago – http://veda.wikidot.com/ancient-city-found-in-india-irradiated-from-atomic-blast

Machu Picchu -Peru -South America http://cdn.media.kiwicollection.com/media/property/PR000846/xl/000846-02-macchu-picchu.jpg

Baalbek – Lebanon https://www.ancient-origins.net/opinion-guest-authors/forgotten-stones-baalbek-lebanon-001865

Baalbek- Lebanon: The Stone of the South' at Baalbek, Lebanon is the largest worked monolith on Earth, weighing in at a staggering 1242 tons. It is even heavier than the 'Stone of the Pregnant Woman' which weighs an estimated 1000 tons, which sits on the other side of the road in the quarry. Neither of these stones made it to the main 'Temple of Jupiter', some 900 metres to the northeast, but some 400-ton and 800-ton stones did make their way to the temple, were raised 20 feet into the air and were placed with machine-like precision into the foundations of this mighty ancient complex. The heaviest slab weighed in at an astounding 3000 tons & was discovered recently at an ancient quarry and never made it out of the quarry – probably due its extreme weight – well that is the official position. or was it that a cataclysm overtook the megalithic ancient builders such as the great flood of Noah?

There are also many spin-offs from these cyclopean ancient structures project for which some would prefer to keep it all hushed up. why? Possibly because it goes against the paradigm used for controlling the opinions of the masses: evolution. according to the science taught in our schools, man is evolving and supposedly getting taller and stronger and smarter.

These massive rocks that we have found formed into cyclopean walls would prove otherwise. It would appear that a race of giants much bigger and smarter than man was on this planet in the very far past who had very advanced technologies such as anti-gravity and levitation. If you want to think they were 'visiting aliens', then that is up to you.

Personally, I believe in the Bible & that there was a Great Flood 4500 years ago. Before the Great Flood, there were massive giants in the lands during

Noah's time. They were the sons of the Fallen Angels according to Genesis 6, and were both much stronger than mankind and also had supernatural powers similar to the demi-gods and gods of old time like Zeus and Hercules, Pan, Hermes etc.

Here below are some of the related topics which I have dug up so far which also confirm things I have written about in my books including the 1st book I about the paranormal: 'Out of the Bottomless Pit' Book I

Cyclopean Giant Structures Under The Oceans:

Tunnels Underground From Scotland To Turkey http://www.outofthebottomlesspit.co.uk/421401449

CHAPTER 12

IS SCIENCE WRONG?

I) Is EVOLUTION the sacred cow of science wrong? We have been taught that man is evolving and getting bigger and stronger and smarter as he evolves but ancient cyclopean structures would paint a totally different picture – that there used to be a gigantic race of people in antiquity (Pre-Flood or more than 4500 years ago) all over the world as mentioned by most cultures.

II) Mankind Is Actually Devolving But Does Not Know IT: https://youtu.be/VzHPqfJrIjE

III) Pre-Flood Wars Using Advanced Technology

Most cultures around the world mention advanced technology in pre-historic times and the ability to levitate large stones such as in the building of the pyramids and other large cyclopean structures. India has some fantastic books such as the VEDA which describe in detail ancient wars using advanced technology like atom bombs and flying machines.

Apparently, this is why there are old walls fused together like glass in countries like Scotland and India as well as other countries. This is exactly what happened in the late forties and fifties when the USA did atomic and hydrogen bomb tests in the Nevada desert. The sand turned to glass at the very high temperatures.

CHAPTER 13

THE PYRAMIDS WERE NOT BUILT BY THE EGYPTIANS

Another import fact is that the Egyptians did not build the pyramids – but they inherited them in their land after the Great Flood. Other cultures which came later all around the world did not build the pre-historic cyclopean structures. However, both the Greeks and Romans built their buildings on top of the massive cyclopean slabs of rock. Man since the Great Flood has not been able to duplicate the cyclopean buildings and structures as it takes exceptional precision, skills in many fields of study and great brute strength – something that modern man simply does not have. The Great Pyramid & similar structures. In using simple maths and physics it becomes quite clear that man could not have built these large structures where sometimes each rock was 20 -100 tons or more. These stones were fitted together perfectly. The Great pyramid is made up of almost 1000 million such stones. How was it done? We can't even do it today in modern times with our massive cranes etc. it is not just the rocks themselves which are fitted together with such razor-blade precision, but they were mostly built without any mortar to hold them together. The amazing thing is that man's modern building like hotels last 30 years before they start to break down and yet the oldest buildings of the planet are still standing. When one sees thee structures up close and personal one stands in awe realizing that we in modern times do not have a rational explanation from these structures which were certainly not built by the Egyptians. They did not have the know-how. Megalithic Structure Built Before Mankind: https://youtu.be/dtxC3oMWp44?t=87

According to Steve Quayle and other experts like Timothy Alberino on the Pre-Flood giants there used to be many different sized giants and some that were over 35 feet tall. A race of giants probably wouldn't have a problem lifting those massive stones.

I am convinced that the giant races used to have a form of levitation or anti-gravity similar to that demonstrated by modern UFO's.

v) this particular location where we discovered these very important ruins are right slap dab in the middle of a known UFO Flap area.

This area was also well used by the Druids in ancient times and there is a lot of spiritual influence in the area or paranormal experiences locally.

It does not surprise me that what we have found is probably an ancient fortress constructed by a race of giants and their slaves over 4500 years ago or in Pre-Flood times.

In doing research one finds that where there are ancient cyclopean buildings from Pre-flood times that those areas are very often UFO Flap areas and where paranormal activity is frequent. Why is that?

We have experienced all those things when visiting this area during the past 12 years. In other words, we have seen UFOs on three different occasions and also seen things that could only be described as paranormal.

Disclaimer by finders of this archaeological site in Scotland: We have deliberately not revealed the exact location of this site on video as we intend to eventually report this find to the proper authorities – in the hope that the archaeological community will be very interested in this site and perhaps get inspired to dig it all up as it could a an tourist attraction if proven to be exactly what we think it is i.e. a massive ancient cyclopean Pre-Flood fortress constructed by a race of Giants. – EARTH ORIGINS: FALLEN ANGELS & THE GIANTS: https://youtu.be/WriGCH83xoQ?t=464

CHAPTER 14

LEY-LINES

All major Cyclopean structures from the Pre-Flood times i.e., > 4500- 5000 years ago were strangely built on Ley-Lines. Why?

(http://www.ley-man.co.uk/

LEY-LINES & THE cyclopean structures. Here in Scotland, we have personally found and discovered some evidence of this. the location is a secret for now! We have found what looks like a giant fortification on top of what was two volcanoes. Most of the giant fortification had been buried by the sands of the great flood and perhaps also in part by lava from the last explosion of the volcano some 3000 years ago according to volcanic records. We will soon publish our archaeological find to the authorities. The whole area needs to be dug up and it looks like the fortifications probably down perhaps hundreds of feet and they also continues laterally for a long distance. Only God himself knows what is inside those ancient giant fortifications? We suspect that it will deliver a treasure trove of artifacts.

After discovering what could prove to be a major 'find' here in Scotland we have subsequently found out that:

1) the location fits all the criteria of ancient structures such as stone henge in England, the pyramids in Egypt and other locations around the world.

2) It is in a volcanic area (or what used to be a volcanic area)

The rocks are made of limestone. Not certain about that one yet. Apparently, the rocks here *are* made of limestone.

3) It is situated on ley-lines: these mountains where the cyclopean structures are found are also on top of a ley-line. This ley-line goes north to south through the UK. Well, it is fairly close to the ley-line when we consider that the next ley-line is 2500 miles to the west of the UK or alternatively 2500 miles to the east of the UK) to be exact: the nearest ley-line is currently about 5 miles to the west of the mountains where we discovered the ancient fortifications. (5000 years of continental drift could account for the 5-mile discrepancy in the position of the ley-line relative to the mountains and the ancient fortifications.)

4) These kinds of Cyclopean Structures are typically found In UFO flap areas

5) Paranormal activities are much more apparent in these areas.

6) Portals are also found in these areas.

7) Baalbek – Lebanon in Baalbek there are massive stone slabs weighing

3000 tons each and apparently some even bigger ones have recently been discovered in Russia.

Map of Ley-Lines: https://www.gaia-legacy.ch/the-ley-lines/

Ley-Lines: https://youtu.be/rgkhLR65qJE?t=98 in Scotland:

http://www.davidfurlong.co.uk/scotland.htm

CHAPTER 15

'ANTI-GRAVITY' AND THE WORLD GRID

WHAT IS THE World Grid? How can it be it mapped? What does it do? Why should we be concerned about it? What does it have to with anti-gravity? In my many travels around the world in search of lost cities and ancient mysteries I have often wondered if there was some link connecting many of the ancient megalithic sites. Some years ago, I discovered that there was no such thing as a coincidence. If the placement of ancient sites was no coincidence, what then was the overall organizing principle for the carefully laid out world-wide pattern?

Earth Grid, based on more primary energy lines, might be like. I say "energy lines" particularly, because one of the most consistent observations readers will encounter in this book is that the geometric pattern of the Earth Grid is energetic in nature. And that this Earth energy, organized into a precise web, was once, and can be again, the source of a free and inexhaustible supply of power, once empowering older civilizations of high technological achievement.

Most Grid theorists state confidently that this Grid technology can be reclaimed again-today.

While UFOs are a very controversial subject, which may contribute to its perennial popularity, some theorists claim that there is a fundamental relation between UFO phenomenon and magnetic-vortex-gravity-anomalies in the Grid.

Furthermore, gravity is as complex a subject as UFOs and the World Grid. 'http://exopoliticshongkong.com/uploads/anti_gravity_and_the_world_Grid_1987_pdf.pdf

IX) Ancient Maps & Grid Lines of Energy

Ex- tending the speculation back further in time, the deluge myth round in the myths of virtually all cultures can perhaps be traced to some (Atlantean?) technological endeavour that caused a partial and devastating collapse of the canopy. Before this collapse, the poles may well have been free of ice (hence the existence of maps such as Piri Reis and Buache). Polar ice caps may have formed relatively rapidly in the period of climatic disequilibrium. In this light, Cyr's Megalithic canopy theory is correspondent with our own findings in analysing Megalithic sites. We have documented in the illustrations of Ireland, Britain, and Europe which follow; a patterned interface of man-made constructions, dating to the Megalithic period, which correspond to our proposed "infrastructure" for the icosa/dodecahedral planetary grid. New evidence that we are just beginning to analyse, and which includes patterns of mounds within the central United States and the curious "lines" of the Nazca area of Peru, exhibits the same close correspondence. This proves to us that past cultures have been aware of, and attuned to, the energies of the UVG 120 Sphere. A second analogy to earth's processes

Ancient civilizations much more advanced than today:

Communication: It is clear to us that Megalithic peoples knew all that we now know about the planetary grid and then some. The stones which they so carefully placed upon ley lines were used to communicate with anyone else linked via common telluric energy flows.

X) The Earth Grid, Human Levitation And Gravity Anomalies

Knowledge of the Earth Grid or "crystalline Earth" is very ancient and has been utilized by a number of civilizations. The pyramids and ley lines are on the power transfer lines of the natural Earth gravity Grid all over the world. The Earth Grid is comprised of the geometrical flow lines of gravity energy in the structure of the Earth itself.

This has been the only known official governmental research program into the Earth Grid system. A considerable number of planes and ships had mysteriously vanished from this region, while many UFO sightings were reported, and other bizarre and unearthly phenomena were noted. (For more information, refer to Hugh Cochrane's Gateway to Oblivion, Avon Books, NY)

Energy Lines? UFO Hot Spots? Disappearances Peculiarities in gravity and magnetism were noted inside these columns, possibly related to a reduction (or weakening) in the nuclear binding forces holding matter together; the nuclear binding forces seemed stronger in the north and weaker in the south. Some of these mysterious columns appeared to be mobile changing location over time.

CHAPTER 16

BERMUDA TRIANGLES – STRANGE DISAPPEARANCES OF PEOPLE: SIGNS 2018-19 –
www.outofthebottomlesspit.co.uk

THE TEN "VILE vortices" originally taken from Ivan T. Sanderson. At these ten areas, theoretically, magnetic-gravitational anomalies take place. Nicholas R. Nelson, in his book, Paradox (1980, Dorrance & Co. Ardmore, Penn.), believes that these vortex areas are entrances to other dimensions. Such "doors" to other dimensions would account for strange disappearances and mysterious vanishings.

Meanwhile in the 20th century, because of numerous aircraft crashes in the Lake Ontario Earth Grid area. Marysburgh Vortex and regarded as "the Other Bermuda Triangle" and "the gateway to oblivion on the eastern end of Lake Ontario"), the Canadian National Research Council and U.S. Navy began Project Magnet in 1950 to investigate the area's magnetic anomalies and possible magnetic utility.

On a planet so determined by gravity, this would be only one of many such gravity-magnetic anomalies present on the Earth Grid. And underlying many of the magnetic peculiarities observed around the Earth is the special principle of diamagnetism, the root of anti-gravity.

Anti-Gravity is essentially a magnetic-neutral zone existing between a north and south magnetic field, which can be exploited for purposes of levitation. As I will indicate below, there are many such "magnetic flow reversal points" on the Earth marked by Grid points.

UFOs are using levitation to build the enormous cyclopic structures around the world:

CHAPTER 17

THE PHILADELPHIA EXPERIMENT

(SEE MY BOOK 'Out of the Bottomless Pit' book I, which talks extensively about this experiment that went terribly wrong!

Background info: the ship the Eldridge was moved in space and time from Philadelphia to the port of Norfolk in 1943 using Einstein's unified field theory.

The unified field theory- Einstein 1926: According to Valentine, Jessup believed he was "on the verge of discovering the scientific basis for whatever was happening." Jessup explained: "An electric field created in a coil induces a magnetic field at right angles to the first, and each of these fields represents one plane of space. But since there are three planes of space, there must be a third field, perhaps a gravitational one. By hooking up electromagnetic generators so as to produce a magnetic pulse it might be possible to produce this third field through the principle of resonance." Jessup thought the Navy had discovered this by accident. This brings up the interesting possibility of a fourth dimension.

'Could it be that the vessel The Eldridge ship in its dematerialized state was actually on this grid line? Could it be that the energy that makes all this possible is a magnetic field transmitted at the correct frequency by the powerful field generators aboard the ship? Maybe it is true that the Navy scientists didn't expect what resulted from their unique experiment; maybe, in fact, the results were terribly counter to the desired effects. If indeed the goal had been just to make the ships invisible to radar (similar to modern day Stealth systems), or to magnetically repel torpedoes, perhaps instead the Navy found something of much greater importance than anyone had ever imagined. It seems to me that the experiment was just that—an experiment. The purpose of the last experiment in the series was most likely the actual transport of the ship, a possibility the Navy might have learned of through earlier tests. But originally, they were looking for radar invisibility or a magnetic torpedo/mine shield. The War was going to be won on the sea and thus the opportunistic Navy exploited Einstein's misgivings about the rise of Nazi Germany to persuade him to assist the U.S. government in developing a passive protection device. In the process they found incredible mysteries regarding pulsating magnetic fields, and through the course of their experimentations, literally led themselves into the dimensional transfer of matter.

Here is my write-up on this Video: True Science: http://www.outofthe-bottomlesspit.co.uk/412513932 (Jessop an important scientist-engineer who was connected with the Philadelphia Experiment of 1943): From there he became a photographer on an archaeological expedition to the Mayan ruins in Central America. Then Jessup went to Peru to study pre-Incan culture. It was in Peru that Jessup, after studying these massive ruins with their incredible exactness and implicit construction skills, speculated that they could have been built only with the aid of levitating devices from sky ships of some sort.

Mr. Allende (who signed his letters "Carl Allen") was markedly interested in Jessops' ideas about levitation and went to great lengths to agree with Jessops' theory--—that many of our megaliths were built using the technique of levitation. In fact, he assured Jessup that levitation was not only scientifically possible but was commonplace on Earth in our recent past.

During the next year Jessup pushed for research into the unified field theory, something Einstein had worked on during the last twenty years of his life. It was this consuming interest that brought the "Philadelphia Experiment" back into the limelight. On January 13, 1956,

CHAPTER 18

TIME CONTROL

WHAT IF THOSE before the Great Flood could 'slow down' time itself making it very easy for them to build the pyramids for example. the blocks would literally 'float around' if time itself was altered in proximity of the stones. the giants having such powers is in fact very likely, because they were the sons of the Nephilim or the Watcher class of angels.

What if they could travel to other dimensions which are not limited by time?

What seems impossible to us in modern times such as lifting megalithic sized rocks and boulders of 10-100 tons weight each could have been like 'kids play' to a tall giant over 35 feet tall. we know for sure that the rocks were not put into place by normal means but by some other means such as levitation or time manipulation? how were the megaliths put into place?

Zero – point energy how the 'speed of light' used to be much greater & time of the universe itself is much shorter: proof of a creator & 6 days of creation – a must see for the scientifically minded people https://youtu.be/wm1fjf7iius?t=2601

Levitation: Tibetan Monks levitate stones by using an acoustic levitation technique with the aid of drams in this 1939 sketch by Swedish aircraft designer Henry Kjeldsen. 'We know from the priests of the far east that they were able to lift heavy boulders up high mountains with the help of groups of various sounds. The knowledge of the various vibrations in the audio range demonstrates to a scientist of physics that a vibrating and condensed sound field can nullify the power of gravitation. Swedish engineer Olaf Alexanderson wrote about this phenomenon in the publication. Implosion No. 13. The following report is based on observations which were made only 20 years ago in Tibet. I have this report from civil engineer and flight manager, Henry Kjeldsen, a friend of mine. He later on included this report in his book, The Lost Techniques. This is his report: A Swedish doctor, Dr Jarl, a friend of Kjeld

CHAPTER 19

SONIC LEVITATION

I BELIEVE THAT there is not much doubt that the Tibetans had posses-sion of the secrets relating to the geometric structure of matter, and the methods of manipulating the harmonic values, but it we can grasp the mathematical theory behind the incident, and extend the application, then an even more fascinating idea presents itself. In my last book I mentioned the flying machines described in ancient records, which flew through the air with a melodious sound, and theorised that the sonic apparatus was tuned to the harmonic unified equations. Now the Tibetans have given us a direct indication of how to construct a sonically propelled anti-gravitational flying machine. All that is necessary is to complete the circle of sonic generators, indicated by the drums, trumpets, etc., and we have a disc which creates an anti-gravitational lifting force at the centre. From this it would appear that a vehicle could be constructed that would resonate at frequencies in sympathy with the unified fields demonstrated throughout this work. It is my opinion that our own scientific establishments are far ahead in this type of research, and that many experimental vehicles have already been constructed. High frequency generators have probably taken the place of the low frequency sonic methods, and electronic systems produced which would allow complete control of movement.

Anti-Gravity and the World Grid

A magnetic field defies mechanical interpretation. In addition, when UFOs do their materializations/dematerializations, intense magnetic disturbances are always present. With these thoughts in mind let's see how the concept of a "World Grid" could be a key factor in the location and function of the alleged Philadelphia Experiment. The Philadelphia Experiment is fantastic because it disturbs our sense of what we think exists in a particular time and space. And when we speak of space and time, we invariably think of Einstein. Jessup believed Einstein's theories held the key to UFO propulsion; after all, Carl Allen had confirmed that it not only was the key, but full-scale research and experimentation of Einstein's mysterious mathematical concepts was already a reality. Researching Naval employment records, we find that Albert Einstein was hired as a scientist for the office of naval research (O.N.R.) on May 31, 1943, a post he maintained until June 30, 1944. Also on July 24, 1943, Einstein met with Naval Officers in his Princeton study—just three months prior to the Philadelphia Experiment.

UFO's Method of Travel: Alter the time paradigm! This is the secret of extra-terrestrial spacecraft; they travel by altering the space dimension by bringing time to zero.

Related: 20-ton Jars in Laos and in India. Who built them and how were they transported from a very distant quarry in ancient times? https://youtu.be/5bqPgO2H4JI?t=45

CHAPTER 20

10 TOES OF DANIEL 2 TURNING FROM CLAY TO IRON

The 'Clay' Governments of The 'Daniel 2 Image' Are All Turning To 'Iron'.

According to the **Daniel 2** prophecy of the **'Image'**, five of the World Empires were described: Gold Head of Babylon, arms and chest of silver was the dual empire of the Medio-Persians, the Chest and best of bronze was the Grecian empire. The legs of iron were Rome. The feet of partly iron and partly clay was the dictatorships and democracies that have existed in the world since the fall of the Roman Empire in around 500 AD. The 10 toes, made partly of iron and partly clay is supposed to be the coming world Anti-Christ government with its 10 world leaders.

This is where it gets interesting, as we can all clearly see that the past year and a half of Great Confusion is polarizing the nations and many former 'democracies' are turning into 'dictatorships' little by little.

It would appear that the clay part of the feet and toes of Daniel 2 are slowly but surely all turning into iron. What does it mean as in regard to Bible prophecy being fulfilled?

The fact that the toes of the Daniel 2 Image are all turning to iron shows that a massive shift has occurred in world politics and noticeably most of all in the west. for example: notice the drastic change in the governments of Australia, New Zealand, Canada and Italy, Germany, Greece, Israel. Sure, we have sometimes seen our governments getting heavy-handed about somethings, but nothing compares to the past 2 years. I suppose the same is also true in hundreds of countries all around the world during the past two years of the covid and vaccine era with all of its mandatory dictates by many governments where they proclaim sudden edicts like an old-fashioned king or queen of old without the permission of their peoples.

If we consider that the feet of iron and clay has been the situation ever since the fall of iron Rome, then 2020-2021 is seeing a worldwide change that has not occurred on such a worldwide scale since the fall of the last world Empire Rome.

What does it mean: Clay governments turning into iron ones. it means that all the nations that came out of the old roman empire which for centuries have mostly been clay in nature or democracies are turning as we speak into iron-fisted governments. Why is this happening? Now that is a very good question.

Iron represents dictatorships and clay. in the book of Isaiah it states, 'Thou art the Potter and we the people are the clay'.

If one takes the time to read about ancient democracies,[The Origin Of Democracies: The Origins of Democracy – Biblical Archaeology Society] it was mostly the Greeks that entertained such disciplines. However, the type of democracies that we have had in the WEST until the past two years are very different in structure than what came in ancient times, and which did not even last very long. In looking at the Image of the feet of partly clay and toes, I was wondering why would the 'ruling elite' decide centuries ago to create democracy? I think that 'they' collectively decided that perhaps if 'they' gave the people the 'illusion' of 'choice' in many areas, that perhaps 'they' could gain even more power, money and control through 'deception', instead of being 'right in the face' of the people as 'absolute monarchs' with their 'dictates' of 'Do what I say or you will be executed, as in the days of 'absolute monarchs'!' So, they started to give the people what they lacked: Free schooling, food, benefits etc- whilst of course they 're-educated the minds of the masses or the 'goyim' to love their 'fake democratic system'. They started the 'illusion' of different political parties – though secretly 'the Powers that' had a 'hand' in all matters. There were the clay democracies in the west, but iron control was still there, in the 'background' and connected to the clay, through seemingly invisible. This way by pretending to be the friend of the poor, the rich could actually rob them much more. that is making it very simple, I know, but if true, then why have the world powers suddenly in the past two years, changed tactics back to 'draconian' controls or 'iron rule', just like the ancient Romans? this explains how 'iron could mix with clay' even if under most physical circumstances that would be impossible!

As you can see 'they' in 2022 are not so successful in certain western countries, as they are in others, as millions of people are 'awake' to their evil shenanigans.] Is it just possible that the covid argument is fast losing steam? Or is it because something else is now in place like 1000's of 5G satellites which were switched on the 7th of January 2022. 'They' don't need so much authoritarian 'control' though covid scare-mongering as they now have satellite 'control':

Proof That People Are Being Murdered By 5-G Combined With Vaccine: 5G Death Towers Activated: Flu-Like Symptoms Will Follow – Forbidden Knowledge TV

Another interesting point is that an image such as described in Daniel 2 could not actually 'stand' on feet and toes made of a mixture of iron and clay, as they are two very different substances that do not mingle together and the image should have fallen over a long time ago if it had been a literal physical image which it is clearly not. If the feet and toes all become iron, then the great image will stand or the 7th and final empire of the Anti-Christ. I don't know if that tiny point has any significance or not. What do you think?

What if? What if the past 2 years is only stage one of the New World Order to take over the world? It would seem in some ways that they have been successful but in other ways they have not been as they simply do not have the confidence of half the population at least.

Could the past 2 years have been a Psych-op? The formula used by the NWO is Problem, Reaction, Solution. The Powers that be do have a major headache right now as they are finding that they cannot control the nations by simple brute force and by mandates. To anyone listening to what has been going on for the past 2 years – the stooges of the Powers that are trying to totally take over the world such as Fauci, Biden, Bill Gates were all trained by Shwaub, The 'Great Reset' guy. Another one is George Soros the front man of the Illuminati. They are all really making their names to stink by all of their lies. What if this is a deliberate ploy of Satan and soon to come Anti-Christ?

According to the scriptures the Anti-Christ is going to start off as Mr Nice Guy and not a monster like the ones we have seen during the past two years who have been trying to impose Vaccine Mandates on all the peoples of the world. Untested Vaccines that can be deadly!

Why do I mention Daniel 2 and in particular the feet and toes? Because we can clearly see that things have changed drastically on the world political scene in only two years of 2020-2021. Something that has never happened before all over the world at the very same time! The feet turning much more into iron as well as the 10 toes would indicate that we are going into the 10 toes of the Daniel 2 Image which toes also represent the 10 Horns of Revelations 13 and the emerging Antichrist One World Government. It would also mark the Last 7 years of man's world history

I believe that Satan himself and even his 'son' the Anti-Christ are currently using psychology on the peoples of the earth. this psychology is also used by intelligence agencies such as the CIA and many other intelligence agencies around the world. firstly, 'they' torture the subject, then eventually give them what they want according to their reactions, and how quickly they are willing to conform to the dictates being enforced at that time.

What have we seen for the past two years of covid mandates? The new world order has bombarded the peoples of this world with misinformation and even conflicting information, and then brought on imaginary crises using their big propaganda machines like the BBC and CNN and rt to lie big time to all the peoples of the world about the covid and the vaccines. Many people have ended up

Being totally confused and not knowing what to do. There have been an exceptional number of suicides during the past year.

Phase two: destabilize the nations economically – take away the supply – famine -threat of nuclear war – weather anomalies – fear, fear, fear. Create an atmosphere where most people are desperate for an answer, even if they do not know what that answer is...

Phase three: bring on 'Mr nice guy' to the rescue!

The revelation of the Anti-Christ as in 2 Thessalonians 2 As many others have already suggested, I also believe that the Revelation of the Anti-Christ will have to be something totally supernatural and not political, as in imitating the 2nd Coming of Christ, so as to totally deceive most people including millions of Christians. As some famous writers have already written, I think it likely that the Anti-Christ will show up in the heavens with a fleet of UFO's showing off his power and claiming that he has come to save mankind from self-destruction. He will also tell mankind that his race is a super race from far away in the galaxy and that mankind was 'seeded' on this planet millions of years ago – which will give the false doctrine of evolution a complete face-lift. Just read 2 Thessalonians 2. It is very strong! Using the Bible scriptures as our complete guide it is stated that the Anti-Christ will reign for 7 years. It is also stated that in the midst of the 7 years the tribulation will begin. The nations will flock to Mr nice guy -the Anti-Christ as he will do many good things for the peoples of the earth and thus deceive them by giving area material gifts to millions of peoples around the globe. Matthew 24.29-31 makes it very clear that after the great Tribulation the Lord returns to take His Bride, the true church up to heaven in the Rapture. The church does not escape to heaven before the Great Tribulation.

2 Thessalonians 2 – The Man of Sin – 'There Shall Come A Great Falling Away First' [Are many people already falling away from their 'faith in Jesus'?] -Then Shall That Man of Sin be Revealed – The Anti-Christ.

As we can all see the past year and a half had been one of '**Great Confusion**' meaning in this case great uncertainty as to 'what on earth is going to happen next?' The powers that be or the new world order clearly want to make the whole world into an iron-fisted dictatorship of some kind. will it be communistic or socialistic or A.I. controlled technocracy?

Daniel 11 'He Shall Tread the Truth to The Ground' [Isn't this exactly what we are seeing in the world today that 'The truth is being trodden to the ground'. All rhyme and reason and logic are overruled, if it does not confirm to the agenda of the NWO and their lackies the main media.]

The 10 Horns of Daniel 7 – '3 of the Horns Ripped Up by The Roots' – Are these nations the USA, UK and Israel? [Israel was part of the Roman empire 2000 years ago, and the USA emerged largely from the UK]

The 10 Horns of Revelations 13 – ''All Ten Horns of Iron – 'Give Their Power unto The Beast'

There seems to be a lot of predictive programming as shown in certain movies. Consider the movie v for vendetta which was made in 2008. In the movie the UK became a dictatorship, and the year was set as 2020! the movie had strong transhuman elements.

In looking at the biblical chapters of biblical prophecy mentioned above, I was wondering if some of it is already happening? or is it at least starting to happen and that the vaccine rollout is a fore-runner of the 'Mark of the Beast', as it is not really a vaccine at all but a type of DNA re-programming.

People have been well prepared in the past year and a half of the 'covid delusion' to be totally subservient to whatever the main media dictates to them is the truth. As George W Bush blurted out when he was president 'The Truth is whatever I say it is'. The arrogance of the Satanic Elite is mind-boggling, to say the least!

Mind-Control Of The Nations: You can see it in the fact that only one view-point is presented about something like the controversial vaccine, which should just a matter of personal opinion and conviction. Now according to all the main media if you don't take the vaccine, you are a menace to society and action should be taken against you. So much for having an opinion about anything! People's minds are largely being made up for them by the emerging One World Government. The Great Re-set is here to the elite's way of thinking.

The leaders of the world are mostly in league with Satan himself: Some years ago, many of the top world leaders were invited to go down to the Antarctic. Who did they talk to whilst down there? Who was giving them future instructions? Apparently, the Pope went down there, as did Putin of Russian and Obama of the USA at the time and many others. The only thing I can think of is that there is some connection to the **Underworld** in the **Antarctic,** or a **Portal** as mentioned by Steve Quayle.

The most highly decorated Admiral in the USA was Admiral Byrd, who claims that he went inside the hollow earth in 1947 and met the **Master of the Underworld** who gave him a message for the leaders of the nations to stop using atomic power as it affected them down inside the earth. Of course, the nations did not listen to Admiral Byrd, and he was largely vilified and ignored by the USA.

The typical unbelief of the nations in the supernatural. Well, it would appear that things have changed in modern times and the nations do know about the supernatural and the paranormal.

As in regard to Satan personified as being a Dragon sometimes and at other times like a snake. Well, what is the difference. As pointed out very well by another writer. When Satan is described as he snake, he is in his deceptive 'behind the scenes spiritual mode'. When he is described as a Dragon, he is right in your face physically ranting and raving and blurting out orders and edicts as in the Emperors of Rome and Pharoah's of Egypt.

This last year and a half we have heard the powers that be openly threatening mankind and ranting and raving and screaming to try and scare everyone to do their evil bidding. The fact that the negative evil spirits are coming more and more to the fore of this physical realm, must show that the world is indeed already getting very dark where everything is twisted to fit the N.W.O agenda.

What is interesting in my opinion is if the feet and toes of the Daniel 2 prophecy given 2500 years ago to God's prophet by the Lord were supposed to be made of partly clay and partly of iron. we know that iron represents the iron-fisted totalitarian governments such as the ancient Caesars of Rome and the satanic pharaohs of Egypt and their terrible oppression of those under them. iron represents dictatorship. clay represents the people in the scriptures and thus the feet being partly clay. Clay governments by the people are the democracies. The Daniel 2 Image showing the feet as partly clay and partly iron represented the fact that in the last days after the legs of Rome, which were built of Iron fell, that from that point in history onwards the governments that emerged from the former Roman empire would be a mixture of both dictatorships and democracies. The fact that the feet and toes were partly clay and partly iron I very interesting when considered from the point of view of politics today. Especially concerning the Western world which mostly came out of the former Roman Empire we are finding countries like Australia which used to pride themselves in being so liberal have turned into a monstrous dictatorship in the past two years. Canada is pretty much in the same boat along with New Zealand. The USA and the UK are also becoming dictatorial. It is interesting because for centuries we have had this mixture of Iron and Clay Governments but all of a sudden that is changing which would indicate that the world is fact-tracking its way to the very end of the world. I expect the 'Rising of the Anti-Christ' to happen shortly and for us to enter into the time of the 10 toes of Daniel which represent the 10 horns from Revelations 13. I would like to point out that what the leaders of this world have done in the past two years is very obviously blatantly arrogant and distasteful, and in many cases plain violent against their own countries. According to the bible the coming Anti-Christ figure will not behave the same way that we have seen the politicians of so many nations behave. Why? It states in the Bible the Anti-Christ shall come in peacefully and obtain the world by flatteries or intrigue. It also clearly states that he will do that which his fathers or ancestors have not done -he will divide the spoil or riches with the poor in order to gain their favour. It is stated in the Protocols of the learned Elders of Zion, that when their man or their false messiah the Anti-Christ shall come to power that they will then remove all traces of their obvious tricks and shenanigans such as you have seen the NWO perpetrate during the past two years with their total confusion and madness of the covid lie and resultant hellish vaccines which are not vaccines at all and worst of all – untested. What we have seen during the past 2 years is what is called in the CIA a psych operation as shown clearly in George Orwell's book 1984 with the 'Ministry of Truth' which actually only tells lies. In order to deliberately cause confusion and to wear down the people by mandates and contradictory information. One week saying one thing and the next week the exact opposite. There is no rhyme and reason or common sense to the behaviour of people like Biden and Fauci. These guys have been clearly taken over by demons or aliens or reptilians as some would say. It would appear that what we have seen in the past 2 years is only stage 1 of the New World Order drama. The next stage will be the rising of Mr Nice Guy the Bible's notorious Antichrist who will be heralded by Israel as the Messiah. Someone who wins the confidence of most people on the planet will have to behave in a very different way that the politicians of the earth have done during 2020 – 2021 during the crisis serious. The crisis of the so-called Covid Pandemic. This is always the formula of the elite. Sometimes they speak the truth and sometimes lies or half-truths depending on what they are after. The media has gotten much worse this past two years and they are generally not reporting what is really going on in the world but are following a 'fixed agenda' or narrative from those 'controllers above them and who own their companies.

War, Famine, & Resultant 'Economic Collapse' On A World Scale to Usher In A 'New Credit System' For The Survivors!

The 4 Horsemen were running rampant with 'Death shots from Covid'.

Now It Is Phase 2: NWO trying to provoke a nuclear war to destroy mankind.

In a world where most of the leaders are insane it would not surprise me, if Famine will be used as a weapon to force the world into the New World Order 'Reset' of tight electronic controls in all areas of human life.

According to Nostradamus circa 1555, he foresaw a terrible 'Famine' starting in the End times in one place, and then becoming 'universal' or all over the world.

In a world where most of the leaders are insane, it would not surprise me, if **War** and resulting Famine will be used as a weapon to force the world into the satanic 'New World Order' of tight electronic control in all areas of life.

The satanic elite, which rule the planet at the present time, do it through their stooges in Power – the bankers and politicians and the very wealthy.

These elite, have proven time and time again, that they have no regard for human life.

Satan has been trying to eliminate mankind ever since the days of Adam and Eve. There is no sanity in Satan, who has been in direct rebellion against God for 6000 plus years.

Satan simply wishes to destroy all of God's Creation by one method or the other.

It is so tragic that the world is heading in the same direction as in Pre-Flood times.

I believe that we will see a return of the Pre-flood gods and demi-gods to the earth.

The world has to get into such a mess that only supernatural intervention can save it!

What if Satan who seems to have been the 'King of empires' throughout all history in possessing some of its most evil leaders such as Adolf Hitler of many during World War II and Nero and Caligula of the ancient Roman empire and many others – what if he manipulates the whole world economic and political systems, and sets it all up so that we will be drowned by serious wars, pandemics, upheavals, confusions, economic collapse, so that he can finally bring on Mr Nice Guy The Anti-Christ.

Finally, a world leader who 'does what he says', and also is kind to the peoples of the earth, instead of being directly cruel and oppressive. Well, at least for a season or around 3 and a half years according to scriptures in both Daniel and the Book of Revelations.

After 3 and a half years he becomes the worst world dictator in history, and the Great Tribulation of 3 and a half years mentioned by Jesus in Matthew 24 shall begin.

SEE MY 7 INSIGHTS BOOKS: WHAT IS GOING ON ?! – www. outofthebottomlesspit.co.uk

'ENOCH INSIGHTS' BOOK – www.outofthebottomlesspit.co.uk

SEE MY 'TEN TOES OF DANIEL 2 CLASS' ON YOUTUBE (3) THE "TEN TOES" IN DANIEL 2 – And the Coming Antichrist – with Steven Strutt – YouTube
BIBLE CLASS ON THE 'CLAY TOES' OF 'DANIEL 2' ALL TURNING TO IRON IN 2020-2022- showing that the 'LAST 7 YEARS of World History' is about to begin – See my webpage: ALL MY ARTICLES BLOG – www.outofthebottomlesspit.co.uk

CHAPTER 21

THE 4 HORSEMEN

1) 1st Horse: Conquering Leadership

And I saw and behold a white horse: and he that sat on him had a bow; and a crown was given unto him: and he went forth conquering, and to conquer'.

2) 2nd Horse: Planned Wars And there went out another horse that was red: and power was given to him that sat thereon to take peace from the earth, and that they should kill one another: and there was given unto him a great sword.

3) 3rd Horse: Wealth Imbalance And when he had opened the third seal, I heard the third beast say, Come and see. And I beheld, and lo a black horse; and he that sat on him had a pair of balances in his hand.

[6] And I heard a voice in the midst of the four beasts say, A measure of wheat for a penny, and three measures of barley for a penny; and see thou hurt not the oil and the wine.

[7] And when he had opened the fourth seal, I heard the voice of the fourth beast say, Come and see.

4) 4th Horse: Death and Hell And I looked, and behold a pale horse: and his name that sat on him was Death, and Hell followed with him. And power was given unto them over the fourth part of the earth, to kill with sword, and with hunger, and with death, and with the beasts of the earth.

It was predicted in 1555 by Nostradamus that a great famine would engulf the whole world.

Luke 21:11 – And great earthquakes shall be in divers places, and famines, and pestilences; and fearful sights and great signs shall there be from heaven.

What to expect in the months and years to come? In a word: famine! there are so many articles showing that at one time famine came because of lack of rain or because of a mini-ice-age or some other natural cause. now, however famine is caused artificially by geo-engineering and by Haarp and controlling the jet-stream. that is just one of the tools in the hands of the 'controllers' The insane 'controllers' get to decide who gets the rain and who gets drought.

That is already a fact and not fiction. Take a look at the following articles along this line of 'controlled famine' or the 3rd and 4th horsemen of the Book of Revelation. the 2nd black horseman of engineered war is already afoot in Ukraine. The 1st horsemen of demonic & insane leadership are leading the whole world into insanity and darkness, which will culminate in the infamous 'Mark of the Beast' of Revelation 13 and destruction – simply put – 'electronic implants' of transhumanism, which will soon be forced upon the citizens of

planet earth. 'The economic forum' along with the un and all of their communist 'stooges' are leading the whole world into famine, poverty and ruin and
complete enforced slavery:

My advice to all apart from being careful with money and not to be extrav-
agant: Be careful with use of water, gas, electricity. Don't go out excessively
using lots of gasoline. Grow some of your own food. Prepare like never before
if you haven't already done so!

If you don't want to be forced to eat bugs in the future:- 'UK School
Children' To Be Fed Bugs To Stop Climate Change: UK School Children To
Be Fed Bugs To Stop Climate Change (humansbefree.com)

It might be a good time to stock up on good survival food and water etc.
The globalists like to boast that we will soon all be eating bugs! The bad joke is
that many of the bees, ladybugs and insects are quickly disappearing because
of chemtrails, and we are personally noticing it!

The Russians also think that the 4 horsemen are already riding forth:
Medvedev (former president of Russia): "The horsemen of the apocalypse
are galloping ahead": **Hal Turner Radio Show – Uh Oh! Medvedev: "The
Horsemen of the Apocalypse are galloping ahead"'**

Control Food And You Control The People': Food Plant Fires,
Explosions, Plane Crashes, Recalls And Ongoing Shortages Are Decimating
Our Food Supply **"Control Food And You Control People" (allnewspipe-
line.com)**

**They Want to Starve Us to Death: Paul Stramer – Lincoln County
Watch: Starve us into submission**

Britons warned of winter blackouts: 'Electricity across the UK could be
rationed as the energy crisis deepens, London says'

'As many as six million British households could be subjected to power
cuts this winter if Russian gas supplies to Europe stop, The Times reported
Sunday, citing a Whitehall document.': Britons warned of winter blackouts
— RT Business News

Amos 8.11 Spiritual Famine: 'Behold the days come saith the Lord God
that I will send a famine in the land, not a famine of bread, nor a thirst of
water, but of hearing the words of the Lord.' Amos 8:11 – Behold, the days
come, saith the Lord GOD, that I will send a famine in the land, not a famine
of bread, nor a thirst for water, but of hearing the words of the LORD:

Amos 8.4-5 Physical Famine: 'Hear this, O ye that swallow up the needy,
even to make the poor of the land to fail, 5 Saying, When will the new moon
be gone, that we may sell corn? and the sabbath, that we may set forth wheat,

making the ephah small, and the shekel great, and falsifying the balances by deceit?

Psalms 107:34 – A fruitful land into barrenness, for the wickedness of them that dwell therein.

Matthew 24:7 – For nation shall rise against nation, and kingdom against kingdom: and there shall be famines, and pestilences, and earthquakes, in divers places.

Proof that there was a great flood followed by a sudden 'freezing' thousands of years ago? The pyramids were made before the Great Flood! – did a portal cause the disappearance of one of the scientific teams sent to the Antarctic in 2012 – just like the infamous Bermuda Triangle!

US marines deployed in the Antarctica to explore ancient pyramids: US Marines deployed in Antarctica to explore ancient pyramids discovered by US and European researchers in 2012

CHAPTER 22

THE HOLLOW EARTH:

(SEE MY YOUTUBE Video Showing That The Earth Might Be Hollow: (34) 'HOLLOW EARTH' & 'HOLES AT THE POLES' – PARANORMAL – -by S.N.Strutt VIDEO 1 – YouTube)

THE EARTH IS IN FACT HOLLOW HOLLOW EARTH? – www. outofthebottomlesspit.co.uk

'You are simply not going to believe this! Now the scientists are finally coming out with things that only were reported before by Stephen Strutt and Steve Quayle and people that I personally know...' (there are probably more people) – on amazing things almost unbelievable -- and they are reporting it like it's "old news" that doesn't surprise the modern scientific community at all! – Comment by John Benjamin

https://www.skywatchtv.com/2019/02/24/did-scientists-just-locate-sheol-hades-mountain-ranges-discovered-400-miles-beneath-earths-crust-bigger-than-everest/

https://www.dailymail.co.uk/sciencetech/article-6709433/Mountains-buried-400-miles-underground-BIGGER-Everest.html

http://www.skywatchtv.com/

HOLLOW EARTH? – www.outofthebottomlesspit.co.uk

'Hollow Earth' Blog: Pact Made To Rule The Outer Earth? Hollow Earth – Blog – www.outofthebottomlesspit.co.uk

CHAPTER 23

THE SPHINX AND THE PYRAMIDS IN EGYPT

The 'Power' Of The 'Sphinx'

WHY THE 'THE Illuminati have no power without the Sphinx – as stated by John Todd?

I found the following link about the '4 Powers of the Sphinx'. [Disclaimer -the following link is from the 'dark side', but it does provide some knowledge and insight]: -The Four Powers of the Sphinx – Temple of the Dark Moon (templedarkmoon.com)

I think the answer to this question might be in going all the way back to the time of the Fallen angels, and their many escapades in the **Book of Enoch** and **Genesis 6** in the Bible.

Initially according to the **Books of Enoch, Jasher, Jubilees** the Fallen angels came down and co-habited with certain human woman.

Not all women, only the licentious daughters of Cain according to '**The Antiquities of the Jews**' by Flavius Josephus.

The Fallen angels had a problem in that they were looking for a realm or a dimension where they could get away from the 'Presence of God', and they wanted to procreate with human women so that they could sire off-spring.

Unfortunately for them as God's blessing was not with them their children by women turned out to be massive Giants and even monsters.

See the **Book of the Giants**. In the **Book of Enoch CHAPTER 9-10**

God told his top angels to incite the Giants to fight the one against the other until they were all slain.

Enoch 10.5 'And Gabriel said unto the Lord 'Proceed against the bastards and the reprobates, and against the children of Fornication, the children of the Watchers from amongst men, and cause them to go forth. Send them one against the other that they may destroy one another in battle. For length of days they shall not have.

THE GREAT FLOOD.

All the Giants and monsters had been destroyed by the time of the Great Flood.

Monsters: The monsters were created by the Fallen ones because when many of the giants died, they found themselves 'trapped' in a lower dimension around the earth or below it. They were crying out to their fathers the Fallen angels to somehow rescue them and bring them back onto the physical plane.

The Fallen angels succeeded to doing many different things to bring back the spirits of the Giants including after the Great Flood at least for a season. This brings up another big topic of 'Portals' which we can discuss later.

The Fallen angels had to find a body that God had simply not created in order to put one of the Giant's spirits into. The Fallen angels found that the answer was in mixing the DNA of humans and animals and birds and many other aberrations.

The Sphinx came into existence in this manner. The Sphinx is part human, part Lion, part bull with the wings of an Eagle.

This creature was not created by God, so that meant that the Fallen angels' sons from before the Great Flood (known as the disembodied spirits of the Giants or what we would call 'demons') could easily possess this creature. It was much easier for the demons to possess a body' or chimera that God simply had not created, and thus were totally under the control of Satan.

Apparently, just before the Great Flood, the world was infested with both Giants and Monsters such as the Sphinx and countless Chimeras.

It is possible that just as Satan was a Cherubim or a type of Chimera, that in his Satanic pyramid structure of leadership that he has certain Chimeras at the very top of his power structure, in the same way that God has his Seraphim and Cherubim. A sort of imitation of sorts of what God does.

In the satanic world, you have Satan at the top, then these strange Chimeras, the Devils (Fallen angels) then their sons the demons.

On earth Satan's top representatives such as the Rothschilds and the Rockefellers and below them the Illuminati.

It is very possible as John Todd stated that the Illuminati get their power from the Sphinx in Egypt because that's where the '7 Satanic kingdoms of mankind' began after the Flood.

1)Egypt followed by 2) Assyria, 3) Babylon, 4) Media-Persia, 5) Greece, 6) Rome and soon the 7) Anti-Christ.

The Sphinx is simply a top part of the satanic structure of leadership of which the brick and stone Sphinx image in Egypt is just an Idol to worship- for the satanists.

The Anti-Christ and the 7th worldwide Empire of man will also have a lot to do with Egypt and its satanic powers of the sphinx

It is interesting that all the 7 world empires all had chimeras as their idols and their gods.

Is this all symbolism or is there a much deeper meaning in that these Chimeras actually exist on a lower satanic plane.

The coming Anti-Christ called the 'Beast' in Revelation 13 also is denoted as a '7- headed chimera', which is given power by a 7-headed Red Dragon of Revelation 12 infamy. The fact that the 7-headed Red Dragon gave the Beast its Power its seat and its authority according to Revelations 13 shows clearly that Satan had been the King of the head of all the 6 World empires of the past and by inference the one that is yet to come.

Look at the chimera Image that was just put outside of the UN main building In New York city. **UN Puts Up Giant Statue in New York That Resembles "Beast" Described in the Book of Revelation – NewsRescue. com**

This image of the Beast is supposed to represent 'World Peace' They have replaced the 'Dove with an Olive branch' in her mouth from the times of Noah and the Great Flood with a monstrous chimera.

I think that a chimera like that one looks like it represents devouring and not certainly peace. it reminds me of the sphinx. she is infamous for asking questions of her potential victims. If they could answer her riddle, then they might live, but if not then she simply devoured them.

EGYPTIAN HISTORY? WHO BUILT THE PYRAMIDS?

Steve Quayle: "Has evidence been uncovered that ties all the earth's pyramids to the fallen angels creating them? This 3,000-year-old carved panel, dated from the China's Genghis Khan era, shows an alien Aztec connection 3,000 years before the Aztec empire! Note the head shape! This is obviously why Spielberg used this head shape in Indiana Jones and the crystal skull. Their giant offspring did settle in Egypt, and this is why the pharaohs wore the conical head pieces they did – and Cairo means city of Mars! These beings also built all of Mexico's pyramids! Note the immense size of the giants and giantesses! This is just a small sample of what I'll be revealing in Branson this year. Don't miss out on these startling revelations."

3,000-Year-Old Carved Panel From China.

To See This Amazing Carved Panel Here Is The Link To Steve Quayle's Website: **https://mailchi.mp/gensix/true-legends-branson-2020-conference-invitation-to-register-967361?e=ea351a08e8**

AMERICA THE GREAT WHORE OF REVELATION 17 & 18

INTRODUCTION: THE FOLLOWING was originally written in the 70's and I think it is still true and very accurate description of the **Great Whore of Revelations 13,17-18** – (the author November 2022.)

Ezekiel 37-38 is mentioned as in regards to **GOG** and Russia invading ISRAEL, in the time of the End. Damascus will be destroyed **(Isaiah 17.1)**. Israel will start **WWIII,** by attacking and destroying Damascus, which will supposedly trigger World War III.

Then the argument is put forth that in order for Russia to attack Israel, first of all Russia will have to destroy the USA, and that they will use an EMF pulse weapon..

However, a little research shows that the military in the USA and in particular all the Deep State, Underground Facilities are all protected from the E.M.P.

They could indeed use the situation to get rid of 90% of Americans, whilst they hide underground.

However, God is not mocked, and we know from **Revelations 17-18** that eventually the **USA** will be totally burned with fire and will be totally destroyed, never to rise again!

God is not the author of confusion. I like the following quote by Bible a prophecy expert: 'Even the Devil himself in the form of the Anti-Christ, will not make such a mess of the world as stupid disobedient mankind has done'. The Devil, in the form of the Anti-Christ does not want the world to be destroyed but wants to have a world to rule over.'

Some scientists try to make the argument, that people will still be able to survive in the USA after an E.M.P, and the last 3rd of the movie is talking about one of the USA'S favourite subjects: Survival, which also is a *real money maker, and preys upon people's fears!*

However, we must face the following facts. What does it *actually say* in the 'Book of Revelation Chapters 17-18?

Talking about the coming *New World Order* and the *Anti-Christ* and his leaders: REV.17:10 'And there are seven kings: five are fallen, and one is, and the other is not yet come; and when he cometh, he (Anti-Christ) must continue a short space.'

REV.17:12 And the ten horns which thou saw are ten kings, which have received no kingdom as yet; but receive power as kings one hour with the beast.

REV.17:13 These have one mind and shall give their power and strength unto the beast.

The total destruction of the USA, however, won't happen according to Revelation 17-18 until the Beast or Anti-Christ is in power, and the 10 leading nations of Europe give their total power and strength to the Beast and turn violently against USA. Nations that today are her allies.

I don't see the USA only being hit by an EMP weapon, but total destruction:

REV.18:8 Therefore shall her plagues come in one day, death, and mourning, and famine; and she shall be utterly burned with fire: for strong is the Lord God who judges her.

Does God tell His people to stick around in the USA and just hope for the best and get survival together? I don't think so.

Once the USA is to be destroyed it will be both total and irreversible. God tells those of his people in the USA to get out of the USA, and not merely try to survive:

REV.18:4 And I heard another voice from heaven, saying, 'Come out of her, my people, that ye be not partakers of her sins, and that ye receive not of her plagues.'

Another important point is to realize that God Himself is in perfect control of world events, one way or the other.

The forces of Evil and even Satan himself are all subject to God's greater will and plan.

Matthew 5.18 'Not one jot or tittle will fail from the law but all will be exactly fulfilled.'

It is the A.C. who gives the order to totally destroy the USA, sometime near the end of the great tribulation and not before.

I'm not saying that a great confusion won't come to the USA prior to the 'rise of the Anti-Christ.' I think it will and will trigger the 'rise of the Anti-Christ'.

all the survivalists in the USA would be much better spending their time and money encouraging all the true believers in Jesus, to get out of the USA, asap!

THE 2ND COMING OF CHRIST:

Sadly, most of the churches teach the False Doctrine of The 'Pre-Tribulation Rapture', which false doctrine just puts most people to sleep spiritually.

As a result of the pre-Tribulation false doctrine, it shows that most church Christians don't even know their bibles! *So how can they possibly be prepared for what is coming?* They can't even notice basic End-time verses about the timing of the Great Tribulation and the Rapture afterwards!

Jesus couldn't have made it easier to understand in Matthew 24-29-31:

MAT.24:29 Immediately *after the tribulation* of those days shall the sun be darkened, and the moon shall not give her light, and the stars shall fall from heaven, and the powers of the heavens shall be shaken:

MAT.24:30 And then shall appear the sign of the Son of man in heaven: and then shall all the tribes of the earth mourn, and they shall see the Son of man coming in the clouds of heaven with power and great glory.

MAT.24:31 And he shall send his angels with a great sound of a trumpet, and they shall gather together his elect from the four winds, from one end of heaven to the other.

THE COMING 'ANTI-CHRIST':

2TH.2:2 That ye be not soon shaken in mind, or be troubled, neither by spirit, nor by word, nor by letter as from us, as that the day of Christ is at hand.

2TH.2:3 Let no man deceive you by any means: for that day shall not come, except there come a falling away first, and that man of sin be revealed, the son of perdition;

2TH.2:4 Who opposes and exalts himself above all that is called God, or that is worshipped; so that he as God sits in the temple of God, shewing himself that he is God.

2TH.2:5 Remember ye not, that, when I was yet with you, I told you these things?

2TH.2:6 And now ye know what withholds that he might be revealed in his time.

2TH.2:7 For the mystery of iniquity doth already work: only he who now lets will let, until he be taken out of the way.

2TH.2:8 And then shall that Wicked be revealed, whom the Lord shall consume with the spirit of his mouth, and shall destroy with the brightness of his coming:

2TH.2:9 Even him, whose coming is after the working of Satan with all power and signs and lying wonders,

2TH.2:10 And with all deceivableness of unrighteousness in them that perish; because they received not the love of the truth, that they might be saved.

2TH.2:11 And for this cause God shall send them strong delusion, that they should believe a lie:

2TH.2:12 That they all might be damned who believed not the truth, but had pleasure in unrighteousness.

THE 3RD TEMPLE IN JERUSALEM

MAT.24:15 When ye therefore shall see the abomination of desolation, spoken of by Daniel the prophet, stand in the holy place, (whoso reads, let him understand:)

MORE ON THE ANTI-CHRIST

DAN.8:9 And out of one of them came forth a little horn, which waxed exceeding great, toward the south, and toward the east, and toward the pleasant land.

DAN.9:27 And he shall confirm the covenant with many for one week: and in the midst of the week he shall cause the sacrifice and the oblation to cease, and for the overspreading of abominations he shall make it desolate, even until the consummation, and that determined shall be poured upon the desolate.

DAN.11:22 And with the arms of a flood shall they be overflown from before him, and shall be broken; yea, also the prince of the covenant.

DAN.11:23 And after the league made with him he shall work deceitfully: for he shall come up, and shall become strong with a small people.

DAN.11:24 He shall enter peaceably even upon the fattest places of the province; and he shall do that which his fathers have not done, nor his fathers> fathers; he shall scatter among them the prey, and spoil, and riches: yea, and he shall forecast his devices against the strong holds, even for a time.

FOR MANY MORE DETAILS CONCERNING THE 14 POINTS OF THE ENDTIME SEE THE FOLLOWING LINK:

http://www.outofthebottomlesspit.co.uk/421198598

BABYLON THE GREAT

REVELATION 16:19 This Seventh Vial is it! The angel says «It is done» when he pours it out. It>s finished; this is the end for the wicked, that is.

Rev 16:18,19 "And there were voices, and thunders, and lightnings; and there was a great earthquake, such as was not since men were upon the earth, so mighty an earthquake, and so great. And the great city was divided into three parts, and the cities of the nation fell: and Great Babylon came in remembrance before God."

Babylon that great city has already been mentioned a time or two, and we have discovered that it is the great false church, both religious and commercial. We know that the destruction of Babylon has to begin in the period of Tribulation because of some other things which are said in prophecy about how the false prophet exhorts the whole world to worship only the Antichrist and only his religion, and he will cause all other religions to be stamped out, including the False Church System and the capitalistic money-worship System.

But the Whore Babylon will still be here, only in another form: That of the Antichrist's worldwide socialist/Communist empire. Many of the cities will still be here, and whether they use money or not, they will still be worshipping materialism and idols such as the Antichrist's Image of the Beast. But here, Under The Seventh Vial, Babylon Finally Gets It For The Last Time, "the cup of the wine of the fierceness of His wrath."

When the cities of the nations fall at the seventh vial, God is completing the destruction of Babylon: destroying the great towers of mammon worship, the cities of man, which are the centres for all of man's materialistic idols,

(**Jer.2:2; Isa.2:18; 30:25**) "For according to the number of thy cities are thy gods.... And the idols He shall utterly abolish...in the day of the great slaughter, when the towers fall."

REVELATION CHAPTER 17 BABYLON: THE FALSE CHURCH SYSTEM

This is one of the most important chapters in Revelation, exposing and analysing for us the relationship between the religious/commercial System and the government, or, as John so aptly describes it, the "fornication" between the "Whore" and the "kings of the Earth." This chapter is mainly `background", giving us an historical analysis of the system so we can understand how God sees it and why He so utterly destroys it in the 16th, 18th and 19th Chapters.

Rev17:1,2 "And there came one of the seven angels which had the seven vials, and talked with me, saying unto me, Come hither; I will shew unto thee the judgment of the great whore that sits upon many waters: with whom the kings of the earth have committed fornication, and the inhabitants of the earth have been made drunk with the wine of her fornication."

Rev. 17.3 "So he carried me away in the Spirit into the wilderness: and I saw a woman sit upon a scarlet-coloured beast (the same beast described in chapter 13), full of names of blasphemy, having seven heads and ten horns."

The Lord is showing us here that you have to drop out spiritually "into the wilderness" if you want to see where the whore, the system, is really at.

And John saw this "woman...arrayed in purple and scarlet colour (royal colours), and decked with gold and precious stones and pearls (precious stones have always represented the power of every economic system from the ancients' "idols of gold and silver" to today's currencies backed by gold and silver), having a golden cup in her hand full of abominations and filthiness of her fornication:

Rev 17.5 and upon her forehead was a name written, mystery, Babylon the great, the mother of harlots and abominations of the earth."

In case you don't know what "to fornicate" means, it means to unlawfully intercourse, and here it means spiritual fornication with the Devil; putting his kingdom (Babylon, the System) first in your life and serving it instead of dropping out of it to serve in God's Kingdom. (New Jerusalem.). As James said, "Ye adulterers and adulteresses, know ye not that the friendship of the world the system, Babylon) is enmity with God?

James 4:4 Whosoever therefore will be a friend of the world (the system) is the enemy of God."

Revelation 17.18 "Is that great city, which reigns over the kings of the earth."

Babel (or Babylon) was the first city man built after the flood and later in this same chapter it says this woman, Babylon, "is that great city, which reigns over the kings of the earth." So, Babylon represents the great worldwide, age-old, capitalistic commercial centres of materialism: the cities of man!

THERE ARE TWO WOMEN IN THE BOOK OF REVELATION REPRESENTING TWO KINGDOMS:

(1) New Jerusalem, the Kingdom of Christ, the Church (Chap.12),

(2) Babylon, the Whore, the System, the kingdom of the Devil. People are working for and building in one or the other.

New Jerusalem is the "glory of god" (Rev 21:11) but Babylon is the glory of man-man's greatest achievements are his cities. That's what he brags about more than anything else, his big buildings and his big cities.

But we agree with Toynbee, the historian who said, "Cities are man's festering sores on the body politic! The curse of civilization is its cities." They have always been the mother of all abominations of the Earth. And it is these centres of commercialism that are responsible for all man's wars which are always fought for the "love of money" or economic purposes and power, the power of possession of other cities.

Jam.4:1 "From whence come wars and fightings among you. Come they not hence, even of your lusts?"

It is these centres of Industrialization based on the production of war goods and idols that have polluted not only the entire Earth, air and sea, but also the hearts, minds and souls of all the inhabitants of the Earth with the "filthiness of her fornication." man's idolatry pollutes everything

1Tim.6:10 "for the love of money (material things) is the root of all evil.

Rev. 17.6 "And I saw the woman drunken with the blood of the saints, and with the blood of the martyrs of Jesus: and when I saw her, I wondered with great admiration."

The Whore has two forms, religious and commercial, but really, it's all the same as they both "go down," "for the love of money." In her religious form she's been responsible for all the martyrs of history, and in her commercial form for all the millions slain in war, as it says in

Revelation 18:24, "In her was found the blood of martyrs, and of saints, and of all that were slain upon the Earth."

When John "wondered" at her, it means he was astonished--the picture really flipped him out. So, the angel said, "Wherefore didst thou marvel? I will tell thee the mystery of the woman, and of the beast that carries her, which hath the seven heads and ten horns."

First, an explanation of the Beast:

Rev 17.8 "The beast that thou saw was, and is not; and shall ascend out of the bottomless pit and go into perdition: and they that dwell on the earth shall wonder, whose names were not written in the book of life...when they behold the beast that was, and is not, and yet is."

Rev 17.9 "And here is the mind which hath wisdom. The seven heads are seven mountains, on which the woman sits."

A beast in prophetic symbolism represents earthly government. Daniel›s vision of the four great beasts arising from the sea in Daniel chapter 7 repre-sented four kings and four kingdoms. (Dan.7:17,23)

Daniel 7:17 'These great beasts, which are four, are four kings, which shall arise out of the earth'.

Daniel 7:23 "Thus he said, The fourth beast shall be the fourth kingdom upon earth, which shall be diverse from all kingdoms, & shall devour the whole earth, and shall tread it down, and break it in pieces."

Rev 17.8 "The beast that thou saw was and is not; and shall ascend out of the bottomless pit, and go into perdition: and they that dwell on the earth shall wonder, whose names were not written in the book of life from the foundation of the world, when they behold the beast that was, and is not, and yet is."

"Was and is not, and yet is"?

This means the Beast is past (was), future (is not, in other words the Beast is not yet complete but will be in the future), and present (yet is).

"The seven heads (of the Beast) are seven mountains."

Mountains represent great world kingdoms. The ancient kingdom of

Babylon during her world reign was called "the destroying mountain" (Jer.51:24,25) and prophecy referring to Christ's earthly kingdom during the Millennium calls it "the mountain of the Lord's house." (Isa.2:2)

These seven mountains, then, are the seven major world powers through which the beast has manifested himself and through which the Whore, by sitting on top, a ruling position, has controlled the world.

"And there are seven kings: five are fallen." at the time when this prophecy was given, 90 AD, five of the seven major world powers had fallen:

1) Egypt,
2) Assyria,
3) Babylon,
4) Medo-Persia
5) Greece.
6) Rome

"And one is": Rome was in power at the time of the prophecy and was the sixth. "And the other is not yet come": This is the final government of the Antichrist, the seventh. "And when he cometh, he must continue a short space." (17:10) This is the short reign of the Antichrist world government, only seven years according to Daniel 9:27. (See our class "Daniel 9")

"And the beast that was, and is not, even he is the eighth, and is of the seven, and goes into perdition." (17:11) The Beast himself is of all seven empires since he bears them up. But what it means by saying the Beast is the eighth is a bit difficult to understand.

It seems to indicate that all seven empires will come and go, and the beast will be the eighth empire just before its `perdition', or destruction.

The only thing I can think that this could possibly mean is that maybe before the great tribulation, before the abomination of desolation, the seventh empire is not yet really the antichrist empire because its leader hasn't been fully possessed by the devil. Though he is the head, or `king', of the seventh world government, he hasn't become the antichrist. But at the point of the abomination of desolation (in the very middle of the last seven years, leaving 3-1/2 years to go) he is fully possessed of the Devil, and he becomes a new man, the antichrist, with a new government, totally of the devil. Although it would be the very same head, seventh head, it would now also become the eighth, and a new government.

The seventh head, however, is already here (though not yet in full power), and it is world communism which is already on the march and is already conquering the world. As the seventh head, it will be the basis of the Antichrist government, because it has all the attributes of that government which are described in both Revelation and Daniel; no other government ever has.

The Beast is red, so is communism (the red flag, red army, the reds, red square, etc.). The most powerful and thorough dictators the world has ever seen have been communists (Stalin, Mao), and the beast is going to be headed up by the greatest dictator of all history. The Antichrist will completely abolish every and all forms of traditional worship--only communism has tried to do this. The beast will destroy the whore--the false religions of man including capitalism, which communism is now working at. It is going to rule the "entire earth": the goal of Communism which they are fast accomplishing.

Finally, in its pursuit of destroying all false religions, the prophecies predict that the Beast will also try to stamp out the true church, which the Reds have tried to do in countries they have conquered. So, if Communism is not the seventh head, then we will have to wait till it passes and another government with exactly the same attributes arises to take its place--which I doubt will happen since there's not enough time!

Rev 17.12 "And the ten horns which thou saw are ten kings, which have received no kingdom as yet; but receive power as kings one hour with the beast."

Since they had received "No kingdom as yet" in 90 A.D., they couldn't have been on any of the first six heads. So, they must be on the seventh, and if they are, then these ten kingdoms must definitely be here today.

In his predictions of these ten Endtime kingdoms, the Prophet Daniel said a little horn, or eleventh horn, rising after the ten horns, will pluck up three of them by the roots, thus taking all of them over.

The conquest of the three horns or kingdoms doesn't mean they no longer exist as separate kingdoms, though. The Communists have been very good at letting conquered countries retain quite a bit of autonomy--so one of these three horns could be the U.S.A., as it is the chief resister to the Red Beast and the Communist world domination. The other two may be Britain and West Germany.

Rev 17.13 "Give their power and strength unto the beast"

Uniting with the Beast, to form the nucleus of the antichrist kingdom. After the conquest of these three horns and the establishing of Communist governments within their countries, they could indeed, as it says here in the next verse. Whoever these ten kingdoms are, though, will become clearer within the next few years.

Rev 17.14 "These (ten horns) shall make war with the lamb, and the lamb shall overcome them: for he is Lord of Lords, and King of Kings: and they that are with him are called, and chosen, and faithful."

When they try to wipe us out is when God is going to wipe them out! The Whore sits:

Rev 17.15, 16,18 "Upon many waters," "the waters...where the whore sits, are peoples, and multitudes, and nations and tongues"--showing the oppressive weight of the system on its miserable masses. "And the ten horns which thou saw upon the beast, these shall hate the whore, and shall make her desolate and naked, and shall eat her flesh, and burn her with fire...and the woman (whore) which thou saw is that great city, which reigns over the kings of the earth."

Now we have said that the whore is the religious/commercial system. We could just as well have said she represented the economic system--because they are both worshipping the gods of mammon, money and materialism. Jesus himself said "no man can serve two masters: for either he will hate the one, and love the other, or else he will hold to the one and despise the other. Ye cannot serve

1) God

2) Mammon (worldly riches)." (Mt.6:24)

Let's face it, organized religion with all its money, buildings and property is pretty well sold out to mammon worship. In fact, it plays quite a big role in the economic systems of all Western countries. For instance, in the U.S., one-quarter of all privately owned land is reported to be owned by the churchianity system! And the Catholic Church is reputed to have a greater income than all top six multinational corporations put together!

The real religion of man has always been "the love of money" and "worship of the works of his own hands." But in the ancient kingdoms it was cleverly disguised in the form of supernatural religion. Even back then materialism was the real god and so-called religion was only the way the rich controlled the masses. In fact, the temple of the god was often the place where they regulated all trade and commerce.

Today the god is still money, but "education" and "science" have replaced spiritual religion with intellectual religion. Together, the god of finance and the religion of education and science make up the modern whore of Capitalism the false worship system. And it is this whore of Capitalism, religious and commercial, that really runs things, not the kings or government!

For instance, in ancient Egypt, which though a dictatorship still allowed property to be privately owned (Capitalism), Pharaoh appeared to be the

Foundation and Fountainhead of all authority and power, but in actuality, authority rested somewhere else.

Pharaoh claimed his authority from his religion, his whore, for the religion taught that Pharaoh was the living offspring of the sun god, RA, who also happened to be the `national god' of Egypt and as such deserving of all Egyptians' allegiance under penalty of law.

The religion taught patriotism and nationalism, which is what kept Pharaoh in power, so actually the religion was in control of the land, not Pharaoh, just as the multinational and international bankers, the high priests of today's whore of Capitalism, control the government of today!

Every great empire has used religion to control their masses. They all had compulsory state religions which taught obedience to the state and were enforced by law! In the ancient kingdoms it was compulsory worship of a national god; today it is compulsory education which teaches you nationalism, patriotism, and how to fit into your slot in the great national worship of the paper pigs of paper money!

So, apparent has this religious influence and control been, that in his study of the same the historian Toynbee said, "If there is ever going to be a world empire it will need a compulsory world religion to keep it in power." Why? Because brute force doesn't make man a willing slave. He has to have something that captures his heart and mind, plays on his fears, self-preservation instincts, etc., and instils a deep-seated patriotism in him so that he is willing to live, fight and die for the state, the Whore's Beast, hence religion, or today, education. So as the prophecy says, the Whore "rules over kings"--for they too have to submit to her if they want to keep their people in subjection.

"And the ten horns" shall destroy the Whore! If the U.S. and other western powers are represented by some of these ten horns, why would they want to destroy their whore? To destroy Capitalism? Well, both Marx and Lenin taught that 'if you leave capitalism alone long enough, it'll destroy itself!' It'll collapse of its own weight, because of its built-in self-destructiveness resulting from its selfishness.

Take America for example, since she is the epitome of the Whore: Right now America is bankrupt and is only kept going by the power of her government, but sooner or later the Crash is going to come, the economic crash and bankruptcy, and it will be brought about by her own selfish, exploitive, wasteful, warmongering economy that has overextended itself in order to keep the rich. Once the Crash comes, though, you know what's going to happen. All those minorities and exploited poor within America that are kept down by her economic system, they're going to go out with their guns and knives and destroy their own rich rulers and their religion, as has already happened in Russia, China and other Communist countries. So, America and Western Capitalism are bringing about their own downfall!

Will this destruction of America and the West finally bring an end to the false, exploitive, capitalistic religions of man? Well, almost but not quite! In Daniel it says the Antichrist government will destroy all forms of idolatry except for one: the abomination of desolation or image of the beast.

What the Communists will eventually do is merely replace many forms of false religion with the worship of one false religion, the worship of this Abomination of Desolation or Image of the Beast. the Whore will still be here, only in another form, and it will so completely control the lives of people that Revelation 13 says no one will be able to buy or sell unless they have been branded with a number in their forehead or hand which will link them up with a worldwide credit system controlled by this Image of the Beast. They will be literally "joined to idols" (Ho.4:17), committing physical as well as spiritual fornication with the Whore and in total bondage to the System!

Yes, the communists are trying to destroy the whore of American capitalism, but they don't know how to do it. They think if they just burn down its buildings and execute its evil leaders and replace its false teachings with the "correct", "scientific" teaching of Marxism, everything will work out all right. But they're going end up right back where they started, only a hell of a lot worse!

What they don't realize is that the system is spiritual, it's based on the big lie of selfishness, pride and rebellion against God, and the only way to fight it is with the spiritual weapons of God's truth, hitting them where it really hurts, in their hearts, really changing people's spirits, bringing them out of the kingdom of darkness into the Kingdom of Light.

BABYLON'S DESTRUCTION

Many of the prophecies of God have intermediate and final fulfilments.

America as the head and leader of world capitalism certainly epitomizes Babylon the whore of Revelation 17-18, and her coming destruction at the hands of the Red Beast can certainly be seen as an intermediate fulfilment of this prophecy about the fall of Babylon the Great.

As we explained before, America will probably still be around even after its conquest by the Communists when much of it will be destroyed. And after the establishment of a Communist Government within the nation:

America may yet have something to do with the final manifestation of

Babylon as fulfilled in the antichrist world empire! However, it works out, one thing is certain: Babylon's final complete destruction occurs at the Coming of Christ. So, it seems that this chapter will have two fulfilments:

1) An intermediate fulfilment in the destruction of America by Communism,

2) A final fulfilment in the destruction of the Antichrist System at the Second Coming of Jesus Christ.

First an angel comes down from Heaven crying with a loud voice, "Babylon the great is fallen, is fallen, and is become the habitation of devils, and the hold of every foul spirit, and a cage of every unclean and hateful bird." (Rev18:2) This shows

The system's complete spiritual fall to total depravity and perversion much like America today, a small foreshadowing of what the A.C.'s System will be like.

"For all nations have drunk of the wine of the wrath of her fornication (the System's wars for commerce, trade wars for the intercourse of Capitalism, over which every war is fought because of the love of money and the lust for power!), and the kings of the Earth have committed fornication with her, and the merchants of the Earth are waxed rich through the abundance of her delicacies." (Rev.18:3)

Every capitalistic system has made rich men of its merchants, but America has enriched the merchants of the whole earth!

«Come out of her, My people, that ye be not partakers of her sins, and that ye receive not of her plagues. For her sins have reached unto Heaven, and God hath remembered her iniquities.» (Rev.18:4,5)

God has always commanded his people to "drop out", to come out of the Whore, and this is still his message to his children caught in the greatest Whore of all time, America, and it is going to be the final message to the Antichrist world empire.

America's "sins" or idols ("idols... which your own hands have made unto you for a sin"- (Isa.31:7), have not only by their spiritual stench reached unto the spiritual heavens, but she has polluted the celestial heavens as well with her Gemini, Apollo and Mariner space idols.

This is certainly a fulfilment of another ancient prophecy,"

Obadiah 1.4 Though thou exalt thyself as the eagle, and though thou set thy nest among the stars, thence will I bring thee down, saith the Lord."

America is not only represented by an eagle, but her manned Apollo space capsule that landed on the moon was called the "EAGLE"-and "Viking I's" landing on Mars (considered a star by the ancients) has given America a "nest among the stars."

The Lord says from "thence will i bring thee down." in other words, once man has reached this point in his idolatry, then God will bring them down. He is only allowing man to go so far then whammy!

Lk.21:25 "Signs in the sun and in the moon and in the stars; and upon the earth distress of nation."

Mars was considered the star of the war god by both the Greeks and romans. Could "Viking i's" landing "in" mars be one of those "signs in the stars" signalling great war upon earth, specifically the destruction of America, which will bring great confusion and "distress of nations"? ("the 'eagle' has landed," the first words radioed from the moon, portended the soon-coming destruction of the USA)

Also, since Russia (the head of world Communism, the seventh head of the A.C. Empire) did launch the first satellite into the heavens and was first in landing on the Moon, it may be that:

This particular prophecy may yet be finally fulfilled in the destruction of the A.C. Empire (seventh head) at the coming of Christ.

"Reward her even as she rewarded you" (with the same cruelties of war and desolation with which she has afflicted the rest of the world), and double unto her double according to her works: in the cup which she hath filled fill to her double." (Rev18:6) Just as Jeremiah's Message had a hand in helping ancient Israel fall to her enemies.

In the final fulfilment of this prophecy, as we return to earth with Jesus at Armageddon, we will literally, physically destroy the antichrist forces who had been our tormentors and persecutors during the Great Tribulation. "Let the high praises of God be in their mouth, and a two-edged sword in their hand; To execute vengeance upon the heathen, and punishments upon the people; To bind their kings with chains, and their nobles with fetters of iron; To execute upon them the judgment written: this honour have all His Saints. Praise ye the Lord!" (Ps149:6.9)

"How much she hath glorified herself, and lived deliciously, so much torment and sorrow give her: for she saith in her heart, I sit a queen, and am no widow, and shall see no sorrow." (Rev. 18:7) That's what America thinks-ask almost any American who voted for Nitler (Nixon). They loved his murders in Southeast Asia; they just didn't like it when he got 'caught' in some moral sins and their hypocrisy was revealed! After only two hundred years, America thinks she's going to rule the world forever--she has a big surprise coming!

Rev 18:8-10 "Therefore, shall her plagues come in one day, death, and mourning, and famine; and she shall be utterly burned with fire.... And the kings of the Earth, who have committed fornication and lived deliciously with her, shall bewail her, and lament for her, when they shall see the smoke of her burning, standing afar off for the fear of her torment, saying, Alas, alas, that great city Babylon, that mighty city! For in one hour is thy judgment come."

Sounds like God is going to make short shrift of America in some sudden deadly blow that will almost totally destroy her with fire! Could this be an atomic strike or sudden sabotage and revolution? Or all three simultaneously? This fiery destruction is a perfect prototype of how Jesus will destroy the AC System,

2Thes.1:7,8 "When the Lord Jesus shall be revealed from heaven...in flaming fire taking vengeance on them that know not God."

Rev 18.11,15-17 "And the merchants of the earth shall weep and mourn over her; for no man buys their merchandise anymore (rich America is the world's biggest market and customer to whom nearly every merchant in the world dreams of selling his goods at the high prices she can afford). The merchants of these things, which were made rich by her (most of Europe and the rest of the world count their wealth in dollars and American customers!), shall stand afar off for the fear of the torment, weeping and wailing, and saying, Alas, alas,...For in one hour so great riches is come to nought."

Sounds like sudden destruction and the end of the American dollar!

"And every ship master, and all the company in ships, and sailors, and as many as trade by sea, stood afar off, and cried when they saw the smoke of her burning. (Sounds like the rest of the world is going to witness her destruction from a distance, as though it would be too dangerous to even get close to her!)...Alas, alas, that great city, wherein were made rich all that had ships in the sea by reason of her costliness! for in one hour is she made desolate." (Suddenly!) (Rev 18:17-19)

"Rejoice over her, thou Heaven, and ye holy apostles and prophets; for God hath avenged you on her...for thy (her) merchants were the great men of the Earth; for by thy sorceries (the deceitfulness of riches and the witchcraft of wealth!) were all nations deceived." (Rev18:20,23) American affluence is the dream of every country the world over, and her luxuries, sins and violence, from her music to her crimes, are imitated by nations around the world!

"And in her was found the blood of prophets, and of saints, and of all that were slain upon the Earth." (Rev.18:24) this false worship system in her religious form has been responsible for all the martyrs of the true church, and in her commercial form has been responsible for the millions of others slain in wars.

America, the epitome of the Whore, has been involved in and to blame for nearly every major war of this century, as well as a good many of the past, and has wrought more destruction of war on the world than any other nation in history, nay more than all other nations combined in all the wars throughout all history! She is the greatest warmonger the world has ever known, and the greatest destroyer they will ever see--and even so shall be her own destruction!

"And a mighty angel took up a stone like a great millstone, and cast it into the sea saying, thus with violence shall that great city Babylon be thrown down and shall be found no more at all." (Rev.18:21)

This is the final destruction of Babylon, "found no more at all", which happens at the Coming of Christ, and Jesus is that millstone, "the Lord...a Living Stone, disallowed indeed of men, but chosen of God, and precious. And whosoever shall fall on this Stone shall be broken: but on whomsoever It shall fall, It will grind him to powder." (1Pet.2:3,4 & Mt.21:44)

CHAPTER 25

CERN & PORTALS

PORTALS & CERN – www.outofthebottomlesspit.co.uk

ANOTHER DIMENSION? JAW-DROPPING photos taken above CERN's Large Hadron Collider led to wild new conspiracy theories and *'prove portals are opening'*

The images were taken as scientists began a new experiment called Awake to change the way particles are smashed together

These incredible photos taken above CERN's Large Hadron Collider (LHC) have provoked dramatic conspiracy theories and stoked fears that "new portals" are being opened.

The images were apparently taken on June 24, the same day CERN scientists began a new Awake experiment to change the way it smashes particles together. The images were apparently taken on June 24, the same day CERN scientists began a new Awake experiment

The film in question – What Portal did CERN open now? Strange Clouds Hover Above the LHC – raises "major concerns" about what the LHC is being used for.

The narrator asks viewers: "How much energy did CERN pull into itself?

"Is this why the weather is so crazy all over the planet?

"There are many other colliders all over the world."

The video showed the CERN schedule for the LCH which included an experiment called Awake, due to commence on June 24.

SOURCE:- (https://www.thesun.co.uk/news/1358274/jaw-dropping-photos-taken-above-cerns-large-hadron-collider-lead-to-wild-new-conspiracy-theories-and-prove-portals-are-opening/)

Image: http://www.breakingisraelnews.com/wp-content/uploads/2016/07/cern-clouds-2.png

This allows scientists to observe subatomic events and has led to discoveries that teach physicists about the universe and its origins. One such subatomic particle discovered at CERN in 2013 is the Higgs Boson, commonly known as the God Particle.

Two weeks ago, the first of a revolutionary series of experiments sent a proton beam hurtling through the Super Proton Synchrotron (SPS) and into an empty plasma cell. This experiment was a test to check the alignment of the magnets on the machine. Named AWAKE (Advanced Proton Driven Plasma Wakefield Acceleration Experiment), it will be the first accelerator of its kind in the world when it is completed at the end of the year.

Some immediately claimed that the experiment delved into unknown territory, opening portals into other dimensions and causing the ominous clouds to appear. A video that has gone viral on YouTube shows an unusual tower of clouds directly over the CERN facility, thread lightning glowing in the clouds.

image: http://www.breakingisraelnews.com/wp-content/uploads/ useful_banner_manager_banners/392-Store_NecklaceMap-600WIDE. jpg

Theories blame the unusual formation on the massive energies involved in running the LHC, listed as the world's largest machine. The 9,600 super-magnets that run the collider generate a field 100,000 times more powerful than the gravitational pull of the earth, leading to fears that such energies could indeed affect the world.

This idea may not be so far-fetched, and actually has support in the scientific community. Even before the experiment began, there was speculation from the scientific sector about extreme and unanticipated side effects. Sergio Bertolucci, Director for Research and Scientific Computing at CERN, briefed reporters in 2009 about some of the possible implications of AWAKE. He speculated that the experiment could possibly open portals into the "unknown".

image: http://www.breakingisraelnews.com/wp-content/ uploads/2016/07/sergio.jpg

Sergio Bertolucci, Director for Research and Scientific Computing at CERN. (Flickr)

"Out of this door might come something, or we might send something through it," Bertolucci was quoted as saying.

Others fear the enormous machine, designed to reveal unknown sub-atomic phenomenon, may bring into existence a microscopic black hole whose enormous gravitational pull would cause the earth to implode. Physicists at CERN admitted that the appearance of such black holes was indeed possible, but "they present no conceivable danger".

The Safety Assessment Group of CERN concluded the new experiments and equipment posed no threat. One person unconvinced by these reassurances was world-renowned physicist Stephen Hawking. In his book "Starmus", Hawking said the Higgs Boson God Particle could become unstable at very high energy levels and have the potential to destroy the universe.

However, Hawking was sceptical that the experiments at CERN could lead to the apocalypse. He estimated that a particle accelerator necessary to achieve the 100bn GeV would be larger than Earth and would not "be funded in the present economic climate".

SOURCE:- http://www.breakingisraelnews.com/71404/physics-experiment-geneva-destroy-universe-one-physicist-says-yes/#LvCZ1tlR1ZvQE2h3.99

CHAPTER 26

MARK OF THE BEAST:

China's Big Development Could Set World Up for Mark of the Beast: (250) China's Big Development Could Set World Up for Mark of the Beast – YouTube

MARK OF THE BEAST: http://www.outofthebottomlesspit.co.uk/412733219

REVELATION 13: A VERY TRAGIC STORY FOR THE MANY WHO TAKE THE 'MARK OF THE BEAST IMPLANT', AND WHO WORSHIP THE BEAST – SATAN INCARNATE

Chapter 13 And I stood upon the sand of the sea, and saw a beast rise up out of the sea, having seven heads and ten horns, and upon his horns ten crowns, and upon his heads the name of blasphemy.

² And the beast which I saw was like unto a leopard, and his feet were as the feet of a bear, and his mouth as the mouth of a lion: and the dragon gave him his power, and his seat, and great authority.

³ And I saw one of his heads as it were wounded to death; and his deadly wound was healed: and all the world wondered after the beast.

⁴ And they worshipped the dragon which gave power unto the beast: and they worshipped the beast, saying, Who is like unto the beast? who is able to make war with him?

⁵ And there was given unto him a mouth speaking great things and blasphemies; and power was given unto him to continue forty and two months.

⁶ And he opened his mouth in blasphemy against God, to blaspheme his name, and his tabernacle, and them that dwell in heaven.

⁷ And it was given unto him to make war with the saints, and to overcome them: and power was given him over all kindreds, and tongues, and nations.

⁸ And all that dwell upon the earth shall worship him, whose names are not written in the book of life of the Lamb slain from the foundation of the world.

⁹ If any man have an ear, let him hear.

¹⁰ He that leadeth into captivity shall go into captivity: he that killeth with the sword must be killed with the sword. Here is the patience and the faith of the saints.

¹¹ And I beheld another beast coming up out of the earth; and he had two horns like a lamb, and he spake as a dragon.

¹² And he exerciseth all the power of the first beast before him, and causeth the earth and them which dwell therein to worship the first beast, whose deadly wound was healed.

[13] And he doeth great wonders, so that he maketh fire come down from heaven on the earth in the sight of men,

[14] And deceiveth them that dwell on the earth by the means of those miracles which he had power to do in the sight of the beast; saying to them that dwell on the earth, that they should make an image to the beast, which had the wound by a sword, and did live.

[15] And he had power to give life unto the image of the beast, that the image of the beast should both speak, and cause that as many as would not worship the image of the beast should be killed.

[16] And he causeth all, both small and great, rich and poor, free and bond, to receive a mark in their right hand, or in their foreheads:

[17] And that no man might buy or sell, save he that had the mark, or the name of the beast, or the number of his name.

[18] Here is wisdom. Let him that hath understanding count the number of the beast: for it is the number of a man; and his number is Six hundred threescore and six.

Revelation 14.9-11 And the third angel followed them, saying with a loud voice, If any man worship the beast and his image, and receive his mark in his forehead, or in his hand,

[10] The same shall drink of the wine of the wrath of God, which is poured out without mixture into the cup of his indignation; and he shall be tormented with fire and brimstone in the presence of the holy angels, and in the presence of the Lamb:

[11] And the smoke of their torment ascendeth up for ever and ever: and they have no rest day nor night, who worship the beast and his image, and whosoever receiveth the mark of his name.

CHAPTER 27

THE BRIDE OF CHRIST

A Vision I Had, In A Dream In 2012
The Bride of Christ will be able to Create!
Many years ago, I had a very vivid dream:

I saw Jesus dressed in white raiment and having a golden band around his chest and having a large golden crown on his head – as described in the Book of Revelations Chapter 1.

He was arm in arm with a very beautiful woman with a crown on her head which was more like a diadem. I immediately recognized her from the Book of Revelations Chapter 12, as the Bride of Christ or a Queen of Heaven having a crown with twelve stars in it.

Magnificent Jesus and his exceptionally beautiful regal Bride were walking past a field, and at the edge of the field parallel to where they were walking, were beautiful hedges and bushes covered in exotic and very colourful flowers. Suddenly, as they were walking along, the scene abruptly changed, and the land that followed on was only desert.

Jesus then looked lovingly at his Bride and said to her as he lovingly squeezed her hand 'It is time for you to create.

Jesus continued "Imagine what you think would be beautiful to be growing along the path and the desert will instantly bloom and be transformed".

Jesus' Bride then pointed her hand to the empty spaces and commanded that beautiful bushes and hedges should continue. And miraculously it started to happen really quick just like as in a cartoon Disney movie.

His Bride was absolutely thrilled that she had been granted the gift of creating things that were alive – just like her husband Jesus who is the Word of God and through whom all things were and are created.

JOHN.1:1 In the beginning was the Word, and the Word was with God, and the Word was God.

JOHN.1:2 The same was in the beginning with God.

JOHN.1:3 All things were made by him; and without him was not anything made that was made.

JOHN.1:4 In him was life; and the life was the light of men.

REV.4:11 Thou art worthy, O Lord, to receive glory and honour and power: for thou hast created all things, and for thy pleasure they are and were created.

THE BRIDE OF CHRIST

REVELATIONS 19:7-9- Let us be glad and rejoice and give honour to him: for the marriage of the Lamb is come, and his wife hath made herself ready.

REVELATIONS 21.2 And I John saw the holy city, new Jerusalem, coming down from God out of heaven, prepared as a bride adorned for her husband.

ISAIAH 54.5 For thy Maker is thine husband; the LORD of hosts is his name; and thy Redeemer the Holy One of Israel; The God of the whole earth shall he be called.

EPHESIANS 5.25 Husbands, love your wives, even as Christ also loved the church, and gave himself for it.

2 CORINTHIANS 11.2 For I am jealous over you with godly jealousy: for I have espoused you to one husband, that I may present you as a chaste virgin to Christ.

JOHN 3.29 He that hath the bride is the bridegroom: but the friend of the bridegroom, which stand and hear him, rejoice greatly because of the bridegroom›s voice: this my joy therefore is fulfilled.

ISAIAH 62.5 For as a young man marries a virgin, so shall thy sons marry thee: and as the bridegroom rejoices over the bride, so shall thy God rejoice over thee.

MATTHEW 25.1 Then shall the kingdom of heaven be likened unto ten virgins, which took their lamps, and went forth to meet the bridegroom.

EPHESIANS 5.27 That he might present it to himself a glorious church, not having spot, or wrinkle, or any such thing; but that it should be holy and without blemish.

MARK 2.19-20 And Jesus said unto them, Can the children of the bride-chamber fast, while the bridegroom is with them? as long as they have the bridegroom with them, they cannot fast.

MATTHEW 25.1-18 Then shall the kingdom of heaven be likened unto ten virgins, which took their lamps, and went forth to meet the bridegroom.

EZEKIEL 16.8 Now when I passed by thee, and looked upon thee, behold, thy time [was] the time of love; and I spread my skirt over thee, and covered thy nakedness: yea, I swore unto thee, and entered into a covenant with thee, saith the Lord GOD, and thou became mine.

The Heavenly Home of the Bride of Christ

REV.21:9 And there came unto me one of the seven angels which had the seven vials full of the seven last plagues, and talked with me, saying, Come hither, I will shew thee the bride, the Lamb's wife.

REV.21:10 And he carried me away in the spirit to a great and high mountain, and shewed me that great city, the holy Jerusalem, descending out of heaven from God,

REV.21:11 Having the glory of God: and her light was like unto a stone most precious, even like a jasper stone, clear as crystal;

REV.21:12 And had a wall great and high, and had twelve gates, and at the gates twelve angels, and names written thereon, which are the names of the twelve tribes of the children of Israel:

REV.21:13 On the east three gates; on the north three gates; on the south three gates; and on the west three gates.

REV.21:14 And the wall of the city had twelve foundations, and in them the names of the twelve apostles of the Lamb.

REV.21:15 And he that talked with me had a golden reed to measure the city, and the gates thereof, and the wall thereof.

REV.21:16 And the city lieth foursquare, and the length is as large as the breadth: and he measured the city with the reed, twelve thousand furlongs. The length and the breadth and the height of it are equal.

REV.21:17 And he measured the wall thereof, an hundred and forty and four cubits, according to the measure of a man, that is, of the angel.

REV.21:18 And the building of the wall of it was of jasper: and the city was pure gold, like unto clear glass.

REV.21:19 And the foundations of the wall of the city were garnished with all manner of precious stones. The first foundation was jasper; the second, sapphire; the third, a chalcedony; the fourth, an emerald;

REV.21:20 The fifth, sardonyx; the sixth, sardius; the seventh, chrysolyte; the eighth, beryl; the ninth, a topaz; the tenth, a chrysoprasus; the eleventh, a jacinth; the twelfth, an amethyst.

REV.21:21 And the twelve gates were twelve pearls: every several gate was of one pearl: and the street of the city was pure gold, as it were transparent glass.

REV.21:22 And I saw no temple therein: for the Lord God Almighty and the Lamb are the temple of it.

REV.21:23 And the city had no need of the sun, neither of the moon, to shine in it: for the glory of God did lighten it, and the Lamb is the light thereof.

REV.21:24 And the nations of them which are saved shall walk in the light of it: and the kings of the earth do bring their glory and honour into it.

REV.21:25 And the gates of it shall not be shut at all by day: for there shall be no night there.

REV.21:26 And they shall bring the glory and honour of the nations into it.

REV.21:27 And there shall in no wise enter into it anything that defiles, neither whatsoever worketh abomination, or makes a lie: but they which are written in the Lamb's book of life.

What does the following verse mean?

ISAIAH 62.5 <For as a young man marries a virgin, so shall thy sons marry thee: and as the bridegroom rejoices over the bride, so shall thy God rejoice over thee.>

Editor: Now that is a very good question. I will try to answer this question in the best way I can.

Most of the verse I think is 'self-evident' with the exception of why does it state 'thy sons shall marry thee', which does seem a bit strange or even distasteful – initially?

This simply means that in 'talking about a whole nation' of spiritual Israel – that there will come a time in the future when there shall be 'great unity' and the Bride of Christ shall finally be truly 'one & united with God'.

As the Bride of Christ we are all different parts of the Body of Christ joined together in love to make the whole Body of Christ in one sense, and in fact the whole body of the Bride in another sense.

One day when God makes things perfect, He is saying in this verse that we shall be truly 'united & one in both the Bride and the Body of Christ.'

Like a beautiful marriage and total union with God Himself in the form of His Son Jesus. Jesus and His Bride.

CHAPTER 28

ANTARCTIC SECRETS

'EMPIRE BENEATH THE ICE': https://dcs.megaphone.fm/
REP9870480875.mp3?key=899716274afc242675439e99cba69806

AUTHOR: I strongly suggest that you all listen to the above podcast as it
is very revealing as to what is going on a world scale and why. Who is orchestrating all the leaders of the world to be imposing tight controls upon their
populations such as we have not seen since ADOLF HITLER and the NAZI
rule in Europe.

I bought Steve Quayle's amazing book 'Beneath the ICE' about the
strangeness of the Antarctic. When it first came out a couple of years ago, I
was amazed by the info it contained as have been many others as well.

'Empire Beneath the Ice' has fantastic information, such as 'Why the
NAZIS didn't lose the 2nd world war!!!

It talks about the NAZIS having experimental UFO's and Portals. It
also mentions that the very 'Throne of Satan' is under the Antarctic some
hundreds of miles beneath the surface of the earth. That would fit in with
the 'Hollow Earth Theory', which I covered in my first book 'OUT OF THE
BOTTOMLESS PIT I back in 2014.

The above interview by Dave Hodges with Steve is 2nd to none in my
opinion.

Why have many political leaders such as John Kerry, who was Barack
Obama's right-hand man, and religious ones like the Pope and the head of the
Orthodox church been invited down to the Antarctic for secret meetings so
far away? Are the Portals in the Antarctic linked to all the planets in the Solar
System and beyond. If so, who made them originally?

Listen to the above interview with Steve Quayle and Dave Hodges to find
out the details.

CHAPTER 29

SUPERNATURAL ENCOUNTERS: MY ENCOUNTER WITH AN ANGEL

OVER THE PAST 45 years as a Christian missionary and as a teacher and now as an author and writer – I have seen many strange things. I have experienced some good supernatural happenings and some bad ones as well.

The first supernatural experience that I can remember happened to me when I lived in Denmark and was 22 years old in 1974.

I had to go out late one night to do some laundry and I went with a teenage friend. We had made the mistake of going very late at night and by the time we had finished and taken a bus we arrived at the end of the road from where we lived – but there were still 3 miles for us to have to walk when there was a foot of snow on the ground and it was around 14C minus – and plus we had two big bundles of laundry to carry, which we had done for a young mother and her two kids.

We didn't know how we were going to manage to get home! So, we did what we always did in a tight situation. We stopped to pray and asked that God would do a miracle for us and send along an angel.

Well, I had hardly gotten the words out of my mouth when a car came along the very same second.

ISA.65:24 And it shall come to pass, that before they call, I will answer; and while they are yet speaking, I will hear.

I don't remember the make and model of the car – but I do remember that something was odd. There was a luminescent covering of light around the vehicle around 1 cm thick. We hitch-hiked the car and it immediately stopped – to our relief. I looked at the driver who had a magnificent smile on his face and I told him where we were going. His response was 'Yes I know – hop in.' We both sensed that this person was in fact angelic, and we both sat in the back seats. My friend mumbled to me very quietly 'Do you suppose that he is an angel?' I replied in a very soft tone 'Of course he is! Well, the strange thing was that although we sat behind this angel that we could feel light coming out of him which was very comforting to both of us, and we knew that it was God's power.

Here is where it gets absolutely amazing. The angel drove us right outside opposite to our house entrance without us even telling him exactly where to stop – as we were quite enthralled by the situation.

My friend Peter got out first, as he was nearest to the pavement. At the same time the driver quickly got our laundry out of the boot and put it on the pavement.

In the short time that it took me to follow my friend out of the 'pavement side' door of the car, I got out and then immediately turned around in order to close the door of the mysterious car.

It was then to my shock that I noticed that: 'Poof' the car had vanished and was no longer there! I literally didn't even get the opportunity to close the door!

Wow! Getting home we sure had tales to tell the other young people there.

It took us around 3 weeks to come done from such a high spiritual experience. I know now that that angel was a Guardian Angel assigned to us at the time.

HEB.13:2 Be not forgetful to entertain strangers: for thereby some have entertained angels unawares

Steve: I have had the above experience of seeing an angel at close range only once that I know of.

Moral of the Story: If you get in a really tight situation ask the Lord to send an angel to help you and your family and I am sure that He will send help in one form or another – even if it isn't as showy as the above testimony.

PSA.42:11 Why art thou cast down, O my soul? and why art thou disquieted within me? hope thou in God: for I shall yet praise him, who is the health of my countenance, and my God.

MAT.7:7 Ask, and it shall be given you; seek, and ye shall find; knock, and it shall be opened unto you:

MAT.7:8 For every one that asks receives; and he that seeks finds; and to him that knocks it shall be opened.

CHAPTER 30

THE 3RD TEMPLE IN ISRAEL THE 3RD TEMPLE
– www.outofthebottomlesspit.co.uk

The Coming 3rd Temple In Jerusalem & The Anti-Christ

THERE ARE MANY aspects as to why that 3rd Temple will be so important, as it will be much more than just an ordinary temple & will be usurped by the coming Antichrist world leader, bringing both the 'Mark of the Beast' implant system and the talking A.I. 'Image of the Beast' of Revelation 13 infamy. (Disclaimer: I personally do not believe in exact 'date setting' -that is in God's hands)

Revelation 13.15 'And he had power to give life unto the 'image of the beast', that the image of the beast should both speak, and cause that as many as would not worship the image of the beast should be killed.

16 And he causes all, both small and great, rich and poor, free and bond, to receive a mark in their right hand, or in their foreheads:

17 And that no man might buy or sell, save he that had the mark, or the name of the beast, or the number of his name.

18 Here is wisdom. Let him that hath understanding count the number of the beast: for it is the number of a man; and his number is Six hundred threescore and six. 666

All these amazing biblical predictions, given 2000 years ago, are about to be fulfilled with the start of the Last 7 Year Covenant of the rising Anti-Christ.

Part 1 To understand the important points as to the 'correct location' of the coming 3rd Temple please see the amazing film The Coming Temple, which was filmed 5 years ago in Israel: (3) The Coming Temple – Full Documentary – YouTube

The Coming Temple documentary gives proof that the Dome of the Rock is not the location of the ancient Temple of Solomon, where the 3rd Temple is destined to be built under the auspice of the coming infamous world leader the Jewish Messiah, who to Christians is known as the Anti-Christ.

Why would any world leader want to build his capital in Jerusalem? Wouldn't it be preferable to build one's capital in the USA or a much richer country? There are important reasons, and even scientific ones, as to the location in Israel and Jerusalem being the very centre of all kinds of things etc.

Why is a 3rd temple even needed? Most people in Israel see no need for a third temple, because they are not of the Jewish faith, and many of them are in fact atheists. Temples are not very scientific and would seem to be very much a thing of the past. So why the change to a great interest in the 3rd Coming Temple?

I don't know the whole picture yet, but God has made the physical location of Israel itself both important to Himself and it is also apparently very important to Satan – why? I will answer that one later – and thus Jerusalem becomes the Anti-Christ's headquarters.

If the world is generally atheistic and less and less people following religion, why should a world leader like the biblical predicted Anti-Christ take a religious stance and not say a scientific stance? The truth is that science and witchcraft are in some extreme cases the same thing. The organized religions are also controlled by mammon or money, and they will play right into Satan's little end-time game. It is all about control of the whole world including every citizen is to be marked with the infamous Mark of the Beast according to Revelation 13.

I think that we are very close to the Revelation of the Anti-Christ as the games of the Western Elite such as at Davos trying to control every citizen of the planet are clearly not working. A lower power from the negative spirit world such as Satan's son the Anti-Christ will be needed to sort out the mess that man has made with all of the financial debts which will very soon cause the Great Whore of Babylon which is epitomized in the USA to crash.

The **Great Whore of Revelation 17-18** infamy will be destroyed by the emerging new world government which will not be the elite of the West who will be destroyed – probably by Russia and China and their allies.

Bible scriptures indicate that Israel will be invaded by Russia.

I said in my recent class on YouTube of the '10 toes of 'Daniel 2 turning from clay to iron' that the emerging New World Government will uproot the current leadership of the USA, the UK and Israel and replace those governments with dictatorial ones who follow the coming One world Government. The real or actual coming New World Order might not be who we think they are. It could be a whole different kettle of fish or a new broom that sweeps clean and gets rid of the old ways and former Anglo-American empire.

There are other very important background details found in the Bible and the apocryphal books as to why Israel is so important, when on the surface it could be seen to world leaders as a seemingly insignificant land of 600 miles long and only a few hundred miles wide, if that.

There are also many reasons why Israel is the actual the centre of the earth

If given the opportunity I would like to tell the audience some supernatural truths about Israel which are also mentioned in the Jewish books in the

Hebrew language.

Will it be the exact centre of something? Is it linked to David Flynn's book Temple in the Centre of Time.

I have that book about time related to distance and time measured from where the temple of Solomon used to stand -uncanny stuff – absolute maths as mentioned by Sir Isaac Newton in the 1600's and first given to Moses on Mount Sinai.

There is an incredible verse in the Book of Jubilees written by Moses stating that there are 3 very sacred mountains all facing each other and I have mentioned it in my Jubilees Insights. I think that info needs to come to light as it is fantastic info and gives background info as to the 3rd Temple has to happen. More for the unbelieving Jews than for the sake of Christians as an above for the false Messiah the Anti-Christ.

I know quite a few of the reasons why the Anti-Christ chooses Jerusalem and what some of the incredible implications are. There is a connection between Jerusalem and the Temple of Solomon's ancient lost location. A mysterious link to the whole planet which I could explain given the time and thus why the location is so important to the AC who could choose any city on earth and any country to be his capital.

Wow! I like the conclusion of the article you just sent me, that once everyone realizes the truth, as to the true location for the 3rd Temple, yet to be built, that it will cause a big uproar in the Middle East, so that there is now no reason why the 3rd Temple cannot be build asap.

I have been writing about this 3rd Temple recently, as I am working on the apocryphal books of the Testament of the 12 Patriarchs.

I will send you the quotes from one of the Patriarchs himself who proph-esied about the 1st Temple and any subsequent temples of man being in one class or what he called the 1st temple. Then he talks about the 2nd Temple as a spiritual temple, which confirms what Jesus said to the Pharisees 'Destroy this temple and in 3 days I will raise it up'.

Because the Jews killed their own Messiah, their old religion is dead, and the 3rd temple will only be 'dead works' according to the Patriarchs or the founders of Israel, who really 'nail the subject in the head', with 'no punches held back', in stating that their descendants, which will come from them, the 12 Patriarchs or 12 sons of Israel, who was Jacob, will kill their own Messiah and thus be disinherited – 'Your house is left to you desolate', as Jesus put it in Matthew chapter 23.

A lot of the truth of some of these matters becomes much clearer when we read the apocryphal books. They sure fill in the gaps of biblical knowledge, like new wine to the thirsty.

I will explain a lot more shortly, but what I am finding out is truly incredible. See 'David Flynn's book temple in the midst of time' which reveals many secrets about Israel and Solomon's Temple as in regard to absolute maths and physics – quite something else and very relevant concerning the coming 3rd temple.

By re-reading David Flynn's amazing book Temple in the midst of Time one can immediately see that like we have done in our videos on YOUTUBE:(4) THE NIGHTLIGHT PODCAST ("Enoch Insights – The Book of the Watchers" – with Stephen Strutt) – YouTube,

He also talked a lot about the Watchers or the Fallen Angels as being responsible for many of the evils on this planet including the gods and demi-gods and all the giants and chimeras of Pre-Flood times and even in post-Flood times.

David Flynn points out that there is an ancient Science and wisdom called the Prisca Sapientia that Sir Isaac Newton who discovered gravity and many other formulae in both maths and physics was searching for.

He goes on to describe the great importance of the location of Jerusalem as being in the direct centre of the world physically, spiritually and dimensionally. What does that all mean?

He mentions that the original Temple of Solomon is a foundation stone to both Time and Distance. He proves that things prophesied that were fulfilled at an exact date can be measured in temporal distance from the original Solomon's Temple to the origin of the event happening in time. For example, the grandson of Nebuchadnezzar saw the handwriting of God on the wall in 539 BC. He was the last of the Babylonian emperors. He was slain that very same day by the Medio-Persians. If one 'takes a line' from Jerusalem to Babylon the distance is exactly 539 miles. David Flynn proves concisely in his books that many of the happenings in Israel was written both in time and distance from the very nations involved in the happenings in Israel at a specific time. Why does this measurement of both distance and time happen using the foundation stone of Solomon's Temple in Jerusalem and not at any other location of the planet? Now that is a valid question!

David also mentions how that when the 'Ark of the Covenant' stood in the Holy Place of the Temple in Solomon's time that it was the link between eternity and the physical plain.

In conclusion – from today's discoveries, Jerusalem is starting to look like an important location for a future 3rd Temple in every sense of the word. One problem for the Jews is that God took the Ark of the covenant back up to heaven because of the disobedience of Israel long before the birth of Christ.

Revelation 11:19 "And the temple of God was opened in heaven, and there was seen in his temple the ark of his testament:

How will the 3rd Temple function without the supernatural Ark of the Covenant? The Anti-Christ won't need the 'Ark of the Covenant' but with use 'scientific witchcraft' instead which will also have powers that govern distance and time to some extent or an imitation of the same by setting up his headquarters in Jerusalem and usurping the Jewish Third Temple for his own nefarious purposes including setting up the 'Image of the Beast' and the 'Mark of the Beast'.

There *is* something supernatural about Jerusalem that would make it perfect for the imitation Messiah or Satan's son the Anti-Christ to set up his rule of the planet for the 'last 3 and a half years of tribulation of all faiths'. It would seem that the coming anti-Christ will have his headquarters in another location for the first 3 and a half years of the 7-year Holy Covenant which He makes with all major faiths in Jerusalem. In the midst of the 7-year covenant he breaks the covenant and declares himself god according to Revelation 13, and 2 Thessalonians 2 and invades and takes over the 3rd Jewish Temple in Jerusalem.

PART 2 The following was just sent to me by those who made the amazing video 5 years ago called The <Coming Temple> which is now on YOUTUBE:(3) The Coming Temple – Full Documentary – YouTube

"But into the second went the high priest alone once every year, not without blood, which he offered for himself, and for the errors of the people."
Hebrews 9:7

Important Differences in Solomon's and Herod's Temples.

There were some extremely important differences between the Solomon›s Temple and Herod's Temple. Since some of the original artifacts were, according to the biblical account, lost after the destruction of the First Temple, the Second Temple lacked the following holy articles: •The Ark of the Covenant containing the Tablets of Stone, before which were placed the pot of manna and Aaron›s rod •The Urim and Thummim (divination objects contained in the Hoshen) •The holy oil •The sacred fire. In the Second Temple, the Kodesh Hakodashim (Holy of Holies) was separated by curtains rather than a wall as in the First Temple. Still, as in the Tabernacle, the Second Temple included: •The Menorah (golden lamp) for the Hekhal •The Table of Showbread •The golden altar of incense, with golden censers. According to the Mishnah (Middot iii. 6), the «Foundation Stone» stood where the Ark used to be, and the High Priest put his censer on it on Yom Kippur. The Second Temple also included many of the original vessels of gold that had been taken by the Babylonians but restored by Cyrus the Great. According to the Babylonian Talmud (Yoma 22b),[2] however, "the Temple lacked the Shekinah, the dwelling or settling divine presence of God, and the Ruach HaKodesh, the Spirit of Holiness, present in the first. "These are major differences since the Ark of the Covenant was the heart and soul of the Jewish faith. This was also how the Jews received forgiveness of sin when the high priest went into the Holy of Holies on Yom Kippur, The Day of Atonement. Some interesting verses to ponder can be found in Ezekiel chapter 10 which was written in approximately 594 BC just eight years before Jerusalem was destroyed and the Ark of the Covenant disappeared. God had been showing Ezekiel the abominations the elders of Israel were committing in the Temple itself. "Then the glory of the LORD went up from the cherub, [and stood] over the threshold of the house; and the house was filled with the cloud, and the court was full of the brightness of the LORD'S glory. Then the glory of the LORD departed from off the threshold of the house and stood over the Cherubims. And the Cherubims lifted up their wings and mounted up from the earth in my sight: when they went out, the wheels also [were] beside them, and [everyone] stood at the door of the east gate of the LORD'S house; and the glory of the God of Israel [was] over them above." Ezekiel 10:4, 18-19 The Spirit of God departed from the Cherubims. Day of Atonement Yom Kippur "The Holy of Holies was entered once a year by the High Priest on the Day of Atonement, to sprinkle the blood of sacrificial animals (a bull offered as atonement for the Priest and his household, and a goat offered as atonement for the people) and offer incense upon the Ark of the Covenant and the mercy seat which sat on top of the ark in the First Temple (the Second Temple had no ark and the blood was sprinkled where the Ark would have been and the incense was left on the Foundation Stone). The animal was sacrificed on the Brazen Altar and the blood was carried into the most holy place. The golden censers were also found in the Most Holy Place." Wikipedia Since sometime before the destruction of Jerusalem in 586 BC these items have been missing and there has really been no atonement for sin although some Jews today say repentance and good works are what really count.

PART 3 The Importance of the exact location of the 3rd Temple

Book of JUBILEES 8.19: And he knew that the Garden of Eden is the holy of holies, and the dwelling of the Lord, and Mount Sinai the centre of the desert, and Mount Zion – the centre of the navel of the earth: these three were created as holy places facing each other.

Here is what my book '**JUBILEES INSIGHTS**' says about the above verse from Jubilees:

C.30 This verse is amazingly revealing: 'Garden of Eden is the 'holy of holies' What is the definition of the Holy of Holies? Strictly speaking and very simplified, it is something inside something else. You know you have the temple and the sanctuary within it and the Holy of Holies is the Inner Sanctum Santorum within the sanctuary. In my opinion, this is in fact stating in so many words, that the Garden of Eden is within the earth where it is 'protected like a baby in the womb' of the earth. This above verse also gives the 'hollow earth' theory credibility in stating: 'Mount Zion' – the centre of the navel of the earth. The word 'navel' implies something inside something else, (hollow earth) such as a baby in the womb.

II EZDRAS: 4.41 And he said unto me, 'In Hades the 'chambers of the souls' are like the 'womb'.

II EZDRAS 5.48 He said to me, 'even so have I given the 'womb of the earth' to those who from time to time are sown in it'

(See my book 'Ezdras Insights' at Amazon.co.uk or Amazon.com)

Why does God Himself call the earth 'like a 'womb' unless He is making a valid point. A womb is hollow in order that it can contain something and that is to say water and a baby, which is similar to Inner Earth. The inner earth contains an inner sun, lands and water as well as Hell and The Lake of Fire in lower dimensions.

Machpelah was the cave where Abraham buried Sarah and it is located in the mountains in Hebron some 20 miles south of Jerusalem. This was no ordinary cave according to the Jewish book of the Zohar but a double cave. The Zohar, and ancient Jewish book of mysticism writes that the Cave is "the very entranceway to the Garden of Eden." The Hebrew word Machpelah means twofold. The Cave is considered "twofold," because it bridges the material and spiritual worlds, linking them by serving as an entrance from one to the other. The name of the city in which the Cave is situated, Hebron, also bears the etymological roots of "connection."

source: https://torah.org/torah-portion/legacy-5768-chayeisarah/

I am of course hypothesizing here that 'if the earth is hollow', which I certainly believe it to be then: The above verse 19 is revealing incredible secrets about the earth and about the inner earth for those who have 'eyes to see' and 'ears to hear'. 'Garden of Eden is the holy of holies, and the dwelling of the Lord, and Mount Sinai the centre of the desert, and Mount Zion – the centre of the navel of the earth: these three were created as holy places facing each other'.

According to modern maps, the distance from Mount Zion in Jerusalem to Mount Sinai in Egypt is around 500 KM or 300 miles. The thickness of the crust of the earth is allegedly around 300 miles also. The distance from Jerusalem to Machpelah, which is in the mountains of Israel south of Jerusalem some 20 miles.

Fascinating mathematical calculations: If one does a little maths drawing a triangle with two sides being equidistant. One side is 300 miles, another side is 300 miles. The long side will be 444 miles. 'These three were created as holy places facing each other.' If all locations are facing each other, then the middle point between them would have to be around 150 miles down in the earth and equidistant from both Mount Sinai and Mount Zion. All these calculations are possible by going through the famous cave systems at Machpelah, where Abraham and Sarah were both buried. A place that represents eternal life and is supposed to be directly above the Garden of Eden according to the Zohar, which is situated on the inner surface of the earth some 300 miles below the caves of Machpelah.

See my book 'ENOCH INSIGHTS': Here is a preview: In the amazing Book of Enoch, Enoch speaks of proceeding to 'the middle of the earth', where he beheld a 'blessed land', 'happy and fertile. He also sees 'many mountains of fire'. The angel Uriel shows him 'the first and last secrets in heaven above and the depths of the earth: There are said to be cavities in the earth and 'mighty waters' under it

Enoch sees an abyss 'opened in the midst of the earth, which was full of fire' There is also a reference to seven great rivers, four of which 'take their course in the cavity of the north' (ENOCH INSIGHTS available at Amazon. com or Amazon.co.uk)

In conclusion: My point today is that we can't fully realize the importance of the 3rd Temple unless you realize that the earth is actually hollow, with interconnecting chambers, as so clearly mentioned in the Book of Enoch chapter 22 and the Book of 2nd Esdras. There are also portals as mentioned in the Book of Enoch connecting the inner surface of the earth with the outer surface of the earth even physically as well as spiritually. These are mentioned as concerning the double-cave of Machpelah where Abraham and Sara were buried in the same cave as Adam and Eve. How was that even possible. See the

Jewish books about the supernatural portal of Machpelah.

See the related '70 Weeks' of the Book of Daniel which also mentioned the 3rd Temple and gives a lot of Bible prophecy which has been amazingly fulfilled. Yet to come soon prophecy fulfilled in the 3rd Temple: THE 70 WEEKS OF THE PROPHET DANIEL – with Joseph Candel – YouTube

Part 4 'Ichabod' & The 'Ark of The Covenant', which disappeared from Israel around 300 years before Christ.

Malachi 4.14-6 For, behold, the day cometh, that shall burn as an oven; and all the proud, yea, and all that do wickedly, shall be stubble: and the day that cometh shall burn them up, saith the Lord of hosts, that it shall leave them neither root nor branch.

² But unto you that fear my name shall the Sun of righteousness arise with healing in his wings; and ye shall go forth and grow up as calves of the stall.

3 And ye shall tread down the wicked; for they shall be ashes under the soles of your feet in the day that I shall do this, saith the Lord of hosts.

⁴ Remember ye the law of Moses my servant, which I commanded unto him in Horeb for all Israel, with the statutes and judgments.

Behold, I will send you Elijah the prophet before the coming of the great and dreadful day of the Lord:

⁶ And he shall turn the heart of the fathers to the children, and the heart of the children to their fathers, lest I come and smite the earth with a curse.

The **Book of Malachi** has 4 chapters, and it is the last book of the Old Testament and was written around 390 BC. It is God's lament against the Levites and priests that they have all gone astray. It appears that God deserted Israel from the End of the Old Testament until the New Testament or for around 300 years or 6 Jubilees. This was also prophesied by one of the patriarchs in the apocryphal book of the Testament of the 12 Patriarchs in around 1700 BC.

These last verses on the last chapter of the last book of the Old Testament predicted that God would send Elijah back to the earth 'before the great and dreadful day of the Lord. Well, that was fulfilled in John the Baptist who prepared the way of the Lord. The Messiah came in the time when Israel was at its worst and sure enough, they killed their own Messiah. As a result just as Jesus predicted in Matthew 23 their temple was totally destroyed as was Israel decimated because of their rebellion against God and their religion was declared defunct as shown with the curtain in the Holy of Holies having been ripped down the centre by God Himself to reveal to all at the time of the crucifixion of the Messiah that the Ark of the Covenant and the Shekinah

Glory was no longer in the temple at Jerusalem.

In fact, the Shekinah Glory (the presence of God) had departed centuries before showing that the spirit of God had forsaken Israel for a season because of its rebellion against God. The point being that God had already taken the ark of the covenant away from Israel. The coming of John the Baptist in the spirit and anointing of Elijah as the prophet who mentioned the coming of the Messiah was the last resort for Israel as Israel killed their own Messiah and today, they are still waiting for the Messiah. Their Messiah will soon come but he will not be a good person but very deceptive and evil and will be the false Messiah known as the Anti-Christ by Christians. Satan in the form of his son the Anti-Christ will again destroy all religions and set up his Mark of the Beast and Image of the Beast right there in the 3rd Temple which is soon to be built in Jerusalem. Since Israel did not want Jesus, they are going to get the Devil instead. Jesus said to the Pharisees 'Ye are of your father the Devil, and his works will ye do. Which of the prophets have your fathers not slain. Fill up your cup of iniquity'-Matthew 23. Meaning: 'you Pharisees are going to kill me also' – your Messiah.

It would appear that the 'Spirit of God' departed from Israel sometime after Malachi had delivered his prophecies or Israel which at least gave the hope that the Messiah would come preceded by John the Baptist. That was Israel's last chance. The Shekinah Glory had disappeared once before in the time of Levi the high priest of Israel when the Philistines captured and took away the Ark of the Covenant in the times of Samuel who became the prophet after Eli around 1100 BC. At the time the Ark of the covenant was taken away by the Philistines. They called that happening Ichabod – which means 'The light of Israel has departed from Israel.' A tragic moment if Israel's history. 1 Samuel chapter 4.11,21-22 The 'Ark of God' was captured, and Eli's two sons, Hophni and Phinehas, died. And she named the boy Ichabod saying, 'The glory had departed from Israel,' because the Ark o God had been captured and her father-in-law and her husband had been killed.

In 70 AD Israel was totally destroyed by the Romans and the 2nd Temple totally torn away as also predicted by Jesus exactly 40 years previously. The Jews were scattered into all the world for the past almost 2000 years until they became a nation again in 1948.

Since the Jewish religion has become nothing but an empty shell of what it used to be, building the 3rd Temple is not going to help Israel but the devil himself will take over because they rejected God's only begotten Son their own Messiah and only hope of Salvation. Satan will take over through his son the Anti-Christ.

Part 5 Expanding on some of the things mentioned in David Flynn's' book 'Temple in the Centre of Time' about the connection between Time and Distance related to people and what they do:

What I have observed in studying both the Bible and Apocryphal books about this topic of time and space being connected: – It is interesting that both in the book of Ezekiel and the book of Revelation, that 'a measuring line' is mentioned.

In the book of Revelation, the angel goes forth to measure the 3rd Temple and the altar and those who worship therein:

Revelation 11.1-2 And there was given me a reed like unto a rod: and the angel stood, saying, Rise, and measure the temple of God, and the altar, and them that worship therein. But the court, which is without the temple leave out, and measure it not; for it is given unto the Gentiles: and the holy city shall they tread under foot forty and two months.

Another verse in the book of Enoch talks about an angel with a 'measuring line' gone forth to measure. In that case the angel was measuring the value of people's souls. Between these verses it shows that there is some link from the physical to the spiritual, and this will also be the case in the 3rd Temple to come.

How can one measure the value of a person's soul with a 'measuring line' in the same vein as measuring the 3rd, Temple?

Believe it or not, the Book of Enoch talks mysteriously about when the wicked and Fallen angels are judged, that all creation 'shall speak against them and their deeds including the nature itself.' I think modern science is very ignorant of the fact that the very planet on which we live seems to be 'alive' and which some say has its own 'consciousness' and observes everything that is done on it both good and bad.

Scriptures seem to indicate the exact same thing. Is it just possible that God Himself uses the earth as a record of all the deeds done on it?

In Conclusion: The 3rd Temple will seem like a good idea at the time of the coming charismatic world leader – the long-awaited Jewish Messiah, but he will be a great deceiver, who has all kinds of evil spiritual powers as mentioned so well in

2 Thessalonians Chapter 2.3-4,9 Let no man deceive you by any means: for *that day shall not come*, except there come a falling away first, and that man of sin be revealed, the son of perdition; Who opposes and exalted himself above all that is called God, or that is worshipped; so that he as God sits in the temple of God, shewing himself that he is God. "Even him, whose coming is after the working of Satan with all power and signs and lying wonders,"

One of his characteristics according to the Book of Daniel is 'he shall think to change times and seasons. Maybe that will be more real that it at first sounds like on the surface?

Daniel 7:25 And he shall speak words against the Most High, and shall wear out the saints of the most High , and think to change times and seasons; and they shall be given into his hand until a time and times and a half time.

(A time is 1 year, and time is 2 years, so it is talking about 3 and a half years of Tribulation for the whole world)

More On The Jewish 3rd Temple: A Christian view of the coming Temple – opinion – The Jerusalem Post (jpost.com)

Comments: The following was my answer to someone who was stating that they thought that the Tribulation would soon begin, and that Jesus would come back in 2026-2027: What we do agree on – is that time is very late and that the past 3 years sound like the Great Confusion. In the class that you sent me, please correct me if I am wrong, as I only briefly looked at it so far, but as far as I can see, there is no mention of the coming 3rd Temple and the 7 Year Pact of the Anti-Christ – which is pivotal when it comes to the Last 7 years according to what we were taught. I will take time to study the whole thing further. I personally do not agree that the 3rd temple is to be only spiritually interpreted.

Jesus made it very clear:

Mathew 24.15 'When ye therefore shall see the Abomination of desolation standing in the Holy place.

Why did Jesus specifically state ' When ye shall see the Abomination. This cannot be interpreted as just talking about people's hearts and souls. It is something both physical and spiritual like most things in life.

In my opinion, the whole point of the coming Third Temple is that if God says He will do a specific thing, such as allow the 3rd physical temple to be built in Jerusalem then it will happen and it will happen when God decides for it to happen and not a day too soon. I don't think that it is important to know exactly when it will happen and doing date setting is never wise and hundreds if not thousands of people have been wrong in date setting time and time again.

One of our goals as missionaries, is to be a Watchman on the wall and warn people, but not be too emphatic about exact dates, as it can be very misleading, as evidenced by the teachings of many of the more radical churches.

I certainly think we will probably see the Rise of the Anti-Christ and the Last 7 years upon us soon, but exactly when? I don't know. Only God knows that.

I believe that we will also see the 'Building of the 3rd Temple' in Jerusalem, which was already years ago as a prefab job waiting to be built at any time the 'powers that be' allow such a thing.

As for timing of the coming of the Anti-Christ? What is holding back the coming of the Anti-Christ or is he orchestrating events at the present time in the very background?

The above is what I recently wrote about the importance of the 3rd Temple, and not dismissing it as purely allegorical, but that it will happen because the prophecies of Daniel said so, whether we fully understand or not'

Another person wrote in and said they didn't believe that there would be a 3rd Temple or even the Anti-Christ. Here was my answer:

'On this particular point of the End-time concerning the Coming 3rd Temple and the Anti-Christ we agree to disagree. I do believe that we will see a 3rd Temple built in Jerusalem during the End time and that the Anti-Christ will soon come on the international scene.

If any point of doctrine is true and valid before the Lord, then it will stand on its own without any one of us tying to 'force the situation'.

As Jesus said, 'Heaven and Earth shall pass away but my words will not pass away'.

Many people seem to be 'getting frantic' about the End-time and what it all means.

It is a time to 'trust in Jesus', and not be worried about the situation. The same with End-time exact date-setting. God is not into date-setting, as it can cause a lot of confusion in itself.

When will the end of all things come? It will come when God says so, and not a day before. We can all but guess, speculate as we do not know.

Why get all worked up about just one small point?!

However, having said all that, there a basic foundation of End-time scriptures that we can depend on. – Jesus exhortation in Matthew 24. Either God's Word is true, and we can trust it, or it is not.

It is not for us to try moving the goalposts so late in the End-time game.

I think we should stick with the guide-stones that the 'fathers have set up', and not listen to some of the more 'so-called' radical churches doctrines of putting all the End-time into the past, for their own convenience and comfort.

Once people start doubting some of the basic foundation stones of biblical prophecy, then where will those doubts end?! The truth is none of us actually know exactly what is going to happen, and especially not exactly when – as it does not really matter.

What matters is that Jesus is coming back the 2nd time, and we all need to be ready for his 2nd Coming after the Tribulation of those days.

Mathew 24.29-31 Immediately after the tribulation of those days shall the sun be darkened, and the moon shall not give her light, and the stars shall fall from heaven, and the powers of the heavens shall be shaken:

[30] And then shall appear the sign of the Son of man in heaven: and then shall all the tribes of the earth mourn, and they shall see the Son of man coming in the clouds of heaven with power and great glory.

[31] And he shall send his angels with a great sound of a trumpet, and they shall gather together his elect from the four winds, from one end of heaven to the other.

Romans 14.1 Him that is weak in the faith receive ye, but not to doubtful disputations.

CHAPTER 31

THE GODS OF EGYPT

I JUST WATCHED this movie 'THE GODS OF EGYPT' which is about two gods – **Horus** & **Set** fighting over who should rule Egypt around 4000 years ago.

I must say that I was very impressed by it – for many reasons. Whoever wrote the script certainly knows their Egyptian history, and more importantly was not afraid to bring out the 'so-called' 'ancient myths' of Egypt. What is fascinating to me, is that the movie made no qualms about the real identities of HORUS & SET, clearly showing them as 'Fallen angels', and not some 'Aliens', as would be the norm these days. In the movie, they could both appear as both as Giants or as Fallen Angels or even as human-animal hybrids. I would not have expected a sceptical generation to have made a movie about the 'ancient gods' of Egypt & portraying them as they really were 'Fallen angels' with many powers of both deception and the abilities to be shapeshifters. This is exactly how I have described the Fallen angels and the Giants in the Pre-Flood times in my **2nd** book **'Enoch Insights'**. http://www.outofthebottomlesspit. co.uk/418666481

The above-mentioned movie 'The Gods of Egypt' does an excellent job of showing that there was a time when the 'gods ruled directly over mankind'. Mankind was afraid of the gods because of their exceptional powers, and they were not just part of some ancient historian's imagination, but they were in fact very real. There is presently so much evidence on this planet to show that man is not alone on this planet, but that even to this day there exist a hybrid race of humans, which are stronger and more intelligent than humans are. These hybrids are an offspring of the original 'Fallen Angels', who still roam the earth today, and still interfere with human genetics. Thus, the case for **'Alien Abductions'**. See my **1st** book **'Out of the Bottomless Pit'** http:// **www.outofthebottomlesspit.co.uk/421556721**

I liked the movie, but as one of the main actors playing as the hero stated' 'You gods don't really care about us humans, but your interest is in deceiving, tricking and abusing us'!

According to history, Horus ends up winning the fight against his nephew Set. Horus ends up as the good guy in the movie and a good god who cares about the people. But is that actually true?

Unfortunately, from all I have studied about the Fallen angels (gods), they are not like the good Angels of God, who do believe in God – that is a God of Love, kindness, curtesy, mercy and the fruits of God's Spirit of Love.

Unfortunately, the Fallen angels (gods) and their sons the Giants (demi-gods), long ago abandoned any human sense of morality and goodness and also long ago descended into 'total madness and chaos and became the Devils and Demons after the Great Flood'. Their only goal is in fact to destroy all human beings and all of God's Creation just like Lucifer (Satan) their lord and master.

The movie does bring out many good points though.

The movie: **'Gods of Egypt'** shows how chaos is being 'held in check' and is not allowed to totally take over the earth. This is indeed correct, at least until the **NEW WORLD ORDER** have fully taken over and many of the ancient gods come back to reign over the entire earth together with their supreme leader Satan in the form of the coming Anti-Christ. Under the Anti-Christ eventually the world will descend into total madness during a period mentioned in the Bible as the Great Tribulation. All the inhabitants of the earth will be required to receive a 'Mark in their right hand or their forehead' in order to 'buy or sell' according to **Revelations 13**. <**http://www.outofthebottomlesspit.co.uk/412733219**>

If they refuse, they will be executed by the 'Image of the Beast' which apparently will be some sort of computerized Android or A.I. You can read about the conditions on earth during this End-time period in my third book **'Ezdras Insights' https://youtu.be/Pl0bkRv0HSM?t=3**

Opinion: It is my own conviction that the true original 'gods of Egypt' idea was stolen from a much earlier time in history from 'Pre-Flood times' when 'Chaos' ruled. In other words, not 4000 years ago, but closer to 5000 years ago, as indicated by the oldest stories about the gods from India. The Sphinx in Egypt shows signs of sea-water erosion proving that the Sphinx was indeed created in Pre-Flood times. The same goes for the Pyramids. The pyramids both in Egypt and many other countries around the world and even on the planet Mars were built in Pre-Flood times, by a very advanced civilization of Giants who were not aliens, but the descendants of the Fallen angels co-habiting with both women and animals making hybrid races.

BACKGROUND HISTORY OF THE GODS: HORUS & SET: THE MOVIE TRAILER: https://youtu.be/IJBnK2wNQSo?t=51

https://www.laits.utexas.edu/cairo/teachers/osiris.pdf

http://www.joanlansberry.com/setfind/set-ram3.html

CHAPTER 32

DWARVES

THE CUBIT AND A SPAN SIZED PHARAOH (2' 6') How is that even possible?

INTODUCTION: WHEN I originally wrote these books of 'JASHER INSIGHTS' books I & II, it was difficult to write 'comments', as the Book of Jasher itself was very big.

For this reason, there were some chapters, where I didn't make any comments or make an analysis, either because the original chapter was self-explanatory and followed the biblical narrative, or else because 'strange things' were written about, about which I had insufficient knowledge.

However, upon re-reading my own books, I have come to learn more about some of the above-mentioned chapters. I realize that in writing the book of 'Jasher Insights' BOOKS I & II, that I have only scratched the surface of the information contained in the Book of Jasher.

I will therefore start to write extra articles about this amazing Book of Jasher.

The Book of Jasher is a gold mine of information, and even more so the **'Jasher Insights'** books, as they both explain difficult parts of the book and also fill in the gaps with inspired explanations of things not fully known before.

Certain things have been made known to me by God's Spirit – as to why the Book of Jasher was made in the way that it was.

It is far more complex than I had at first imagined!

In General, in a nutshell, those who have read the 'Book of Jasher' think that the 'Book of Jasher' is a book of interesting adventures: of Fallen angels, Fallen women such as the daughters of Cain, and resultant Giants. Later on, came the Hybrids and Chimeras. A lot is mentioned about Abraham and Jacob and his 12 sons and their frequent wars against the Canaanites. Not to even mention very detailed stories such as the Tower of Babel and Nimrod and many other interesting adventures.

Now in this chapter 77 we find the origin of Dwarfs. It is very interesting in that; all the above-mentioned creatures are what famous writers like R.R Tolkien put into his books of Lord of the Rings and C.S. Lewis into the Chronicles of Narnia.

Disclaimer Warning: This First Part of Chapter 77 Is Not For The Squeamish!

Why the fascination about these strange creatures by those famous writers? It turns out that the creatures they wrote about, are in fact real and not imaginary -at least very similar creatures. Both those writers were Christians and wanted to get things put in a story that would be very interesting for children. Well, it turned out that the adults were also very interested in their stories.

Why did they write about Dwarves and Giants and Ogres and Chimeras of all kinds both Human and Animal kinds? Because the stories involve supernatural creatures and things which we were taught in school are only myths and imagination.

What we were taught in school turns out to be a lie. Those creatures do exist and come into existence under very special evil circumstances as is evidenced by this book of 'Jasher insights' Book II.

Some woman wrote to me recently and said that she thought that some amazing movies could be made from the contents of the amazing adventures in the Book of Jasher.

Up until now I knew how the giants came into existence, but I had no idea how the Dwarves came into being.

The dwarf Pharaoh mentioned in Jasher 77 is only two and a half feet tall which would on the surface seem totally impossible, but is it? And yet these types of mythological creatures both small and big have been reported countless times throughout the full length of time itself. Steve Quayle mentions them in his book Little Creatures. – [www.stevequayle.com]

It is very interesting to me that it states in this 77th chapter of Jasher, that there was a Pharaoh who was only two and a half feet high and that he had a beard growing all the way down to his feet. Just like a dwarf. The Dwarf Pharoah, is described as being in height a cubit and a span. (A cubit is a maximum of 25 inches and a span is the size of the length of a man's hand. (6 inches) 25 + 6 would make it about two feet and six inches high. Dwarfs are famous for growing their down to their feet.

Now if this story is to be believed, as something credible, then how did the dwarf come into being?

The interesting thing is how did this this dwarf come in to being if he was the son of Pharaoh and his wife, both of whom were presumably normal to average height? How could their DNA be altered into going into their dwarf son?

Pharaoh had many sons and daughters. On his deathbed he chose his dwarf son to be the next Pharaoh, as he said that he was very intelligent (in darkness)

The father of the dwarf Pharaoh was a very evil Pharaoh and ruled for a very long time according to the story. (90 years). God struck him down with leprosy for 10 years, until he died because he was exceptionally cruel to the children of Israel.

He actually is recorded as having slaughtered hundreds of innocent Israelite babies, and used their blood on his leprosy sores in the hope of curing them. Of course, it did not work as God simply did not bless him for his satanic vicious actions and horrific treatment of the children of Israel in the captivity of Egypt.

We know that the giants conceived before the Great Flood were created by Fallen angels having sex with human women. The fruit was hybrid giants who had supernatural strength and other super-human powers. It did happen again also after the Great flood. After the Great flood it was not so prevalent as before the Great Flood and the giant offspring were much smaller. Giants before the Great flood were over 35-45 feet high. After the Great flood they were from 9 feet to 25 feet in general. (**See Steve Quayle's website about GIANTS**) How did they manage to come back after the Great Flood and what has happened to them ever since?

What about dwarves? How did they come into being? How could the DNA of both pharaoh and his wife be altered in such a way that they had one dwarf son. On the surface and to our limited science today that would seem absolutely impossible! But is it? From what I have researched, they are truth to both witchcraft and sorcery and even lycanthropy. You know what I mean – werewolves etc. One of the ways to corrupt the human DNA is by dark arts – human sacrifice and the deliberate spilling of human blood. The Pharoah did exactly that. He did both witchcraft and sorcery and spilled the blood of the innocent children of Israel – mere little babies and as a result his wife gave birth to a very evil Dwarf, who became Pharaoh according to the 77ᵗʰ chapter of Jasher.

How evil was the satanic dwarf, Pharaoh? Well according to the book of Jasher he was even worse than his very demented father. He ordered that the Children of Israel had to produce bricks without straw. He also then got worse and said that if the Israelites did not complete their daily quote of bricks in the wall, then the Egyptian soldiers would go and take their youngest child and use him as a human brick in the hole in the wall and place cement over the top of him while he die screaming. Thus reads the 77ᵗʰ Chapter, 270 children died in this horrific manner.

It was shortly after this that Egypt was totally destroyed.

It is very easy now to understand why! When you realise how satanic the Pharaohs really became at the time of Moses, it is no wonder that God brought on the **10 Plagues of Egypt** and totally destroyed Egypt. According to the Bible there have been 6 major world empires starting with Egypt. **1) Egypt 2) Assyria 3 Babylon 4) Medio-Persia 5) Greece, 6) Rome.**

According to the book of Daniel there will be a 7th worldwide empire of the Anti-Christ who will be totally satanic in nature, and eventually will be possessed by Satan himself.

Such evil as has gone on before the Great Flood is returning in the form of the Nephilim or the Fallen angels along with Satan himself and all the spirits of the Giants of old (the disembodies spirits of the Giants) which are also known as the demons of hell.

There are many evils on this planet today which could be classified as human sacrifices, and thus very strange creatures could also start appearing because of the extreme evil of some.

In the book of the Septuagint in the book of Isaiah chapter 13 is stated 'Giants coming to fulfil the Wrath of God'. There has been evidence that when races on the earth do things as depraved as cannibalism that giants come and take revenge as in the case on the Azteks and many other Indian tribes who were cannibalistic. The Anastasi tribes were apparently devoured suddenly by giants which came out of the ground according to Steve Quayle's website.

Wars are human sacrifices, and there will be the Devil to pay for all those people who cause the innocents to die in wars. Another form of Human sacrifice are abortions.

All I know is, that 'whatsoever a man soweth that shall he reap'. God is however very merciful & forgiving, and when people repent, and get saved through the blood of the Messiah and Saviour Jesus Christ then God can forgive anything. As long as people are sincere.

More Comments: ANCIENT T. COMMENTS – www.outofthebottomlesspit.co.uk

CHAPTER 33

ALIEN ABDUCTIONS & ADVANCED MEDICAL SURGERY – IN THE PRE-DILUVIAN WORLD

(Not for the squeamish)

THE FOLLOWING LINK shows 1000's of stone figurines in Peru -South America – depicting humanoid creatures dissecting human beings and doing complicated surgeries such as heart surgery.

Question: Are these ancient beings who lived in Central & South America – thousands of years ago actually performing ancient medical practises or were they in fact making human sacrifices?

It would seem that the races who came later in time such as the Azteks and Incas etc – saw what these ancients had done and started imitating them thinking that what they had done were human sacrifices, when in fact they had been operating on humans for whatever nefarious reasons.

The Azteks saw the ancient races as the ancient 'gods' of old from the 'Golden age of the gods' when Atlantis existed and ruled over much of the earth – from Pre-Flood times.

These stone figurines are said to be many thousands of years old and I as a Bible believing Christian would state that they were probably made before the Great Flood of Noah's time.

HERE IS THE LINK TO THE MUSEUM OF HORRORS:

https://www.ancient-origins.net/opinion-guest-authors/professor-cabrera-s-cabinet-horrors-secret-chambers-and-shocking-artifacts-020981

I have to admit that this sounds strikingly very similar to the modern phenomenon of 'Alien abductions' where people have reported being taken underground by aliens and abused in in one form or another – many times sexually.

Why have alien entities had access to the use and abuse of human beings for many millennia?

It has been proven that anyone being abducted by strange humanoids can simply rebuke these forces in the name of Jesus the saviour and they will immediately disappear.

I have personally confronted some of these beings 'face to face' – beings like these mentioned above – whilst out witnessing as a missionary many years ago.

See my book 'OUT OF THE BOTTOMLESS PIT' BOOK 1' about the Paranormal. [www.amazon.com/author/777.7]

CHAPTER 34

THE CANOPY

Inner Earth & The Hollow Earth – My Own Theory About The Original Creation

MY OWN CREATION theory, (which needs yet to be proved), is that not only was there a layer of water above the atmosphere *before the great flood,* as other creation scientists have speculated, but that also above the inner earth, around 50-100 miles above the surface of the inner earth there was also an ‹inner earth› canopy of water for the same reason, which made the inner earth also like a greenhouse and helped protect the earth from all kinds of cosmic and UV radiation which caused the ageing process.

Before the Great flood people lived to be up to 900+ years old. After the great flood the age of mankind kept dwindling down until it was around 70 years old at the time of King David 3000 years ago. It has stayed around the same ever since.

I think it likely that the 'outer waters' above the earth acted like a change-able lens, and the inner earth waters acted like a perfect internal mirror.

There were portals in the earth or better said dimensional gates, which allowed light to get through the surface of the earth in selected places around the world in perfect order. At least 12 portals that we know of.

Unfortunately, since the Flood, those portals no longer work the way they used to in Pre-Flood times, and in modern times they have become dangerous areas known as the 12 Bermuda Triangles around the world, where ships and planes and even high-altitude satellites get caught in the dimensional voids or areas between dimensions, which we call Bermuda Triangles.

Here is a verse from my book '**EZDRAS INSIGHTS**' which is taken from the Jewish Book of **2nd Ezdras** about the Portals:

2 EZDRAS Chapter 6.1 ‹And he said unto me, "At the beginning of the 'circle of the earth', before the portals of the world were in place, and before the foundations of paradise were laid, ... and before the powers of movement were established, and before the innumerable hosts of angels were gathered together, and before the heights of the air were lifted up, and before the measures of the firmaments were named, and before those who stored up treasures of faith were sealed.›

SEE MY VIDEO ABOUT 'EZDRAS INSIGHTS': https://youtu. be/Pl0bkRv0HSM?t=58

There are apparently five Bermuda-like triangles in the Northern

Hemisphere and 5 in the Southern Hemisphere.

The two so-called Poles of the Earth, would have also conceivably been light sources to the inner earth as they are today in modern times. A total of 12 portals.

I propose that God's original creation was far more fantastic and beautiful than He is given credit for.

What if Adam and Eve were indeed placed in the Garden of Eden inside the earth.

They might have been able to see the inner sun, but what about all the beautiful Cosmos of stars, not to the mention the Sun and the Moon, which normally one could only see from the outer surface of the earth?

God would certainly have created the earth in such a way, that his first children Adam and Eve could clearly have seen His magnificent creation of the Sun, the Moon and the stars!

Obviously if that 1st assumption is correct, then God must have arranged the planet in such a way that Adam and Eve could still easily see the beautiful stars and the sun and Moon and planets even being inside the earth, but how was that even possible?

The Bible tells us that God is the 'Father of Lights',

JAM.1:17 Every good gift and every perfect gift is from above, and cometh down from the Father of lights, with whom is no variableness, neither shadow of turning.

I put it to you that the earth was in the beginning both like a projector with moveable lenses, and a mirror and original light sources.

I propose that what was seen of the universe by Adam and Eve on the Inner Earth in the Garden of Eden was a perfect internal reflection.

The waters above the earth acted as a giant moveable lens, letting in the light. The inner waters above the inner earth acted as a perfect mirror.

There are invisible portals (today known as Bermuda Triangles) which sometimes, act as dimensional gateways, which before the flood allowed the light to travel through the very surface of the earth.

Today 10 of the Bermuda Triangles (Gateways) are at around 30 degrees Latitude, in 5 points equidistant in the Northern Hemisphere, and 5 points equidistant in the Southern Hemisphere.

Strangely enough, in modern times these Bermuda Triangles are mostly listed as to the immediate right of a land mass.

I propose that as Enoch mentioned in his book, that there used to be a lot less water in the seas of our planet.

Originally, all the "light portals" or "Bermuda Triangles" today, would have, for convenience been on the land area, and not in the sea.

The light then focused on the waters above the inner earth surface, which was like a perfect mirror, which reflected all the light of the cosmos and the sun and moon and stars back down onto the inner surface of the inner earth.

When it comes to light, water itself has amazing qualities and has been known to sometimes act as a lens, and sometimes act as a mirror, and at other times as a magnifying glass.

Whether acting as a lens or a mirror or magnifying glass would depend on different factors, but primarily on the temperature of the waters.

Amazingly enough, I have just found some evidence to support my theory of the Inner Waters & Outer Waters. The inner waters acting more like a perfect mirror in order to reflect the light perfectly onto the surface of inner earth. The light would have come through the portals (Bermuda Triangles).

Today I was reading a very famous book called, 'Flying Saucers from The Earth's Interior (1960) by Raymond W Bernard. He was talking about many different explorers & scientists who have descended through the North Pole (Northern Aperture) and have tried different experiments to show that the earth is in fact Hollow.

One of the amazing things that the scientists and explorers mention is that in going through the hole at the north and on their way onto the under surface of inner earth, at some point the sky acts very odd and appears as a mirror in the sky, which he stated that no one, at that time, understood the cause of this phenomenon. Although scientists suspected ice-crystals.

Well when I read this, I was completely blown away, as one would say, because my theory above, is that there used to be a layer of water above the outer surface of the earth, which acted more like a lens and sometimes like a magnifying glass, and another layer of water above the Inner Earth, which because of the uniform temperature, somehow acted more like a perfect internal mirror, allowing for total internal reflection.

The fact that scientific observers have found one area of the sky where this mirror effect is still evident and formed by water in the form of ice-crystals is very encouraging.

Apparently, this connecting Northern Aperture which directly connects our outer world with the inner world, is the only remaining location on the entire planet, where the mirror waters in the sky are yet still working!

It is stated time and again that the Inner Earth today has a uniform temperature of around 73 degrees F by all reports.

I also think that God being the amazing and incredible creator that He is, that He created the outer-earth waters above the earth, as a giant changeable lens.

When night-time came, the stars and in fact the whole universe would have been seen as being much closer to the earth

At night-time, somehow the waters above the earth, acted as a giant magnifying glass.

If the above theory is correct, then at different times of the year, Adam and Eve could have clearly seen the 12 Astrological Star arrangements in the sky from Aries to Taurus, as though they were all very close-up.

It must have been absolutely both spectacular and astoundingly beautiful, and breath-taking.

The curse of the Bermuda Triangles wouldn't even exist today, if man hadn't been so rebellious, destructive, violent and perverse, in the first place, which resulted in the judgement of the Flood, and also unfortunately, caused the destruction of the giant projector of the earth, mentioned above.

All we apparently have left of that original light projector, is the defective "Light Portals" (Bermuda Triangles)

After Thoughts by the author: If my theories which I wrote in my book 'Enoch Insights are true – then many other things would have been possible in the original creation.

I propose the following additional possibilities using the information above:

1) The Inner Earth temp is mentioned to be a constant by the highly decorated Admiral Byrd and other famous explorers.

2) the outer surface of the earth is affected by night & day

3) water has incredible light refraction and reflection qualities – depending on the temperature.

Here are the new things that I propose:

1) As we do know scientifically from observation by many explorers and scientists – the inner earth being of constant temp would also explain how that if and when the inner earth had a canopy of water above it before the great flood it would have always acted as a mirror because of the exact constant temperature of 73 degrees f.

2) The canopy of waters above the outer earth were subject to night and day being only approx. 100 miles above the outer earth's surface, which if compared to a 'globe of the planet' is only just above the surface and in a very

thin layer. This would mean that the outer canopy of water would indeed be influenced by some sort of gradual temp change at night-time.

3) God being the perfect creator that he is, made sure that the sunlight in the daytime was not too bright! Therefore, i propose that he made the waters above the earth act as a perfect lens in the daytime just letting all the light come in from outer space.

4) At night-time it could have been very different. Even if the water temperature of the 'water canopy' around the earth only went down by a few degrees, it could have been possible that the lens effect was amplified into a magnifying effect.

5) This would mean that God himself could come along 'in the cool of the day' and visit Adam and eve and he could have taught them about the stars.

6) I propose that at night-time Adam and eve could see the constellations and the planets and stars as if they were close- up and unlike today in modern times, when it takes a powerful telescope for the average person to see the constellations, planets and stars.

7) The inner earth of our hollow planet was used by God himself as a cradle for the first human beings – Adam and Eve – literally the cradle of civilization.

Is it just possible that:

1) The original 'Garden of Eden' was located inside the earth. 2) Then, after the flood, mankind came to live on the outer surface of the earth.

There is evidence that not only are there cities inside the earth, but that also there are the remains of ancient cities, built long before the great flood. In the book, 'Journey to Gragau' by Alan Trenholm, Alan states that he went on a spirit trip down through the crust of the earth whilst riding a horse.

He travelled widely inside the earth, and visited both paradise and hell.

Whist riding the horse down into hell, through the many strata of the earth's crust, just before entering the inner earth, he states that he felt a clammy hand reach out and grab his leg, which was presumably one of the inmates of hell itself.

His spirit guide explained to Alan that the "clammy hand" that he felt, was belonging to one of the "rock people". When Alan asked his very first question;

"who are the rock people?' the explanation given is what gives it all away concerning when man moved from the inner earth to the outer earth! She explained that the "rock people" were spirits of the people from before the flood, who were buried in the rubble of their former cities, and in imprisonment in the strata of the earth, because they didn't honour God.

Instead they honoured themselves, and their cities, often built with the price of human blood and sacrifice. The incident mentioned about a being that grabbed Alan's leg, happened just before he entered the inner surface of the earth, howbeit, in the lower dimension of hell. The important point here that it

shows that "being" was buried in the rubble of cities on the inside of the earth and not the outside.

From this we can indeed deduce that as the first cities of man were built on the inner surface of the physical earth, that it is more than likely that mankind first came onto the outer surface of the earth where we live today after the flood at Noah's time. This is just one example concerning cities inside the earth, and the rubble of ancient cities.

See the dramatic, amazing and insightful book, "Journey to Gragau" by

Alan Trenholm. Alan's "spirit trip" down to hell, which he claims was 100% real: 'Journey to Gragau' – www.amazon.com

This could also explain why much of the book of Enoch, & the topography of the earth as described by Enoch sounds like, that when he was actually describing the earth, most of the time like he was actually talking about the inner earth, because that is where he lived before the great flood.

Remember that Enoch has talked about dinosaurs and dragons, and large creatures and both sea and land monsters. He also talks a length about the land of a 'thousand mountains', often volcanic in nature, and something that simply does not exist today; at least not on the outer surface of the planet, as we now know it today. He has also described trees as being exceedingly high and unlike the trees in our modern world. He also went to the ends of the earth and saw the northern polar entrance. Enoch stated that the seas only occupied one seventh of the earth's surface.

Sounds like a very different world being described by Enoch. Today the outer surface of the earth, where we live is 80% seas. What a contrast that is!

I believe that Enoch also visited the uninhabited outer surface of the earth where we live today. We know from Enoch's book, that he also visited both the higher dimensions of heaven itself, as well as the lower dimensions of both hell and the lake of fire.

To learn a lot more about these fascinating topics, i highly recommend the above-mentioned book by Alan Trenholm, about hell, the lake of fire, demons and fallen angels, as it gives an amazing amount of insightful information about the lower worlds and the future of our planet.

Conditions Before & After the Flood

Let's compare conditions on the earth before the flood and after the flood. Before the flood people lived up to almost 1000 years. Noah lived to be 950 years old. Noah died 350 years after the great flood. (Around 4000 years ago or 2000 BCE) Shem the son of Noah 600 years old. Son of Shem Arphaxad 438 years. Only 90 years later Arphaxad's great-grandson Peleg lived 209 years. Another 90 years later Peleg's great grandson Nahor only lived to be 148 years (Noah was still alive when Nahor '8 generations' after Noah, had already died!) Isaac lived to be 180 years

Jacob died at 147 years. Joseph died at 110 years

(There were 13 generations from Noah to Joseph and a total of 640 years)

Less than 800 years later in 1000 BC, King David stated that a man's life was 70 years.

Something was very different about the surface of the earth and the heavens above the earth, after the Great Flood.

God had cursed man at the time of the Flood and stated that a man's life would be 120 years only.

Why did men live to be almost 1000 years old before the Flood and less and less after the flood and their ages dwindled down from 950 to only 70 years in only 1600 years.

I propose that before the flood mankind lived inside a very 'protected earth'.

After the Flood mankind now lived on the outer surface of the earth, which was no longer protected as greatly as before the Flood.

The earth lost its protective shield of water about the earth.

We started to feel the influence of cosmic rays, which reduced the length of people's lives.

Conclusions: I believe that not only is the earth Hollow, but also the moon, and the sun and the stars, as hollow objects are much easier to cause to spin. Solid objects are not. Because of centrifugal forces, when one puts clothes in a washing- machine, all the clothes that occupied the centre of the machine, once put in the centrifuge, all material is flung to the sides of the machine. The same is true of the earth and all other astral bodies.

One of my theories is that the entire universe down to the earth, within earth, & Hell & Tartarus below that, consists of globes and circular orbits.

1) The Earth is the centre of the universe

2) The Earth is hollow

3) All astral bodies are hollow

4) The sun and the moon rotate around the earth and not the earth around the sun.

5) The universe is not oval or ovuloid but is actually global in shape, with the earth at the very centre of it.

6) Before the Flood, the Earth was protected by a layer of water around 5-15 metres thick, 100 miles above the earth's surface all away around the earth.

(Apparently 100 miles up in the atmosphere, is where both gravitational and centrifugal forces which are in opposite direction to each other, cancel each other out.) This caused the earth to act like a green-house and was the reason why the vegetation grew to be so big.

7) The protection above the earth, also acted like a "pressurized hyperbaric oxygen chamber", and thus large creatures like dinosaurs, which today scientists can't understand how they could have been breathing with such small lungs.

Well, there's your answer: the earth had a much higher oxygen content than today, and it was also pressurized, thus making it much easier to breath for the dinosaur.

Bible verses about the Hollow Earth

PHI.2:10 That at the name of Jesus every knee should bow, of things in heaven, and things in earth, and things under the earth.

EPH.4:9 (Now that he ascended, what is it but that he also descended first into the lower parts of the earth?

EXO.20:4 Thou shalt not make unto thee any graven image, or any likeness of

anything that is in heaven above, or that is in the earth beneath, or that is in the water under the earth.

GEN.1:6 And God said, 'Let there be a firmament in the midst of the waters, and let it divide the waters from the waters.'

ISA.40:22 It is he that sits upon the circle of the earth, and the inhabitants thereof are as grasshoppers; that stretches out the heavens as a curtain, and spreads them out as a

tent to dwell in:

AMO.9:2 Though they dig into hell, thence shall mine hand take them; though they climb up to heaven, thence will I bring them down:

PHI.2:10 That at the name of Jesus every knee should bow, of things in heaven, and things in earth, and things under the earth;

EZE31:16 I made the nations to shake at the sound of his fall, when I cast him down to hell with them that descend into the pit: and all the trees of Eden, the choice and best of Lebanon, all that drink water, shall be comforted in the nether parts of the earth.

(See my book 3rd Book 'EZDRAS INSIGHTS' for a lot more about the Hollow Earth or the 'Womb of the Earth' as God Himself calls the inside of our planet in **II EZDRAS.**)

I have just placed these articles from my book '**ENOCH INSIGHTS**' today **01/09/19** in answer to a question sent to me by a gentleman in China just today: Here is his message:

'Concerning the hollow inner Earth, I am very intrigued! Is it possible that once one is inside the inner Earth, the relative size increases, so as to accommodate an inner Sun? Perhaps something like the Tardis effect (Dr Who), where the outside is small, but the inside is very large. I am just speculating. Thus, once inside the inner Earth, one can see another universe!'

MORE COMMENTS FROM THE PUBLIC ABOUT THE HOLLOW EARTH

http://www.outofthebottomlesspit.co.uk/443397541

According to the Zohar the Jewish book of Mysticism along with the Torah the Garden of Eden exists inside a 'Hollow Earth' which I explained about in my 1st book 'Out of the Bottomless Pit': eden.pdf (koshertorah.com)

Comments: From The Public: Is The Earth Hollow? – Or Is It Flat? – Or Is Round? Solid Or?

Rachel from Brazil asked the following question: If the earth is Hollow then did Noah start inside the earth in Noah's Ark at the time of the Great Flood? Then he would have to have sailed through a Portal, right?

I agree with you. There are many reasons why I hold to the Hollow Earth Theory. Please read my book 'Out of the Bottomless Pit Book I' as well as 'Enoch Insights'

Those who do believe in the biblical Flood as well as the Hollow Earth Theory are divided on this issue as to when mankind came out from the centre of the earth. Some say at the time that Adam and Eve were kicked out of the Garden of Eden and others at the Great Flood. Which is correct?

If you read my 8 books including the '7 INSIGHTS' books based on the apocryphal books you will find that they all mention that the earth Is hollow.

1) I personally hold to the view that mankind came out from the inner earth at the time of the Great Flood. Again, there are many reasons why I hold to the view. I will try to expand upon this given time:

2) It is true that both the Northern and Southern openings where the

poles are supposed to be are also 'portals'. What does this mean? Well, similar to the Bermuda Triangles, one minute apparently, they are there, and the next minute you can't detect them, as fantastic as that might seem. I covered this topic in my 1st book 'Out of the Bottomless Pit.'

The Bible verses that you quoted:

3) THE FLAT EARTH THEORY:

Isaiah 40.22: He sits enthroned above the circle of the earth, and its people are like grasshoppers. He stretches out the heavens like a canopy, and spreads them out like a tent to live in.

Proverbs 8.27: When he prepared the heavens, I was there: when he set a compass upon the face of the depth:

Job 26.10: He hath compassed the waters with bounds, until the day and night come to an end.

You mentioned:

4) The earth does not spin:

Psalms 104:5 "Who laid the foundations of the earth, that it should not be removed for ever."

Psalm 93:1 The LORD reigns, he is clothed with majesty; the LORD is clothed with strength, wherewith he hath girded himself: the world also is stablished, that it cannot be moved.

I Chron 16.30: Fear before him, all the earth: the world also shall be stable, that it be not moved.

Psalm 96.10: Declare among the nations: "The LORD reigns!". The world is firmly established; it cannot be moved; He will judge the peoples with equity. King James Bible. Say among the heathen that the LORD reigns: the world also shall be established that it shall not be moved: he shall judge the people righteously.

5) Limits of the earth:

Deuteronomy 28.49: The Lord shall bring a nation against thee from far, from the end of the earth, as swift as the eagle flies; a nation whose tongue thou shalt not understand.

What I don't see clearly is why it looks like in the future we're not going to use the under Earth, save to locate the rebels and hold them there until they repent.

Wouldn't it be simpler and more beautiful to have the Garden of Eden on the surface of the Earth?

It's my quest after reading some of your ideas.

- Andres NV

My Response to Andre: 04/09/19

Dear Andre,

Great hearing from you as always.

In Answer to Your Very Good Question: That is indeed a very good question. Well, if those of us who theorize that the earth is indeed Hollow then I would imagine that eventually all areas of the original creation will be made perfect once the Heavenly City comes down at the end of the Millennium. By that time there won't be any more evil and both Hell and Death will have been thrown into the Lake of Fire.

According to Jewish book the Zohar – the Garden of Eden was located originally in the centre of the Earth – however just like it says in the Book of Revelation that God Himself took the 'Ark of the Covenant' up to Heaven, maybe God could have also taken the 'Garden of Eden' back to Heaven?

The only problem with that is that Jesus Himself mentioned to the guy on the cross next to him.' 'Tonight, you shall be in Paradise with me'.

Where did Jesus go that night? Scriptures say that he descended into Hell to witness to the people down there – inferring that Paradise was inside the earth.

Not that it matters that much – as eventually the earth which has been usurped by Satan in its entirety at present, will be totally cleansed and therefore the whole earth both inside and outside will become a paradise – Garden of Eden and not just one small, protected area – the whole planet. wow!

TYSVM for your article. You email only has option for me to reply to all, that's why I need to reply in a new message. Thanks for taking the time to answer on flat earth theory. I have just started reading and you caught my attention with 12 Bermuda **Triangles.** Oh my! – Rachel

HOLLOW EARTH -SNS – www.outofthebottomlesspit.co.uk & HOLLOW EARTH COMMTS – www.outofthebottomlesspit.co.uk

CHAPTER 35

A DRAGON & A PHOENIX
(Aurora' Appeared in the Sky Over Iceland on 22/02/19)

IT IS QUITE amazing to me, that any clear shape could randomly form itself in the upper atmosphere, and also be part of the amazing colourful Aurora Borealis over Iceland on the 22nd of February 2019.

What are the chances that another clear shape was also spotted on the very same day? The 2nd shape was that of a Phoenix. Now assuming that both phenomena are not proven to be hoaxes, which is highly unlikely, as the source is from NASA https://www.livescience.com/

This is more than coincidental, and some would say that it is simply impossible! And yet, there are the two very distinct pictures.

Furthermore, both of the pictures are of what is classified as 'supernatural beings' and 'mythological creatures'. Why were the shapes exactly these two mystical supernatural creatures?

Why not a sheep and an owl for example?

Is there a reason for these two pictures to have been painted in the sky? Who painted them onto the Aurora Borealis?

Was it God himself that painted these pictures as a warning of things very soon to come, upon the entire earth?

Are these clear pictures, what many would call ' a sign in the heavens' or even a 'sign of the times'?

Let's look at what is the significance of both a dragon & a phoenix?

I find it absolutely fascinating that these particular shapes have appeared in the sky over Iceland at this particular time and I will go on to explain why.

The Meaning of the Mythological Creature the Dragon:

The Dragon has always been known as a supernatural creature and dragons have been seen upon occasions even in modern times. The Bible talks about a dragon 22 times in the Book of Revelations.

The Dragon is symbolic of Satan or the Devil himself. The Dragon is also mentioned 20 more times in the rest of the Bible.

REV.12:3 And there appeared another wonder in heaven; and behold a great **red dragon,** having seven heads and ten horns, and seven crowns upon his heads.

REV.12:4 And his tail drew the third part of the stars of heaven, and did cast them to the earth: and the dragon stood before the woman which was ready to be delivered, for to devour her child as soon as it was born.

REV.12:7 And there was war in heaven: Michael and his angels fought against the dragon; and the dragon fought and his angels,

REV.12:8 And prevailed not; neither was their place found any more in heaven.

REV.12:9 And the great dragon was cast out, that old serpent, called the Devil, and Satan, which deceives the whole world: he was cast out into the earth, and his angels were cast out with him.

REV.12:10 And I heard a loud voice saying in heaven, Now is come salvation, and strength, and the kingdom of our God, and the power of his Christ: for the accuser of our brethren is cast down, which accused them before our God, day and night.

REV.12:11 And they overcame him by the blood of the Lamb, and by the word of their testimony; and they loved not their lives unto the death.

There is another **monster** in **Revelations 13** Which is describing The Coming <New World Order>s> <One World Government> led by a Dragon – Satan.

REV.13:1 And I stood upon the sand of the sea, and saw a beast rise up out of the sea, having seven heads and ten horns, and upon his horns ten crowns, and upon his heads the name of blasphemy.

REV.13:2 And the beast which I saw was like unto a leopard, and his feet were as the feet of a bear, and his mouth as the mouth of a lion: and the dragon gave him his power, and his seat, and great authority.

REV.13:3 And I saw one of his heads as it were wounded to death; and his deadly wound was healed: and all the world wondered after the beast.

REV.13:4 And they worshipped the **dragon** which gave power unto the beast: and they worshipped the beast, saying, Who is like unto the beast? who is able to make war with him?

THE MEANING OF THE MYTHOLOGICAL CREATURE THE PHOENIX:

The Phoenix Was A Very Unusual And Supposedly Mythological Spirit-Being with the form of a fabulously beautiful large scarlet and gold-coloured bird similar to the flamingo, with a very melodious voice.

It Appears Throughout The Religions Of The Orient, all the way from Egypt to China, but is particularly associated with Egypt and the Arabs, especially the sun worship of ancient Egypt, whose principal magnificent temple was a Heliopolis, near Cairo.

The Phoenix Was Considered A Good Omen of prosperity, benign rule and the active principle of life in nature. It also represented resurrection, life after death and eternal immortality.

Its legendary life lasted hundreds of years, at the end of which it built a nest of aromatic spices, set it on fire and was consumed in the flames, from the smoking ashes of which it immediately rose to life again to live a new life of many more hundreds of years! Its presence was considered a blessing, but its departure was a warning of impending doom!

The phoenix was also symbolic of the eternal spirit which cannot be destroyed, but, despite seeming death, shall always rise again. Birds in the Holy Scriptures, or bird-like creatures, particularly in the Prophetic Scriptures, usually represented spiritual beings, angels, supernatural powers, spirits and even the Holy Spirit of God!

In Egyptian religion, the phoenix was the soul of Osiris, god of the sun, and was said to have appeared in the sunrise from Arabia.

It is also identified with Venus, the morning Star, which in Revelation 22:16, Jesus says that He Himself is--"the bright and Morning Star"! Christ also speaks of His Own Second Coming in the End Time as the rising of the Day Star," or again the Morning Star! (2Peter 1:19)

The early Greek Christians considered the phoenix definitely as a symbol of Jesus, "Who came down from Heaven with wings full of fragrant perfume, His divine words!" He did indeed build a nest of spiritual spices, and then offered Himself in death for us, only to rise again from the ashes of the grave to live forever!

What an accurate symbolism! Could he indeed have been represented in ancient mythology by the peerless Phoenix? Even the Phoenix' royal colours of scarlet and gold, its graceful form and lovely voice remind us of Him!

In Malachi 4:2, Jesus is spoken of as "the sun of righteousness" which shall "arise with healing in His wings ... unto you that fear My Name"!

I am convinced as I have said before that many of the ancient mythological characters, events, and religions had some original bases in actual facts, spiritual personalities and past battles, struggles and occurrences in the spirit world, between both evil spirits and good and evil spirits, the angels of God and the demons of Satan!

In the process of time and through lack of specific recording or the loss of written records, some of these accounts became considerably contorted, distorted and embellished by word of mouth into some of the odd tales which we have in mythology today which have been handed down to us from thousands of years ago.

If Christ himself, therefore, is likened unto the sun, and his bride the church unto the moon, only reflecting His glory, and the stars as angels, gods of the heavens, is it any wonder that some of the ancients through the passage of time and the darkness of ignorance of the full truth of God, and for lack of His Holy Scriptures, became confused and misled and began to worship the sun, moon and stars themselves as symbols of their Creator?

No wonder in their spiritual wandering he became to them the sun god, Egypt's Osiris, god of all nature and the life-giving Nile, ruler of the spirit world, lord of resurrection and new life, the best, greatest and most beneficent of all Egyptian gods!

His wife became the virgin ISIS, the good, beautiful goddess of west, justice, truth and judgment who introduces the departed spirits to Osiris in their second life in the spirit world!

And could not that feathery plume she bore on her head have been significant of our own dear phoenix, the very soul of Osiris, indeed his own son? In fact, she is often pictured with that plume alone as her very head! What a picture of the Wife of God, the church, with Christ as her Head, our beloved Phoenix, Jesus! Interpreting these things is like interpretation of dreams and visions which God has given me, Praise His Name!

Them that trust in the Lord thy God shall be saved and shall rise again like the phoenix from the ashes of defeat by the miracle-working power of God, like a resurrection!

They shall rise again, even from the ashes, the smoking ashes of defeat, o god, like the phoenix of thy power, the phoenix of thy resurrection, the phoenix of thy spirit! By the Spirit of God, they shall rise again for Thy Glory

'There shall be a very great shaking in the land, and the Lord himself shall come, and He shall utter His voice in the heavenlies, and the powers of the heavens shall be shaken, and the earth itself shall tremble, and the high places shall be destroyed and brought low! All those high places! Those towers! And only them which call upon the Name of the Lord shall be saved!'

A 'Possible' Interpretation:

The real question is: why such a display in the skies over Iceland on the 22/02/19 in the aurora borealis at this particular time in history – as a green dragon and a blue-green phoenix?

The colours in the sky probably are not the important thing as the aurora borealis tends to be these colours anyway.

Having said that, in revelation 6 it mentions the green horse of death & hell. Maybe that is where the Dragon comes from.

If we know that the Dragon represents Satan and that the Phoenix represents Jesus, then what could the signs in the sky mean, if anything at all?

These two amazing depictions in the sky really couldn't be any clearer. It is talking about the warfare between Jesus and Satan.

Rev.12:7 and there was war in heaven: Michael and his angels fought against the dragon; and the dragon fought and his angels,

It is also indicative that Satan is about to come on the world scene in the form of his son the Anti-Christ who will rule the whole world for 7 years. In the midst of the 7 years will start 3 1/2 years of Great Tribulation.

According to the Bible, Satan will fall to earth, and it shows him as a great red dragon. He will persecute all religions and especially Christians. He will reign for 7 years upon the earth and try to totally replace Jesus & God. In the soon to be built 3rd temple in Jerusalem, he will set up an image of himself, and cause all on the earth to receive a Mark in their right hand or their foreheads, without which they won't be able to buy or sell. In other words, Satan makes everyone on earth his slaves or at least he attempts to by force of arms.

The Anti-Christ & The False Prophet

REV.13:5 And there was given unto him a mouth speaking great things and blasphemies; and power was given unto him to continue forty and two months.

REV.13:6 And he opened his mouth in blasphemy against God, to blaspheme his name, and his tabernacle, and them that dwell in heaven.

REV.13:7 And it was given unto him to make war with the saints, and to overcome them: and power was given him over all kindreds, and tongues, and nations.

REV.13:8 And all that dwell upon the earth shall worship him, whose names are not written in the book of life of the Lamb slain from the foundation of the world.

REV.13:11 And I beheld another beast coming up out of the earth; and he had two horns like a lamb, and he spake as a dragon.

REV.13:12 And he exercises all the power of the first beast before him, and causes the earth and them which dwell therein to worship the first beast, whose deadly wound was healed.

REV.13:13 And he doeth great wonders, so that he makes fire come down from heaven on the earth in the sight of men,

REV.13:14 And deceives them that dwell on the earth by the means of those miracles which he had power to do in the sight of the beast; saying to them that dwell on the earth, that they should make an image to the beast, which had the wound by a sword, and did live.

REV.13:15 And he had power to give life unto the image of the beast, that the image of the beast should both speak, and cause that as many as would not worship the image of the beast should be killed.

REV.13:16 And he causes all, both small and great, rich and poor, free and bond, to receive a mark in their right hand, or in their foreheads:

REV.13:17 And that no man might buy or sell, save he that had the mark, or the name of the beast, or the number of his name.

REV.13:18 Here is wisdom. Let him that hath understanding count the number of the beast: for it is the number of a man; and his number is Six hundred threescore and six. 666

CHAPTER 36

WHO WILL BE THE ANTI-CHRIST: IS IT PUTIN?

IS THERE SOMETHING Unique About Putin? Will He Become A 'World Leader' – Like The 'Anti-Christ', Or Will He Be Killed By The Rulers And Controllers?

When Putin speaks, America should listen. Really! :When Putin Speaks, America Should Listen. Really! – The Burning Platform

The above speech by Putin just a few days ago is unusual, if just for the fact that Putin the president of Russia, genuinely seems to care for the peoples in his country by putting forth definite plans for progress under the present difficult circumstances of Russia fighting a war in Ukraine against the western backed Nazi Party of Ukraine.

I have not heard of any Western politicians who show a definite concern and interest in their peoples.

Most politicians have been lying through the teeth all through the last few years of Covid and Vaccines.

It amazes me that the so-called Elite don't realize that millions of people can see right through their lies and deceptions.

Many of the elite are running scared when the slightest thing does not go according to plan and go hiding in their underground bunkers. What a bunch of cowards!

Putin's invasion of Ukraine seems to have 'upset' the basket of apples, as far as the Great Reset is concerned.

I think that it is a possibility that the 'elite' will try and assassinate Putin just like they did Gadhafi and for the same reason.

Gadhafi like Putin also offered an alternative to using the almighty $, and has turned to the Russian Rubel, as a currency backed up by gold. The West is now 'hopping mad' at Putin's Rubel, and it is reflected in all the newspapers every day in calling Putin every name on the book and none of them good names. What is the truth about the situation in Ukraine right now?

I am not saying that I know exactly how the future will play out, but the truth is that the Elite are in a big fix right now! Why? They have the money and the power and the weapons and their underground bunkers and secret bases,

BUT something is most definitely missing in their plans for a new world order take-over of the world. Otherwise, why are they acting so frantic? It would appear that Klaus Schwab, Bill Gates and George Soros all thought that they had both Russia and China in their bag of a rising 'New World Order'.

However, both Russia and China seem to prefer to keep their own national identity instead of going for Globalism.

Those pushing Globalism seem to all be a bunch of 'old men' and totally nuts!

Their control of the Media shows clearly that they are afraid of what Putin is doing, as he is operating independently of their wishes.

Yes, it is true that Putin was originally trained by the Illuminati, as was the former KGB or Secret Police of Russia of which Putin used to be the head, but it would appear that something has changed in Russia. Why is that?

Many of us have up until now been thinking that Putin and China are all part of the New World Order plan, right? What if that simply is *not* the case? Or at least not anymore.

Concerning Bible Prophecy -The Bible predicts that one day a very smart man will come on the world scene who is known in the Bible as the Anti-Christ but to the people in the world he will be the most charismatic world leader ever to have lived. I will give a rundown of his charismatic personality which will end up winning the nations to his way of thinking!

I personally do not think that the existing Elite of the West are going to succeed in making their New World Order.

I believe that those on a higher spiritual plane than the Illuminati will actually betray them and bring on the world scene something very different in order that the coming Anti-Christ will be proclaimed as Mr Nice Guy and not a monster such as the Western newspapers and TV all paint Putin at present.

Another interesting Bible verse about the Anti-Christ states' 'He was wounded to death and his deadly wound was healed.' What does that mean?

Revelation 13:3 And I saw one of his heads as it were wounded to death; and his deadly wound was healed: and all the world wondered after the beast.

Another point: It is said about the coming Anti-Christ world leader that he will '*destroy them that put him in power.*'

Look how the Nazis' ended up killing the very people who helped Hitler and themselves to power – the 'Brownshirts' – Why? Hitler did not like any competition, and neither does Satan of his son the Anti-Christ. The communists did the same with many of their so-called sympathizers after they gained power.

All throughout the history of the planet, just when one world power seemed totally invincible and their leaders became unbearably arrogant and cocky and over-confident that is exactly when they fell and their world power was totally destroyed such as Egypt, Assyria, Babylon. Medio-Persia, Greece and Rome.

Now the USA thinks that it is totally invincible and guided by the UK imagines that it will rule for the next 1000 years through the almighty god the $. I don't think so.

I think it more likely that a new world power is emerging, and that is likely to be Russia along with China.

Looking at Bible Prophecy about the End-times: If we consider Daniel 7 in the Bible it is talking about a Beast that has 10 horns and that a little horn comes up after the other 10 and overcomes and pulls out by the roots 3 of those horns.

Does Russia have the power to destroy 3 nations such as the USA, UK and Israel. These are the nations that are giving Putin and Russia the most trouble right now!

Look at the spiritual powers mentioned in the Bible behind the coming Anti-Christ and his world government:

Daniel 7.7-8 After this I saw in the night visions, and behold a fourth beast, dreadful and terrible, and strong exceedingly; and it had great iron teeth: it devoured and brake in pieces and stamped the residue with the feet of it: and it was diverse from all the beasts that were before it; and it had ten horns. 8 I considered the horns, and, behold, there came up among them another little horn, before whom there were three of the first horns plucked up by the roots: and, behold, in this horn were eyes like the eyes of man, and a mouth speaking great things.

Revelation 13.1-2 And I stood upon the sand of the sea, and saw a beast rise up out of the sea, having seven heads and ten horns, and upon his horns ten crowns, and upon his heads the name of blasphemy. 2 And the beast which I saw was like unto a leopard, and his feet were as the feet of a bear, and his mouth as the mouth of a lion: and the dragon gave him his power, and his seat, and great authority.

Revelation 12.3-4 And there appeared another wonder in heaven; and behold a great red dragon, having seven heads and ten horns, and seven crowns upon his heads. 4 And his tail drew the third part of the stars of heaven, and did cast them to the earth: and the dragon stood before the woman which was ready to be delivered, for to devour her child as soon as it was born.

By comparison to the above Bible verses, and its vivid description of End-time rulers, the so-called elite of today are simply 'out of their league'! Something much greater has to happen, with much smarter leadership, who initially will try to win the peoples of the world, instead of openly crush them as in Canada and Australia, & as we have seen under the tyranny of the Covid laws, vaccines and mandates. Covid was just the 'elite' of the world's feeble attempt to gain total control of every citizen of the planet and to force everyone into their Global mould, which means first of all getting rid of 90% of the world's current population, by hook or by crook – known as eugenics.

Well, Hitlers plans failed to set-up a 1000-year rule of the 3rd Reich.

Communism's plans have also failed miserably leaving its people poverty stricken.

Only the coming Anti-Christ, according to the Bible, will be a Mr Nice Guy, (at least in the beginning of his reign) who actually does many good things for the peoples of the earth.

Now you are probably thinking, surely Putin cannot be the predicted Anti-Christ, as Mr Putin claims he is just interested to keeping his own country safe, and with safe national borders and without interference for the Elite of the West.

Is Putin for real? Does he really genuinely care for Russia and its peoples? Is so, he is very different than all the other politicians in the West, sad to say! Most of them just are puppets of the elite.

It is too early to say, but I think that we should all keep an eye on Putin and pray that he does not end up like poor Gadhafi – slaughtered by the Western powers.

It is just incomprehensible how that the West can say they want to try Putin for war crimes etc when the West has slaughtered the peoples of Iraq, Libya and many other nations which Putin mentions in his speech.

Putin also mentions how that World War I & II were artificially created by the Powers that be or the Illuminati in order to cull the nations.

Related: My other articles that mention **Putin: MY ARTICLES 2 –** **www.outofthebottomlesspit.co.uk**

The Anti-Christ & The Last 7 Years: SIGNS of the TIMES – www.outofthebottomlesspit.co.uk

More on the Last Seven Years – Open or Secret Covenant?

Over the years I have received a lot of questions about when the Antichrist confirms or signs the 7-year covenant will this be open & in the news for all the world to see or would the 7-year covenant possibly be done in secret behind the scenes?

And another frequent question will the Antichrist be in some sort of prominence or position before he signs the Last Seven Year Covenant?

When the Antichrist Confirms the Covenant we know that this event will clearly mark the start of the Antichrist's seven-year reign and the last seven years before Jesus' Second Coming and the Rapture.

Some people speculate that the Seven-Year Covenant could be signed secretly from behind the scenes & we may not know when the covenant is signed. Whereas others suggest that the Seven-Year Covenant could be signed openly & that we'll recognize the covenant & therefore know exactly when the last seven years begins. Will we be able to recognize the Seven Year Covenant & when it starts?

We know that in the last seven years the Antichrist will certainly be in power, but it seems highly unlikely that he would have enough power to get the World to sign the seven-year Covenant unless he were already in some kind of power & prominent in some way, & with enough power & influence to persuade them to sign that Covenant!

He doesn't just suddenly pop out of the woodwork, someone that nobody ever heard of & says, "Here's the solution to your war & the economic problems!" He's not just some nobody, unheard of, a little diplomat in the U.N. who suddenly stands up & offers the World the solution on a silver platter just like that, without already certainly being known & having some influence & some power! Otherwise, they wouldn't even listen to him!

So, it would seem the Antichrist has got to get into some position of power before that & from reading Daniel 11:21-23 it sounds like he rises to power peaceably:

But then uses force or war to crush his opposition and strengthen his position.

So, it seems that the Antichrist is quite prominent even before he confirms the 7-Year Covenant that signals the start of the last seven years before Jesus' Second Coming and the Rapture.

The covenant appears to be a peace accord, as well as some sort of religious pact-possibly one that tackles the thorny issue of coexistence between Jews, Muslims, and Christians in the Mideast, and by which Jerusalem could be declared an international city with free and equal access guaranteed to people of all faiths. (Daniel 9:27; Daniel 11:28,30)

This covenant could also clear the way for the Jews to finally be able to rebuild their Temple on Jerusalem's Mount Moriah and resume animal sacrifices on its altar-something that hasn't happened since the last Temple was destroyed in 70 A.D. It certainly seems that confirming the 7- Year Covenant by the Antichrist would be World-famous news or it wouldn't do the antichrist any good, because that's great public relations, he's made peace with the religions! So, it's likely going to be an open public event.

CHAPTER 37

'CHANGES' FROM 1999-2022
SIGNS OF THE TIMES: "SIGNS" – www.outofthebottomlesspit.co.uk

LUK.21:9 But when ye shall hear of wars and commotions, be not terrified: for these things must first come to pass; but the end is not by and by.

LUK.21:10 Then said he unto them, Nation shall rise against nation, and kingdom against kingdom:

LUK.21:11 And great earthquakes shall be in divers places, and famines, and pestilences; and fearful sights and great signs shall there be from heaven.

Here is another bible verse mentioning the kind of conditions that we can expect in the time of the end:

Joel: 2:2 'a day of darkness and of gloominess, a day of clouds and of thick darkness.'

Introduction: back in 1999 in August, I happened to read what has turned out to be an amazing and very accurate prophecy. What was said was that *'with the turn of the century (the year 2000) the world would start to descend into greater darkness and that governments would become even more corrupt. The intensity of evil deeds would increase dramatically. We would also see a drastic increase in the signs of the times as mentioned by Jesus in Matthew 24, & Luke 21. The prophecy went on to say that the descent into evil would culminate in the rise of the Anti-Christ and a one world government along with a 7-Year Pact, and eventually the great tribulation.*

Added: 06/03/19: the following is from a new book that I am currently writing called 'Jasher insights'. The world today reminds me of pre-flood times or is very close to it. As Jesus himself said 'as in the days of Noah, so will it be in the days of the coming of the son of man.' here is the quote from chapter 4 of my book 'Jasher insights', which should come out in a few months' time:

'This gradual descent into madness, darkness, violence and depravity was caused by the influence of the 'fallen watchers' or 'fallen angels'. Once God had removed Enoch from the earth, who was a great spiritual influence over the peoples of the earth to remain loyal to God, then gradually the fallen angels were able to influence mankind more and more until the point that within 200 years of the death of Enoch, mankind had totally rejected the ways of the lord.'

'23 Years of Signs of the Times'

1999 New Year's Eve: Putin takes over as leader of Russia. 20 years later he is still in power. Russia has been transformed from a weak country to a very strong and formidable one in those last 20 years.

2001 'Twin towers' 9/11 Muslims are blamed, in order to give the USA the green light to go and attack Muslim countries!

Twin towers 9/11 http://www.outofthebottomlesspit.co.uk/412454018

2001 Bin Laden and the Muslim fanatics are blamed! Both are eventually killed, even though they were not guilty of 9/11 http://www.outofthebottomlesspit.co.uk/420916542

2004 Tsunami hits Indonesia with terrible loss of life: 300,000 people lost their lives.

2004 Saddam Hussein is killed by USA forces in Iraq.

2008 Devastating financial crash on Wall Street

2009 The economy of the world goes down.

2011 Devastating tsunami in Japan and nuclear power station melt down resulting in the total pollution of the pacific ocean and the destruction of a large portion of the aquatic creatures in the sea.

2011 Arab Spring: Muammar Gadhafi the president of Libya is allegedly killed by the friends of USA because he suggested to use the gold dinar instead of the $ as currency for all African countries.

2013 Devastating hurricane in the Philippines: great loss of life: 30,000 lives lost

2014 2000 demolition experts made a movie in the USA explaining how that 9/11 twin towers was a demolition job plain and simple. Https://youtu.be/0y8hgzkv9us?t=135

2016 Donald Trump unexpectedly becomes president of the USA. He is a billionaire. He has become famous in Israel

2017-2018 Devastating fires raging through northern California. Proven to be caused by lasers from above. In other words, deliberately caused. Why? To drive people out of Northern California, as the elite want the masses in the cities only, so they are driving the people out of the countryside: http://www.outofthebottomlesspit.co.uk/412590896

2018 Donald Trump is the first American president to declare Jerusalem as the capital of Israel. The Israelis are so happy they are calling trump like unto Cyrus the emperor of Persia and have made coins with trump's picture on it.

The 3rd Temple the Jews see Donald Trump as having a lot to do with the start of the Jewish 3rd temple being built in Jerusalem.

2018 the Jewish messiah. Israelis believe that Donald trump is helping to bring the 'messiah' into power in Israel. Of course, in the Christian religion we would see the Jewish 'messiah' as the foretold Anti-Christ, who will sign on to a '7-year peace pact'.

2019 18th February: Dragon & phoenix in the aurora borealis the very same day! Does it signify something important? http://www.outofthebottomlesspit.co.uk/413325062

2019 Destroying the planet through HAARP, chemtrails and geo-engineering which are ruining the climate of our planet deliberately. Chemtrails: http://www.outofthebottomlesspit.co.uk/412291091

In the USA this winter of 2018-2019 has been totally engineered with ice-nucleation where temps have been forced down to minus 50c or the coldest temps on record. Https://usawatchdog.com/dane-wigington-we-face-abrupt-climate-collapse/

Here in the UK this winter has been the mildest on record as the weather machine or HAARP situated in Wales has been on most of the time, to drive away the cold weather by moving the jet-stream to the far north of the UK. Apart from a few frosts we have seen no winter to speak of, at least here in the UK. Why? Because simply put, many of the elite who run the planet, live in southern England, and they don't want their roads and airports blocked by snow, so they have the power and influence to get the military to 'switch on' the chemtrails almost every day along with the hellish 'H.A.A.R.P. Weather machine. Http://www.outofthebottomlesspit.co.uk/412291091

2019-2020 5G Cell towers – 20,000 telecommunication satellites to be put in space over the next year, to bring in the mini-micro-waves. Cell towers to be placed every 250 meters in the towns. These microwaves according to some sources, will be devastating to our health, causing brain cancer, skin cancer and Alzheimer's and other mental illnesses.

Why would anyone in their right mind opt for putting this insane microwave system right over our heads.

In a word: **Eugenics**. Or better said 'to get rid of the useless eaters' as stated by the illuminati or the elite of this planet: http://www.outofthebottomlesspit.co.uk/412561137

Volcanic activity & earthquakes have increased dramatically over the past 20 years and many 'sleeping' or even 'extinct' volcanoes have come roaring back to life.

Pollution on the planet has increased in many ways and the greatest danger if from Fukushima in Japan as hundreds of tons of nuclear wastewater are continually pouring into the Pacific Ocean killing all the sea creatures.

Poisoning the water, we drink: http://www.outofthebottomlesspit.co.uk/413438756

Global cooling for the last 20 years and not global warming. Many scientists state we are heading into an ice-age, although there is certainly no sign of that in the UK.

However, as I mentioned above, we can't judge by the deliberate 'climate change warming' in the UK, as the 'powers that be', apparently keep the UK winters much milder than normal. why? Probably to give the appearance of 'global warming'.

There is a major problem and that is if the sun itself has gone into 'quiet phase' with next to no 'sun-spots' then all the global weather machines are not going to be able to stop an ice-age.

Ice-age. http://www.outofthebottomlesspit.co.uk/420939961

'GLOBAL WARMING':https://www.telegraph.co.uk/news/worldnews/australiaandthepacific/australia/11591193/Australia-PM-advisor-says-climate-change-a-UN-led-ruse.html

TRANSHUMANISM & A.I. are accelerating exponentially. **SOURCE: https://www.infowars.com/humanity-replaced-by-ai-robots-and-human-animal-hybrids/**

CERN COLLIDER is up to no good and is trying to open 'Gates to Other Dimensions' **CERN: https://youtu.be/dO7EdBRALqE?t=612**

CERN, UFO'S, WATCHERS & GIANTS: https://youtu.be/dO7EdBRALqE?t=289

'ALIENS & ALIEN ABDUCTIONS' During the past 20 years one of the Signs of the Times is the fact that man is pushing the agenda through Hollywood films that mankind was seeded here on the planet by benign aliens from distant galaxies.

ALIENS VERSUS FALLEN ANGELS & HUMAN ABDUCTIONS : https://youtu.be/4SAg5xHbD-w?list=PL9SHD8shR4ZNmcDkjQ8D6l MN8Z3qzqGRW&t=143

HOLLOW EARTH: The truth is that it is much more likely that our Earth is not solid but hollow and is full of all kinds of critters, including demons, as well as Reptilian Races and other humanoid races. **http://www.outofthebottomlesspit.co.uk/421040248**

We are told that they have a much more advanced technology than mankind, but then, why do they hide underground?

Has God Himself forced them to remain below ground? So rather than them being advanced races from other planets who 'seeded' mankind on this planet millions of years ago, as part of the failing and erroneous teachings of Evolution, they are in fact nothing more than masquerading devils and demons, and their offspring through abductions of human beings to the underground world. Why the human abductions? Because the races below the earth are often infertile and thus, they need humans to procreate for them!

Corruption, Violence & Perversion on a scale never seen before in history, or let's say since the destruction by God himself of Sodom & Gomorrah, and the Tower of Babel.

1000,000,000 babies aborted since 1960. 50-60 million abortions every year! Abortion is now the no 1 cause of death in the whole world! New York just voted in a new law to allow abortions up until the moment of delivery. just another eugenics policy. murder the innocents!

Abortion Was No.1 Cause of Death in 2018: https://www.breitbart. com/health/2018/12

/31/abortion-leading-cause-of-death-in-2018-with-41-million-killed/

Emasculating of the men by chemicals and high estrogenic levels. the population of the planet is no longer increasing. the average number of children born is 2.4 / couple worldwide. it used to be 6.0 back in the 1960'. western Europe & the USA are dying out as so few people have children any longer.

Many of the men have a 'low sperm count' and many of the women are infertile. How has this happened? Well, it has been planned by the Elite for a very long time. It is called 'chemical castration' of the men and 'forced infertility' on the women.

Too many chemicals in our water supply and too many heavy metals in the atmosphere dropped through the Chemtrails all over the world. http://www. outofthebottomlesspit.co.uk/412291091

I have observed that many people that I know today of the younger generation consider themselves infertile. Why is this?

The fertility rate of the planet has gone down 60% in the past 40 years! What has happened to our planet? Are we are being deliberately eradicated by the eugenic plans of the elite, which were put into effect many years ago.

Apparently, the elite with all these eugenics plans intend to 'reduce world population' from 7 billion to 500,000,000 over the next 5 years.

Robots And Robotics Are Replacing Humans And Therefore The Elite 'No Longer Need So Many' Human Beings. Well that's the way they see it, but I think God Himself might disagree with them.

Wars & Rumours of Wars: No End Of These As Long As The Military Industrial Complex in the U.S.A is handed $1.4 trillion for 'weapons and war' in the USA. The military industrial complex create wars if there isn't one, and that's how they make their money. The Bible calls them the merchants. One day soon they are all going to go down!

UFO Sightings Have Increased Drastically In The Past 20 Years As Signs Of The Times:

UFO's Evidence By The Military: https://www.wanttoknow.info/ufocover-up10pg

Leaders Of The World Are Non Human- or better said some of them are demonic.

When one takes all the above into account, it is very obvious that those running the planet do not care about the welfare of our planet or of its people and in fact they are 'bent on destroying God's Creation altogether'.

This shows the leaders of this planet are strongly led by demonic forces who are still in total rebellion against God and their goal is to destroy all of god>s creation including both the nature and all the people on the planet.

Conclusion: I have only mentioned a very few of the important and even devastating events over the past 20 years.

The frequency of the 'signs of the times' as mentioned by Jesus himself in Matthew 24 is increasing in every sense of the word.

Jesus will have to come back soon to rescue this planet before it is totally destroyed.

Faith in God. It is so important to have faith in Jesus for our salvation. The truth is that only Jesus' return can ever fix the monstrous mess that our planet is currently in!

Don't worry, all the biblical books that i have ever studied, predict the total destruction of the wicked merchants who run this planet. They will all be cast into Hell by Jesus himself when he returns, and some of them will eventually be cast into the lake of fire if they don't repent.

'There was a *rapid descent into great spiritual darkness* once the Nephilim (fallen angels) and their sons the Rephaim (giants) had returned to the earth. So, shall it also be in man's last days on earth when pandora's box of total evil will again be opened as it was in the 500 years leading up to the great flood of Noah's time.

Total evil will rule in the 'reign of the satanic Anti-Christ for 1260 days, according to the book of revelations & the book of Daniel in the time marked as 'the great tribulation.'

'At the time just after the 'great flood' 'those people described as building the tower of babel, sounded more like drones of a beehive, in other words mindless zombies. So, shall it also be in man's last days upon earth, when eventually all order will break down and total chaos will descend and consume the whole earth in the time when mankind is forced to be branded with the 'mark of the beast' implants and thereby making him a mindless zombie. A time when a man shall not regard his neighbour or relative, but it shall be every man for himself. A spirit of unrest will come upon the whole earth:

Mark of the Beast: http://www.outofthebottomlesspit.co.uk/412733219

II EZDRAS 15.19 'A man shall have no pity upon his neighbours but shall make an assault upon their houses with the sword and plunder their goods. Because of hunger for bread and because of great tribulation'.

In conclusion: I am sure some of you are wondering why I would list all of these 'Signs of the times 1999-2019'. Why bother, you might say? Well, the truth is that everything is intensifying, and the world is moving faster and faster, and unfortunately so many people hardly have the time to even think about things, as to what is really important.

CHAPTER 38

VAMPIRES & BLOODSUCKERS
Scientific Vampires: TRUE SCIENCE
– www.outofthebottomlesspit.co.uk

JUBILEES 6.12 AND Noah and his sons swore that they would not eat any blood that was in **any flesh**, and he made a covenant before the Lord God for ever throughout all the generations of the earth in this month.

EDITOR: Why did God make a covenant with Noah in making Noah and his family swear that they would not drink the blood of an animal or any creature, including mankind? Was it just possible that 'drinking blood' alters the D.N.A of people and actually makes them into vampires or even 'eventually cannibals' as happened to the Giants, the sons of the Fallen Watchers before the Great Flood.

We know that since this time the dark side of the spirit world often require 'human sacrifices' to 'curry the favour of the gods' so to speak. Maybe there is a lot of truth to that ancient concept. For this reason, God made strict laws concerning the blood of both humans and animals, in the hope that mankind would not slip back into the type of depravity that had happened before the Great Flood.

More from ‹Jubilees Insights›:
Conditions Before The Great Flood?
The 'Fallen Angels' Came Down To Earth And Seduced The Women And Their Children Became Giants In The Land. When The Giants Died They Became The 'Disembodied Spirits Of The Giants' Also Better Known As The 'Demons'.

After the Great Flood of Noah, Noah began to admonish his sons about the danger of the 'disembodied spirits of the Giants', otherwise known as 'demons ', coming to seduce and harm his descendants, especially if they gave in to ‹demonic influences› of ‹shedding blood›, ‹eating or drinking blood ‹ and ‹idol worshipping›:

JUBILEES 7.27 For I see and behold the demons have begun (their) seductions against you and against your children and now I fear on your behalf, that after my death ye will shed the **blood** of men upon the earth, and that ye, too, will be destroyed from the face of the earth.

JUBILEES 7.28 For whoso sheds man›s blood, and whoso eats the blood of any flesh, shall all be destroyed from the earth.

JUBILEES 7.29 And there shall not be left any man that eats blood, or that sheds the blood of man on the earth, nor shall there be left to him any seed or descendants living under heaven; For into Sheol (Hell) shall they go, And into the place of condemnation shall they descend, And into the darkness of the deep shall they all be removed by a violent death.

Editor: I was just reading about how the wealthy can buy young people's blood by the litre to drink – for $8000/L. Why do they want to drink this blood? They believe that it will help them to stay younger!

SOURCE: <http://www.exposingsatanism.org/ blood-of-young-people-8000-will-get-you-a-bag/>

< https://www.extremetech.com/extreme/181818-vampirism-is-real-scientists-find-that-old-animals-can-be-rejuvenated-with-the-blood-of-the-young-and-innocent >

Drinking Blood Can Kill You (*Not* Controlled And Screened Blood-Transfusions): https://www.livescience.com/15899-drinking-blood-safe.html

This reminds me of an article where the author had a hellish nightmare about exactly what is happening today! It was written back in the 1970's and is called 'the blood-suckers-the scientific vampires':

'**But The Next Scene Was More Like A Nightmare!** They were rounding us all up in this huge barn like warehouse--there must have been several hundred of us inside like prisoners. But our captors seemed to be trying to avoid the impression that we were prisoners but that were voluntarily taking part in some kind of experiment, a scientific experiment, and they were asking who'd like to be next to volunteer to demonstrate somebody's new scientific discovery some kind of physical regeneration. I remember the scientist's name was definitely mentioned and so was the name of the new method, but I can't remember either one of them now.

Some Girl Was Then Strapped Onto This Slanted Operating Table it was slanted at about a 45-degree angle from her head down to her feet on a sort of platform, apparently so we could all see, and the small tubes about the size of your little finger were running from various parts of her body into this little machine which seemed like a pump. And these two very well dressed but cruel-looking, almost bestial-looking men were sitting on either side of the machine at her feet, with similar tubes in their mouths, each one with one tube running from the machine into his mouth. And the scientist said,

"Are We Ready To Begin The Experiment? Be sure all the windows are closed, and doors are locked so we won't be disturbed." But I had the feeling we were being locked in more than that others were being locked out, and that we were actually captives, and these so-called scientists were our captors.

Anyway, the demonstration began, and we were all supposed to watch while the scientist lectured on what was going on. He said,

«You Will See Now That As We Start The Pump The Blood Is Being Drained From The Subject Slowly, first from her brain and head as she is gradually losing consciousness quietly and peacefully, so that she no longer even knows what>s happening. It is all very painless and pleasant, and she no longer has anything to worry about." And sure, enough as we watched, right before our horrified gaze the blood was draining from her head, and her face went white, and she obviously became unconscious! Then her neck went white, and her shoulders and the whiteness seemed to move down her naked body from her head toward her toes.

Meanwhile We Could See These Two Men Sitting At Her Feet Sucking On These Tubes From Which We Could See Her Blood Flowing Into Their Mouths! They both seemed to get almost demonically gleeful expressions of great exhilaration and excitement, becoming very excited and as though they were exploding with energy! And I thought to myself, "My God, what a horror! How awful! They're killing her right before eyes and drinking her blood right in front of us and claiming this renews their energy and their life forces and helps them to live longer by drinking human blood like vampires but making it all look very scientific and sound very humane!" I thought,

«My God, We>ve Got To Get Out Of Here Somehow Or They>re Going To Kill Us All And Drink Our Blood So They Can Live!» So I began looking around for a possibility of an open unguarded window through which some of us might jump. But the scientist, almost as though he had read my mind, spoke to some of the men who were standing around the doors and windows obviously as guards, he called out again, «Be sure all the doors and windows are shut tight so that no one can interrupt our demonstration.» But I knew what he meant of course: So that nobody could get out and get away from the demonstration! And I just can>t remember any more right now. It seemed like then I woke up and remembered the whole dream.

I Was So Horrified It Woke Me Up! You know how sometimes when you have a nightmare you get to the most awful scariest part and mercifully you awaken! I was so thankful that it wasn't really true, it wasn't really happening!

CHAPTER 39

UNDERGROUND BASES, UFO'S, GREYS, REPTILIANS, DULCE WARS, MIND CONTROL, UNDERGROUND FACILITIES, ALIENS FROM INNER EARTH

A Dulce Base Security Officer Speaks Out

THE FOLLOWING IS a list of questions that were directed to former *Dulce Base Security* officer Thomas Edwin Castello approximately a year before his death [or disappearance].

They are followed by his responses:

The references to the Dulce base here deal mainly with the upper levels, not the extreme lower levels which include vast natural caverns and, some believe, very ancient tunnel systems as well. This would include the tunnels illuminated by phosphorus pentoxide which the alien greys avoid, and the origin of which is unknown. In fact, sources have informed us that some of the underground NORAD facilities of Colorado were constructed within already-existing cavern systems, suggesting that Ray Palmer and Richard Shaver were correct when as early as the mid-1940's they wrote about the government's search for ancient underground cave and tunnel systems to be converted for their own use.)

Carlsbad caverns and especially the adjacent Lecheguilla caves are 'officially' among the largest and deepest in the world, with several 'leads' that remain to be explored by professional speleonauts -)

I believe Thomas Castello is referring to the 'joint-operational' fleet. From combined sources however it appears as if Dulce is absolutely surrounded on all sides by 'alien' bases, and that Archuleta peak – although apparently the central nexus of the entire underground network – is nevertheless just one part of an overall complex that some claim is nearly the size of Manhattan!

One source has indicated that there are chambers a few hundred feet below the very town of Dulce itself that are part of level one of the facilities. This close proximity may explain why it has usually been described as the 'Dulce Base'. Apparently even with his high-security clearance, Thomas Castello was only familiar with one part of the overall mega-complex which underlies the area. Whatever amount of activity is taking place there, different sources seem to indicate that the town of Dulce nevertheless lies over a major crossroads, convergence or 'intersection' area of alien activity even though the 'core' of alien activity has been extended to Los Alamos.

Los Alamos and the mountainous regions east and southeast of it in and around the Santa Fe National Forest seem to be the MAJOR 'nest' of Reptiloid/Gray forces in North America, although there is also a large number of 'dens' scattered throughout the underground networks between Dulce and Area 51.

Dulce seems to be a major 'through' point for Exterran and subterrains reptilian activity, a central 'infiltration' zone for surface operatives, as well as an operational base for abduction-implantation-mutilation agendas and also a major convergence for sub-shuttle terminals, UFO ports, and so on.)

Thomas mentioned several areas surrounding Utah – Colorado, New Mexico, Arizona, Nevada and Idaho, where there are 'connections', but little on Utah which according to some sources lies directly over one of the largest natural cavern systems in North America, one that is said to reach deep beneath the Western Rockies as well as beneath the Bonneville basin.

There have been many rumours of ancient 'tunnel' systems being inter-sected during the excavations of sub-basement levels below major industrial and mall areas in downtown Salt Lake City. Various stories surrounding these tunnels include:

There is a famous story which is not openly talked about – there are two versions... both may be true. In one version a Mormon Temple worker penetrated an underground tunnel below the 'square' in downtown Salt Lake City and travelled for some distance through a series of underground catacombs until running into a 'lizard' like man.

The creature attempted to attack him, but the man escaped and managed to find his way back to the surface. He began telling other people what had happened and soon afterwards the 'government' arrived in the area and went in and closed off many of the tunnels leading to the sub-basements of the Temple. Presumably there was some heated debates over how much of the underground system this denomination was allowed to control.

A similar dispute apparently occurred to the southwest where the LDS church maintained a large storage facility under Granite Mountain in Little Cottonwood canyon, within the upper levels of a vast network of caverns. Fascist CIA elements and the Greys came in and took control of the larger caverns deeper within the mountain and ordered the 'vault' workers to stay out of the 'forbidden' areas – and stated that the "U.S. Government" was now using them for "National Security" purposes and that it was their "patriotic duty" to maintain the secret.

The other version concerned a custodian who entered a tunnel near the cinemas area below the Crossroads Mall across the street and to the south from the temple square, while excavation was being carried out in a that part of the mall. The worker entered the tunnel and before long encountered a 'serpent' type man, beat a hasty retreat, and told his fellow workers what he had seen. The FBI and/or the local police soon arrived and sealed the tunnel.

Another story involved a young man who, along with a friend, had used a chain tied to his pickup truck to rip-up a manhole cover in the area near the 'Mall' and the 'Square'. They navigated through a maze of sewer passages underneath and came to a shaft that descended in a series of 5 small 'rooms' one below the other, and from the bottom room a tunnel led south into a large chamber wherein they saw a seemingly bottomless shaft, a large south-west tunnel strung with lights and 'large enough to drive a semi through', and the footprints of some type of three-toed bi-pedal creature.

Other sources imply that early pioneers and settlers of the area who explored these tunnels came in contact with and in some cases even joined with some of the Telosian-Agharti-Melchizedek-Mayan underground colonies below the Salt Lake Flats, the Salt Lake Valley and the Western Rockies.

These Subterraneans had formerly established territorial agreements with the Reptiloids and Greys before the aliens begun invading their subterra-nean lands below the intermountain west en-masse in the early 1900's. The treaties were part of an attempt to stave off a possible inter-species conflict, as skirmishes between the humanoids [Teros] and reptiloids [Deros] within the cavern networks of North America had been increasing since the 1920's, 30's and 40's.]

Because of a somewhat non-exclusive collective mind with which these humans interacted, it was decided that one possible way to 'convert' the reptil-ians into becoming beings of emotion and compassion was to allow them access to the group consciousness. The reptiloids however, once given access, immediately began taking advantage of the collective and used it to 'control' the humans on a subliminal basis.

The ease with which this occurred may have been enhanced by the fact that the Reptiloids and Greys were already operating as part of a collective or group mind, one which was far more complex than the Ashtar or Astarte collective itself which many of the 'Aghartians' depended on.

This suggests that the reptilian 'collective' or hive itself is absolutely void of any and all care, concern or compassion for human beings. Individual reptiloids operating distinct from the draconian collective might however be 'tamed' by other collective-free humanoids in some cases – as some have reportedly been 'tamed' by the Andro-Pleiadean worlds.

If the non-humans could be severed from the 'collective' they might be deprogrammed and reprogrammed so-to-speak and even attain individual awareness and a degree of emotionalism. In such cases it would not be advisable to give these creatures equal standing among humans, and absolute subservience and monitoring should be enforced even if means were found to sever them from the collective mind network.

When dealing with the reptilian forces, unconditional surrender should be first offered, and if this is not accepted than direct military action would be justified especially in light of the many permanent 'abductees' whom the Greys and Reptiloids have taken captive [those who are still alive] to their underground systems.

Most of the treaties that the humanoids had made with the reptiloids 'down under' have since been broken... especially following the Groom Wars of 1975 and the Dulce Wars of 1979, during which time much of the underground U.S. base networks [which were funded by American tax dollars by the way] were taken over by the Greys.

Some sources have implied that the aliens took advantage of the chaos especially during the Dulce wars and commenced to invade and conquer several of the older underground colonies. This apparently led to a rift in the 'Ashtar' collective, with many humanoids and hybrids splitting off and joining with the Andro-Pleiadean Federation non-interventionists, and many reptiloids and heartless humanoid agents splitting off and joining with the interventionists of the Draco-Orion Empire.

The Sirius-B system which – aside from Arcturus and Sol – has been the major centre of 'Ashtar' activity, has since been shaken by this split between the two opposing Ashtarian factions and war had reportedly raged through the Sirius system for several years, according to some 'contactees'... an apparent reflection of the division within the underground networks of North America between the Pleiadean-backed Sirian humanoids and Orion-backed Sirian reptiloids which both had maintained operations within the underground levels before the "Dulce Wars" broke out.

The Dulce wars were just the mere tip of the proverbial iceberg when we consider that the overall events which happened at Dulce had a chain reaction effect throughout this whole sector of not the galaxy. Before the division occurred, the reptiloids were invited to take part in 'peace talks' in Telos and elsewhere as an act of good faith, but the reptiloid-grey collectivists were more interested in expanding their empire and feeding their insatiable appetite for conquest than they were in making peace, although they agreed to peace treaties that they never intended to keep for 'Trojan horse' manipulation purposes.

There is a remnant collaboration such as that taking place in the underground facilities near Paradox Nevada where collectivist humanoids and reptiloids from Sirius and Sol still maintain a collaboration of necessity – in order to establish a global control system, however a large number of humanoids within the underground systems are at war with the collectivist-interventionist Reptilian infiltrators who would otherwise 'assimilate' these humanoids into their collective through deception, espionage and mind control.

Now several contactees like Alex Collier, Ray Keller, Stan Johnson and others are claiming that the conflicts in Sirius between the Andro-Pleiadean backed Ashtar forces and the Draco-Orion backed Ashtar forces – which were infiltrated and commandeered by Draco-Orion agents – have now spread to the Sol system, as both stellar superpowers have focused on this most strategic system, intent on protecting their respective 'interests' here from being subverted by the other side.

Whether or not the reigning 'King' of the Agharti realms at the time had benevolent or other motives, subjecting America to an outside super-power without Congressional consent would be considered high treason. Although unelected/appointed 'individuals' working within the Executive-Military-Industrial branch of 'government' might choose to do so of their own volition without Congressional or Senatorial consent, such an act cannot apply to the 'America' which is based on the Declaration of Independence, the U.S. Constitution and the Bill of Rights. There are apparently two 'nations' occupying the United States,

the traditional grassroots 'America' established by the founding fathers and led by the 'Electorate' government, and the fascist Bavarian-lodge 'underground nation' led by the 'Corporate' government which is contesting the original 'America' on its own soil.

Some predict an inevitable civil war between the Electorate/Constitutional/Surface government of the U.S., and the joint humanoid-reptiloid Corporate/National-Global Socialist/Underground New World Order government, which incidentally was bought and paid for by American taxpayers and other unsavoury money-making projects. This war will apparently provoke an armed United Nations / New World Order invasion of the U.S.A. which, according to George Washington's famous 'vision' at valley forge in 1777, will ultimately end with an American victory as a result of Divine Intervention.

Something like this may be inevitable if freedom is to be preserved on this world, and beyond. We should never forget however that the NWO corporate elite and their draconian masters intend to 'depopulate' the surface of this planet and the underground systems as well. According to one Navy intelligence source the 33-plus Masons [there are allegedly several degrees above the 33rd degree which interact directly with the Draconians and are part of the interplanetary initiatory lodges] intend to set the left-wing caverns and the right-wing caverns against each other in order to depopulate the underground realms so that they can impose absolute Bavarian-Draconian global control of 'both' worlds.

The 33+ and higher degrees according to this source intend to ride out the inferno in super-secret fortified caverns while the 33rd and lower degree masons and their respective left-wing and right-wing armies will be left to die in the surface and subsurface wars. It may be that some of the 33+ Masons intend to ride-out the holocaust in their Alternative-3 bases on the Moon and Mars. If those bases are still active. Remember, the roots of both the 'right-wing' national socialist and the 'left-wing' global socialist agendas trace back to Bavaria. isn't it interesting that the legendary 'dragon' has two 'wings' – a right wing and a left wing – both of which are controlled by a single 'beast'?

In essence, when it comes right down to it the war is between the Judeo-Christian based Constitutional Republic of America and the Luciferian-cult-based Socialist empire of Bavaria. Both the right- and left-wing movements are Machiavellian extremes created by the Bavarian Black Nobility ['Black' here being a reference to something hidden that cannot be seen, and not skin colour] in order to foment global chaos.

There are several claims that the collaboration with the Reptilians began with the Luciferian cults of Bavaria, and was later brought into America via the infiltration of the Scottish Rite and the fascist core of the NSA-CIA. There may have nevertheless been a reptilian presence below North America within the caverns that dates back several centuries, however a massive reptilian infestation of these underground systems seems to have begun near the beginning of the 20th century. 'Mt. Archuleta' might be considered the 'capital' of the alien segment of the 'secret' [Bavarian-Draconian] New World Order government in America – with the deep underground systems beneath the Denver International Airport being the 'capital' of the human segment of the secret government. .

This question is based on the assumption made by some researchers that many of the Masonic lodges were, beginning about 1776, infiltrated by the

Bavarian Illuminati. Much of the Masonic world is ultimately controlled by the Bavarian-lodge-backed 33+ degrees of Scottish Rite Masonry, a 'Rite' which according to early Masonic authority Rebold can be traced back to the Jesuit college at Clermont in Paris – a rite which advocates the destruction of national sovereignties in exchange for world government, the destruction of religious and especially Judaeo-Christian movements, and the destruction of the family-structure to be replaced by 'state' control of children, etc., as opposed to the more traditional protestant-Christianised York rite of masonry which the Scottish rite has attempted to subvert since its inception into Masonry.

This question was also based on claims from a former 33rd degree Mason, James Shaw, that the Scottish Rite headquarters in the "House of the Temple" (click image right)-- which lies at the northern apex of the pentagram-like street layout of Washington D.C. – is filled with all kinds of indications of serpent worship in the form of murals, carvings, statues, etc., depicting serpentine figures.

Actually, from what my sources tell me, not only are there degrees beyond the 33rd degree, but the 33rd degree itself is made up of two cores, an inner and outer core, the 33rd degree and the 33+ degree. In the past when the 33rd degree initiation was reached a potential initiate might have been given a Bible or a Cross and asked to spit on it or desecrate it in some manner.

If they refused to do this, they were told that they had made the "right decision" and remained in the outer core of the 33rd degree, thinking that they had finally 'arrived'. If they did or do commit this form of blasphemy then they are told that they have made the "right decision", and they are sent on to the inner core of the 33+ degree, which is the springboard to the higher levels which interact with the joint humanoid-reptiloid Ashtarian lodges or branches of the 'Serpent Cult' on other planets, within underground cities, and possibly even other dimensions.

One source informs me that former president George Herbert Walker Bush – who was at one time the head of MJ-12 – had attained to the 42nd degree, however he may have attained to even higher levels since that time. I would guess that the one who holds the highest level of initiation would be the 'dragon-king' of Draconis himself, or whatever appellation the leader or the leaders of the Draconian Empire may go by.

Perhaps we should have referred to the CIA's superior agency, the NSA, whose personnel reportedly pilot the "black-budget UFOs" between the Luna and Dreamland bases. –

A letter from R.J.M.' of Pennsylvania dated 1-31-91 stated: "...I have a lot of UFO videos. I also have 'the secret land' [1947]. It shows bunger's oasis and says they discovered warm land at the south pole. One German author claims the Nazi's had a photo-finish fight with Byrd. At the end of the movie, it says: 'Byrd's Intrepid 4,000 met and defeated Antarctica's toughest Battalions.' I don't think they were talking about the weather."

Another source has stated that there were loses on both sides, and the battle for Antarctica against the Nazi's "Last Battalion" – which had fortified themselves in underground bases below the mountains of Neu Schwabenland, Antarctica – ended in a stalemate.

Question: Why would Adolph Hitler and Eva Braun commit suicide after Hitler had spent so much energy executing over 5000 Nazi officials whom he 'suspected' were behind his assassination attempt at the 'Wolf' bunker, especially if he had a way out via a secret Nazi South Polar base? The March 18, 1994, issue of the plain dealer [Cleveland, Ohio] carried an ap story titled "doctors find burnt body could not be Hitler's".

Excerpts include:

This is also interesting when we consider that the well-known 'abductee', Barney Hill, remembered the following experience under regressive hypnosis as recorded in the paranormal encyclopaedia, "mysteries of mind, space & time". barney and his wife betty were abducted by grey-skinned humanoids "from zeta Reticuli".

However, one of the 'beings' on the craft was described by barney hill under regressive hypnosis in the following words which are taken from p.1379 of the encyclopaedia: "Another figure has an evil face. He looks like a German Nazi. he's a Nazi. His eyes! his eyes. I've never seen eyes like that before!"

Remember that this occurred nearly 15 years after Europe had supposedly been "de-Nazified". There seems to be an Antarctic connection with the Dulce scenario as well as other possible 'Nazi' connections:

German 'tourists' scouring New Mexico, exploring mines and caves and buying up land and mineral rights just before the outbreak of WWII; The Nazi-connected CIA's involvement and their placement of several Nazi S.S. agents – who had been brought into the U.S. via Project Paperclip – within the Dulce and other underground facilities; the involvement of secret 'Bavarian' lodges at Dulce. and the possible Antarctican-Dulce connection to 'Alternative 003'.

Another interesting connection is the fact that the secret Nazi teams involved in the construction and operation of the underground bases below the mountains of Neu Schwaben land and elsewhere in Antarctica were called ULTRA teams. ULTRA is also the code-name for the DULCE base!

Also there seems to be a direct connection between the Dulce base and the Montauk base in Long Island – which was/is[?] reputedly jointly operated by the Draconian Reptiloids, Orion Greys and the Bavarian Thule Society which had backed the Nazi agenda. –

Take note of the similarity between this scenario and the NBC mini-series "V", which is now available on video cassette after years of non-availability. I have it on good authority that the original author of the "V" idea was an investigator who knew Thomas Castello on a personal basis.

He had connections in Hollywood and had written a motion picture script, which was in turn seen and 'borrowed' without permission by an NBC employee and re-written as a mini-series. The show was based on reptilian humanoids from Sirius-B who had come to earth under the guise of benevolent human-like space brothers to bring a new order of universal peace. In reality they had a secret agenda to rape planet earth of her resources and steal her people for biological sustenance.

This agenda was being contested by a human resistance who refused to fall for the reptilian's facade, and these resistors were in turn working with a secret fifth-column of reptilians who did not agree with their leaders' agenda for planet earth. Could this mini-series have had an actual basis in a bizarre reality?

If Thomas Castello is correct in his assertion, then based on his overall revelations, as well as the revelations of others such as Robert Lazar, Phil Schneider, etc., the Dulce Wars were the result of at least five overlapping factors or scenarios which converged at more or less the same time or played into each other.

This may have also involved a conflict of interest within MJ12 itself, and apparently involved different security forces including the Delta Force, Black Berets, Air Force Blue Berets, Secret Service, FBI Division Five, CIA stormtroopers and Dulce Base security.

The various factors which seem to have played into the Dulce Wars would include animosity towards the Greys for their slaughter of several scientists and security personnel in the Groom Wars below Area 51 three years earlier as described by,

- former MJ12 Special Studies Group agent Michael Wolf
- accidental [?] encounters between aliens and human construction workers and security forces near Dulce as described by Phil Schneider

- an attack on the Dulce base 'resistance' that was apparently ordered by die-hard collaborators in deep-level intelligence as described by Thomas Castello
- an attempt to rescue several of our best scientists who had been captured by the aliens after they had discovered the "Grand Deception" involving a violation of the established treaties, that is the permanent abduction of thousands of humans to the Dulce and other bases for God only knows what purposes, as described by John Lear – could it be that MJ12 / PI40 was unaware of these abductees, yet their superior agency the BLACK MONK / MAJIC agency was aware and had agreed to an actual exchange of human life for technology?
- and another factor would involve a dispute over whether human security personnel could carry flash guns as opposed to machine guns

All of these were apparently contributing factors to the 'altercations' which raged throughout the Dulce Base beginning in 1979.

It may be conceivable that some of the higher security clearances are used for the joint human-alien interstellar projects. For instance, Whitley Streiber described an abduction to another planetary sphere where he encountered ancient ruins, aliens and human personnel dressed in military kackies and carrying camcorders, automatic weapons, etc.

Obviously, such personnel would have to possess an extremely high security classification, such as "Universal Military Service" for instance? The joint alien-illuminati " alternative-3" projects have reportedly taken part in joint offensive operations against the peaceful residents of other worlds, this according to a couple who 'defected' from the alternative-3 movement after an agent from the 'Federation' warned them about such atrocities. –

According to many abductees, the reptiloids are not above eating human flesh. It has been said that they prefer flesh that is young enough to be free of toxins, yet old enough to be imbued with a lifetime of accumulated "emotional energy residue" which is resident within the human body. Some abductees claim that certain reptilian factions have such complex biotech-nologies that they are able to remove a human's soul-energy-matrix and place it in a containment 'box' and use the controlled 'body' for whatever purpose they choose.

Some abductees also insist that in some cases the reptiloids can create a cloned duplicate of a person in a short amount of time through time warping and replace the soul-energy-matrix of a person back into the new cloned body if their disappearance from society would otherwise create too many problems. This way they can ingest the emotional-residue-imbued original body without the abductee realizing [in most cases] that their soul-memory-matrix has been transferred to a cloned body, because they would have experienced a total 'soul-matrix' energy transfer and a suppression of any memories relating to the transfer process.

The cloned bodies do not possess the integrated emotional residue that the vampirialistic reptiloids apparently crave and find intoxicating in a similar manner as a human on earth who is addicted to hard drugs.

This may tie-in with the reports of certain remote-viewing «astral spies» who claim to have «projected» into underground facilities like Dulce New Mexico or Pine Gap Australia, only to have close encounters with these astral containment fields, or have been captured by the same and released after being 'interrogated' via super-sensitive electronic equipment. In one case an Australian remote-viewer was probing the Pine Gap facility where he also «saw» three other astral spies.

The magnetic or astral body of one of these people had been captured by such a containment field, which really disturbed him. This man, Robert, also saw Greys and Reptiloids operating in the deeper levels of Pine Gap and also Nordic-type humans who were apparently captives and who did not seem to be very happy about being there. –

Naturally this may be true, however through genetic bioengineering and gene-splicing this has apparently been accomplished to some extent.

The Hollow Earth theory is one that was postulated by various well known individuals, including Marshall B. Gardner, Raymond Bernard, William Halley – discoverer of Halley's comet, Edgar Allen Poe, Edgar Rice Burroughs, John Cleves Symmes, John Uri Lloyd and others.

Basically, the thesis involves what one might refer to as the Geo-concavitic sphere theory, or that as the earth was forming in its molten state the planetary spin created a hollow or concavity within the centre similar to the hollow created by the centrifugal force of a horizontal washing machine following a spin cycle. The theory, which has been postulated in para-geological theories, in adventure novels, and in some cases even in alleged visits to the "inner world", states that the 'shell' of the earth averages between 800-1000 miles thick, with an interior surface consisting of oceans and land illuminated perpetually by a sphere of electromagnetic and/or nuclear energy suspended at the very centre of the "empty space".

There are reputedly funnel-like openings near the polar regions, perpetually concealed by mist created by the collision of cold air from the outside and hot air from the inside, which permits ingress and egress to and from this inner 'world'.

The theory states that the inner surface has its own gravity, yet slightly less than the outer surface gravity. One side-theory is that between the inner and outer surface where gravity is nullified there exists a layer of weightless or low-weight caverns in an eternal state of chaos where minerals, liquids, gases and chemicals continually slam together from the earth's rotation, causing intense magmatic activity, a virtual inferno, or "bottomless pit".

Some have theorized that – based on the Apocryphal book of Esdras, chapter 13, which contains non-canonized Jewish legends – that the 10 'lost' tribes of Israel disappeared beyond the river Sambatyon and to a place in the far north where humans never lived before called 'Arzareth'. In the last days, a path would be made through the ice and waters of the north and the lost tribes would Return. There are three tribes accounted for as of this writing, or rather two tribes and two half tribes: Judah, Benjamin, half of the Levite tribe, and apparently half of the tribe of Dan if we are to believe the Ethiopian 'Jews' who claim to be descended from Dan.

The '13th' tribe would be accounted for by the fact that the two Josephite tribes of Ephraim and Manasseh are considered distinctive tribes in and of themselves. As for the 'giants', some believe that these have a direct connection to the 10-12 foot tall 'Anakin' people mentioned in the Old Testament who were driven out of Palestine, following which the Torah gives no further details as to their fate, although there have been many reports of such 'giants' being encountered in large cavern systems below Alaska, Oregon, California, Utah, Texas and Mexico, and also reports of ancient gravesites in the western U.S. and elsewhere where the remains of human giants have reportedly been discovered. Most often they – like the fifth dimensional "Sasquatch people" themselves – have been described as being benevolent, unless provoked.

Apparently, according to another source, these lower 'Bigfoot' type creatures – having more of a resemblance to apes than to the more "human-like" faces and features of the much friendlier Sasquatch people who frequent the surface – dwell in wild cavern systems some 6 or more miles deep, along with other very large and dangerous insectoid and quadruped or serpentine reptilian life forms reminiscent to something from out of a Haden nightmare.

This is according to a report I investigated some years ago of a group of speleonauts who reportedly broke into a vast underground labyrinth west and northwest of Cushman, Arkansas, where they encountered these types of creatures as well as friendly blue-skinned humans who claimed to be descended from a family that had survived an ancient global deluge by taking refuge within a large ship. These ancient people claimed that their ancestors had come to the Americas and discovered the cavern 'world', wherein they commenced to establish their hidden civilization.

Presumably including the original two 'planetoids' that arrived in geosynchronous orbits around earth at 400 and 600 miles up in 1953. This reportedly led to an NSA project which successfully communicated with the Grey aliens and resulted in a contact-landing-treaty scenario involving president Eisenhower and other Executive-Military-Industrial officials at Muroc/Edwards/Holloman Air Force Bases in 1954

For instance, hiding entrances to underground bases beneath religious shrines, federal buildings, mining works, malls, libraries, lodges, hotels or basically areas that one would consider the least likely places to hide or accommodate an entrance to an underground facility. The underground New World Order 'FEMA' facilities throughout the United States apparently utilize this type of concealment with many of their bases. **Source:** UNDERGROUND BASES – www.outofthebottomlesspit.co.uk https://www.bibliotecapleyades.net/branton/esp_dulcebook11.htm

CHAPTER 40

ALIEN TECHNOLOGY, TUNNEL-BORING MACHINES & THE GREYS.

(The following video is definitely very scary, and not for everyone.)

However, in the fight against Darkness, it is good to know your Enemy and how he operates.

For "we wrestle not against Flesh and Blood, but against Principalities, against Powers, against the Rulers of the Darkness of this world (Satan and his Fallen Angels), against spiritual wickedness in high places."

Find out how the USA government wastes 28% of the USA's yearly income on "black operations" alone. They steal the money from the Budget, with total arrogance and disregard for the laws of man. They treat the man on the street as a complete nobody, who doesn't deserve to know the truth.

So much information, about a myriad of important technologies are deliberately hidden from the general public, with the very arrogant attitude of those in charge of the black budgets. They spend money on many things, for which they should be arrested for serious crimes against the laws of the USA. They act as if they are the untouchables, and that they are above the law!

NUCLEAR TUNNEL-BORING MACHINES
200 UNDERGROUND CITIES IN THE USA ALONE
UNDERGROUND HIGH SPEED TRAINS travelling at MACH 2 (Twice the speed of Sound) using Alien Technology.

In this video, you will hear about all kinds of beings far under the ground who are physical and very dangerous and beguiling and who eat human flesh.

It explains why so many unaccountable persons have disappeared from the face of the earth for good, and who ended up as lunch to these sickening Hybrid Reptilian races.

A lot of very interesting details on this video. I have just mentioned but a few of the interesting details

Well worth watching, for those who can handle it!

Let's keep up the fight against the evil deception that is trying to take over the planet, in the form of the new world order, who are totally in league with the above-mentioned sickening demonic Reptilian Races.

Even if they are physical, they have a lot to do with demons and Fallen Angels, and are the resultant Hybrid Races, formed from mixing DNA collections from humans in so-called Alien Abductions, which actually happen underground and not in space.

Source: UNDERGROUND BASES – www.outofthebottomlesspit.co.uk

CHAPTER 41

HEAVEN IS REAL

I JUST WATCHED this movie with my wife and teen daughters, and we all liked it very much as we have had a large family of 11 children & have experienced some of the sorrows brought out in this movie such as losing a baby. In this movie their son has a near death experience after being operated on for a burst appendicitis. The boy describes heaven in great detail after his traumatic operation ordeal.

Truly a wonderful Near-Death Experience which has already inspired millions of people around the globe to realize that heaven is real, and that Jesus is real as well as angels and that more than anything else God is love and is very forgiving. A truly a beautifully heart-wrenching tear-jerker of a movie. Best True-Life Drama film in many years.

NEAR DEATH E EXPERIENCES

What heaven's really like – by a leading brain surgeon who says he's been there: Read his testimony before you scoff. It might just shake your beliefs

By Dr Eben Alexander 18 October 2014

When I was a small boy, I was adopted. I grew up remembering nothing of my birth family and unaware that I had a biological sister, named Betsy. Many years later, I went in search of my biological family, but for Betsy it was too late: she had died.

This is the story of how I was reunited with her — in Heaven.

Before I start, I should explain that I am a scientist, who has spent a lifetime studying the workings of the brain.

Dr Eben Alexander says he was taken 'on a voyage through a series of realms' after he went into a coma when he was diagnosed with meningitis

My adoptive father was a neurosurgeon, and I followed his path, becoming an neurosurgeon myself and an academic who taught brain science at Harvard Medical School.

Although nominally a Christian, I was sceptical when patients described spiritual experiences to me.

My knowledge of the brain made me quite sure that out-of-body experiences, angelic encounters and the like were hallucinations, brought on when the brain suffered a trauma.

And then, in the most dramatic circumstances possible, I discovered proof that I was wrong. Six years ago, I woke up one morning with a searing headache. Within a few hours, I went into a coma: my neocortex, the part of the brain that handles all the thought processes making us human, had shut down completely.

Dr Eben's Alexander's 'heaven' was filled with music, animals, trees, and colours and was extremely vivid

At the time, I was working at Lynchburg General Hospital in Virginia, and I was rushed to the emergency room there. The doctors ascertained that I had contracted meningitis — a rare bacterial strain of E coli was in my spinal fluid and eating into my brain like acid. My survival chances were near zero.

I was in deep coma, a vegetative state, and all the higher functions of my brain were offline. Scans showed no conscious activity whatever — my brain was not malfunctioning; it was completely unplugged.

But my inner self still existed, in defiance of all the known laws of science.

Magical: He said he found himself as a speck of awareness on a butterfly wing, among pulsing swarms of millions of other butterflies

For seven days, as I lay in that unresponsive coma, my consciousness went on a voyage through a series of realms, each one more extraordinary than the last — a journey beyond the physical world and one that, until then, I would certainly have dismissed as impossible.

For thousands of years, ordinary people as well as shamans and mystics have described brief, wonderful glimpses of ethereal realms. I'm not the first person to have discovered that consciousness exists beyond the body.

What is unique in my case is that I am, as far as scientific records show, the only person to have travelled to this heavenly dimension with the cortex in complete shut-down, while under minute observation throughout.

There are medical records for every minute of my coma, and none of them show any indication of brain activity. In other words, as far as neuroscience can say, my journey was not something happening inside my head.

Plenty of scientists have a lot of difficulty with this statement. My experience undermines their whole belief system. But the one place I have found ready acceptance is in church, where my story often tallies with people's expectations.

Even the deep notes of the church organ and the glorious colours of the stained glass seem to echo faintly the sights and sounds of Heaven.

Here, then, is what I experienced: my map of Heaven.

After the blinding headache, when I had slipped into the coma, I gradually became aware of being in a primitive, primordial state that felt like being buried in earth.

It was, however, not ordinary earth, for all around me I sensed, and sometimes heard and saw, other entities.

It was partly horrific, partly comforting and familiar: I felt like I had always been part of this primal murk.

I am often asked, 'Was this hell?' but I don't think it was — I would expect hell to be at least a little bit interactive, and this was a completely passive experience.

I had forgotten what it was even to be human, but one important part of my personality was still hard at work: I had a sense of curiosity. I would ask, 'Who? What? Where?' and there was never a flicker of response.

After an expanse of time had passed, though I can't begin to guess how long, a light came slowly down from above, throwing off marvellous filaments of living silver and golden effulgence.

It was a circular entity, emitting a beautiful, heavenly music that I called the Spinning Melody. The light opened up like a rip in the fabric of that coarse realm, and I felt myself going through the rip, up into a valley full of lush and fertile greenery, where waterfalls flowed into crystal pools.

There were clouds, like marshmallow puffs of pink and white. Behind them, the sky was a rich blue-black.

This world was not vague. It was deeply, piercingly alive, and as vivid as the aroma of fried chicken, as dazzling as the glint of sunlight off the metalwork of a car, and as startling as the impact of first love.

I know perfectly well how crazy my account sounds, and I sympathise with those who cannot accept it. Like a lot of things in life, it sounds pretty far-fetched till you experience it yourself.

Despite scans showing his brain was not functioning, Dr Alexander had a vivid experience

There were trees, fields, animals and people. There was water, too, flowing in rivers or descending as rain. Mists rose from the pulsing surfaces of these waters, and fish glided beneath them.

Like the earth, the water was deeply familiar. It was as though all the most beautiful waterscapes I ever saw on earth had been beautiful precisely because they were reminding me of this living water. My gaze wanted to travel into it, deeper and deeper.

This water seemed higher, and purer than anything I had experienced before, as if it was somehow closer to the original source.

I had stood and admired oceans and rivers across America, from Carolina beaches to west coast streams, but suddenly they all seemed to be lesser versions, little brothers and sisters of this living water.

That's not to denigrate the seas and lakes and thunderstorms that I've marvelled at throughout my life. It is simply to say that I now see all the earth's waters in a new perspective, just as I see all natural beauties in a new way.

In Heaven, everything is more real — less dense, yet at the same time more intense.

Heaven is as vast, various and populated as earth is ... in fact, infinitely more so. But in all this vast variety, there is not that sense of otherness that characterises our world, where each thing is alone by itself and has nothing directly to do with the other things around it.

Nothing is isolated in Heaven. Nothing is alienated. Nothing is disconnected. Everything is one.

I found myself as a speck of awareness on a butterfly wing, among pulsing swarms of millions of other butterflies. I witnessed stunning blue-black velvety skies filled with swooping orbs of golden light, angelic choirs leaving sparkling trails against the billowing clouds.

Those choirs produced hymns and anthems far beyond anything I had ever encountered on earth. The sound was colossal: an echoing chant that seemed to soak me without making me wet.

All my senses had blended. Seeing and hearing were not separate functions. It was as if I could hear the grace and elegance of the airborne creatures and see the spectacular music that burst out of them.

Even before I began to wonder who or what they were, I understood that they made the music because they could not contain it. It was the sound of sheer joy. They could no more hold it in than you could fill your lungs and never breathe out.

Simply to experience the music was to join in with it. That was the oneness of Heaven — to hear a sound was to be part of it. Everything was connected to everything else, like the infinitely complex swirls on a Persian carpet or a butterfly's wing. And I was flying on that carpet, riding on that wing.

Above the sky, there was a vast array of larger universes that I came to call an 'over-sphere', and I ascended until I reached the Core, that deepest sanctuary of the Divine — infinite inky blackness, filled to overflowing with indescribable, unconditional love.

There I encountered the infinitely powerful, all-knowing deity whom I later called Om, because of the sound that vibrated through that realm. I learned lessons there of a depth and beauty entirely beyond my capacity to explain.

During this voyage, I had a guide. She was an extraordinarily beautiful woman who first appeared as I rode, as that speck of awareness, on the wing of that butterfly.

I'd never seen this woman before. I didn't know who she was. Yet her presence was enough to heal my heart, to make me whole in a way I'd never known was possible. Her face was unforgettable. Her eyes were deep blue, and her cheekbones were high. Her face was surrounded by a frame of honey-brown hair.

She wore a smock, like a peasant's, woven from sheer colour — indigo, powder-blue and pastel shades of orange and peach. When she looked at me, I felt such an abundance of emotion that, if nothing good had ever happened to me before, the whole of my life would have been worth living for that expression in her eyes alone.

Dr Alexander became a neurosurgeon and an academic who taught brain science at Harvard Medical School

It was not romantic love. It was not friendship. It was far beyond all the different compartments of love we have on earth. Without actually speaking, she let me know that I was loved and cared for beyond measure and that the universe was a vaster, better, and more beautiful place than I could ever have dreamed.

I was an irreplaceable part of the whole (like all of us), and all the sadness and fear I had ever suffered was a result of my somehow having forgotten this most central of facts.

Her message went through me like a breath of wind. It's hard to put it into words, but the essence was this: 'You are loved and cherished, dearly, for ever. You have nothing to fear. There is nothing you can do wrong.'

It was, then, an utterly wonderful experience.

Meanwhile, back on Earth, I had been in my coma for seven days and showing no signs of improvement. The doctors were just deciding whether to continue with life support, when I suddenly regained consciousness. My eyes just popped open, and I was back. I had no memories of my earthly life but knew full well where I had been.

I had to relearn everything: who, what, and where I was. Over days, then weeks, like a gently falling snow, my old, earthly knowledge came back.

Words and language returned within hours and days. With the love and gentle coaxing of my family and friends, other memories emerged.

By eight weeks, my prior knowledge of science, including the experiences and learning from more than two decades spent as a neurosurgeon in teaching hospitals, returned completely. That full recovery remains a miracle without any explanation from modern medicine.

But I was a different person from the one I had been. The things I had seen and experienced while gone from my body did not fade away, as dreams and hallucinations do. They stayed.

Above all, that image of the woman on the butterfly wing haunted me.

And then, four months after coming out of my coma, I received a picture in the mail.

As a result of my earlier investigations to make contact with my biological family, a relative had sent me a photograph of my sister Betsy — the sister I'd never known.

The shock of recognition was total. This was the face of the woman on the butterfly wing.

The moment I realised this, something crystallised inside me.

That photo was the confirmation that I'd needed. This was proof, beyond reproach, of the objective reality of my experience.

From then on, I was back in the old, earthly world I'd left behind before my coma struck, but as a genuinely new person.

I had been reborn. And as I shall reveal on Monday, I am by no means the only one to have glimpsed the afterlife — and the wonders it holds. (Source: – www.peopleofthekeys.com)

Heaven Is Real, As Well As Incredibly Beautiful & A Very Happy & Fulfilling Place, Where Your Deepest Dreams Will Finally Be Fully Realized.

CHAPTER 42

SERAPHIM VISITS OUR GARDEN

THE OTHER DAY on Wednesday 07/09/16, my wife and I, and family, who live here in Scotland, (UK), had the privilege of being visited by a very beautiful Seraphim bird, which we found out later originated from the USA.

I have put the history of this bird and how it got its name, which we have traced back to North America below.

Whilst sitting in our garden yet again, this time we had a beautiful experience, in seeing a rare bird arrive in our garden.

We had never seen such a bird before, and though looking like a cross between a dove and pigeon, it had extremely feathered feet.

My granddaughter quipped, that it looked like it had a rooster's feet.

The bird flew from our garage roof into the big tree in the centre of our small garden. It then flew onto one of the 2nd-floor windowsills. It appeared to be reasonably tame. It then finally went, and perched on the top window to our bedroom, and promptly tucked its head in and went to sleep. Not surprising the timing as, it had just started raining outside. We didn't have the heart to close the window, as long as this beautiful and gentle bird, was still perched on our window-frame, so we simply just left the window wide open all night.

When we awoke the next morning, the beautiful bird was still there. Then she awoke, and flew away, and we thought that was the last we would see this wonderful bird.

But lo and behold, about half an hour later, the bird returned & flew right back onto our bedroom windowsill.

Our 7-year-old granddaughter, who happened to be visiting from Spain with our daughter, her mother, really enjoyed this adventure with this rare bird.

We decided to call for expert attention, and we called Scotland's only charity for the preservation and protection of birds.

They sent a young man who was obviously an expert with capturing escaped birds. He told us that it was very good that we had called them right away, as the bird was under-nourished. They promised to take good care of the bird and to re-house it with a good new bird-keeper.

We took the fact that my wife and family were visited by such a beautiful and rare bird as a very good Omen of Blessing, which is much appreciated by us at the present time, when my wife has been in a wheelchair for the past 10 months, due to a very severe concussion, and I myself have recently been very sick with severe anaemia.

SERAPHIM

ISA.6:1 In the year that King Uzziah died, I saw the Lord sitting on a throne, high and lifted up, and the train of His robe filled the temple.

ISA.6:2 Above it stood seraphim; each one had six wings: with two he covered his face, with two he covered his feet, and with two he flew.

ISA.6:3 And one cried to another and said: «Holy, holy, holy is the LORD of hosts; The whole earth is full of His glory!»

ISA.6:6 Then one of the seraphim flew to me, having in his hand a live coal which he had taken with the tongs from the altar.

Seraphim or Seraphs

The word Seraphim (one seraph, two or more seraphim) means "burning ones" or nobles. They are also sometimes called the 'ones of love' because their name might come from the Hebrew root for 'love'. Seraphim are only fully described in the Bible on one occasion. This is in the book of the prophet Isaiah, when he is being commissioned by God to be a prophet and he has a vision of heaven 1.

So, these types of heavenly beings have six wings, but they only use two of them for flying. It sounds strange to use wings to cover your face and feet. They may well cover their face because, being so close to God, they would witness His full glory which would be too powerful to behold. Feet are considered 'unclean' and so not worthy to be shown to God. (Some scholars also think that 'feet' could actually mean 'genitals'.) We're not told how many Seraphim there are, but it's more than one.

Their position is flying above God's throne, unlike the Cherubim who are beside/around it. Their primary duty is to constantly glorify, and praise God and they may also be the personal 'attendant' angels of God. Their eternal song "Holy, holy, holy is the LORD Almighty; the whole earth is full of his glory." has been used by Jews and Christians for thousands of years to join with the angels in praising God. In Hebrew, to use the same word three times to describe something means that the person/object is utterly like the word. So, calling God Holy three times means that God is utterly and perfectly holy.

In Jewish folklore, and some later Christian works, the Seraphim are said to be the highest rank of angel. This is probably because of their very close proximity to God.

In art, Seraphim are often red (because of their names 'burning ones') and are shown holding a flaming sword with the words 'holy, holy, holy' on the blade.

The coal in Isaiah's vision, which touches his lips, is used to signify that

Isaiah is now purified and fit to be a prophet. The coal came from the altar in heaven, so would have been very powerful. Fire is also used in many religions and faiths as a way of purifying and cleansing something.

Cherubim or Cherubs

When most people think of Cherubs they'll think of pudgy little baby-like creatures, with two little wings, who are rather cute. However, that's not how the Bible describes them! Cherubs (the correct plural is Cherubim) are described in two books of the Bible, Genesis and Ezekiel (a Jewish prophet).

1.In Genesis they guard the Garden of Eden, following Adam and Eve's banishment from the Garden, and are described holding flaming swords

"God drove out the man and He placed cherubim at the east of the Garden of Eden, and a flaming sword that turned every way to guard the way to the tree of life' (Genesis 3:24)."

2.The prophet Ezekiel has a vivid vision of heaven where he sees many angelic beings. His description of the Cherubim is powerful – almost frightening

3. Not your average cute little angel! These are powerful heavenly beings with four faces and four wings. The Cherubim are also described in the construction of the 'Ark of the Covenant'. (Yes, the one out of the Indiana Jones film!) The Ark was the dwelling place of God with the Israelites during their exodus in the desert

4. The ark was placed in the Jewish Temple, when it was built in Jerusalem. The holy part of the Temple (where the ark was placed and where the highest alter was located) also featured statues of Cherubim

5. In Ezekiel's vision he also describes another type of angelic beings that seem to be associated with the Cherubim. Their description is even more strange, to our eyes

6. Certainly, an amazing scene. Ezekiel's vision might seems strange, it might well be that human eyes and senses just can't properly describe the wonder of heaven. The Bible doesn't say how many Cherubim there are, but we're told that Ezekiel saw four – and there may be more than that! Their role is to guard God's Holy domain and presence from any sin and corruption. They are sometime known as the throne angels as they are seen to be around the throne of God

7. In Jewish folklore the 'Throne Angels' are known as Merkabah. Having four faces on four side of their heads and being arranged in a square, they can travel in any direction without having to turn. The word Cherub may come from a term 'to guard' which would fit well with their role. Nowhere in the

Bible are the Cherubim actually called angels! So far from being cute, cuddly creatures, the Cherubim are the mighty and powerful guardians of God.

EZE.1:4 Then I looked, and behold, a whirlwind was coming out of the north, a great cloud with raging fire engulfing itself; and brightness was all around it and radiating out of its midst like the colour of amber, out of the midst of the fire.

EZE.1:5 Also from within it came the likeness of four living creatures. And this was their appearance: they had the likeness of a man.

EZE.1:6 Each one had four faces, and each one had four wings.

EZE.1:7 Their legs were straight, and the soles of their feet were like the soles of calves› feet. They sparkled like the colour of burnished bronze.

EZE.1:8 The hands of a man were under their wings on their four sides; and each of the four had faces and wings.

EZE.1:9 Their wings touched one another. The creatures did not turn when they went, but each one went straight forward.

EZE.1:10 As for the likeness of their faces, each had the face of a man; each of the four had the face of a lion on the right side, each of the four had the face of an ox on the left side, and each of the four had the face of an eagle.

EZE.1:11 Thus were their faces. Their wings stretched upward; two wings of each one touched one another, and two covered their bodies.

EZE.1:12 And each one went straight forward; they went wherever the spirit wanted to go, and they did not turn when they went.

EZE.1:13 As for the likeness of the living creatures, their appearance was like burning coals of fire, like the appearance of torches going back and forth among the living creatures. The fire was bright, and out of the fire went lightning.

EZE.1:14 And the living creatures ran back and forth, in appearance like a flash of lightning.

EZE.1:15 Now as I looked at the living creatures, behold, a wheel was on the earth beside each living creature with its four faces.

EZE.1:16 The appearance of the wheels and their workings was like the colour of beryl, and all four had the same likeness. The appearance of their workings was, as it were, a wheel in the middle of a wheel.

EZE.1:17 When they moved, they went toward any one of four directions; they did not turn aside when they went.

EZE.1:18 As for their rims, they were so high they were awesome; and their rims were full of eyes, all around the four of them.

EZE.1:19 When the living creatures went, the wheels went beside them;

and when the living creatures were lifted up from the earth, the wheels were lifted up.

EZE.1:20 Wherever the spirit wanted to go, they went, because there the spirit went; and the wheels were lifted together with them, for the spirit of the living creatures was in the wheels.

EZE.1:21 When those went, these went; when those stood, these stood; and when those were lifted up from the earth, the wheels were lifted up together with them, for the spirit of the living creatures was in the wheels.

EZE.1:22 The likeness of the firmament above the heads of the living creatures was like the colour of an awesome crystal, stretched out over their heads.

EZE.1:23 And under the firmament their wings spread out straight, one toward another. Each one had two which covered one side, and each one had two which covered the other side of the body.

EZE.1:24 When they went, I heard the noise of their wings, like the noise of many waters, like the voice of the Almighty, a tumult like the noise of an army; and when they stood still, they let down their wings.

EZE.1:25 A voice came from above the firmament that was over their heads; whenever they stood, they let down their wings.

EZE.1:26 And above the firmament over their heads was the likeness of a throne, in appearance like a sapphire stone; on the likeness of the throne was a likeness with the appearance of a man high above it.

EZE.1:27 Also from the appearance of His waist and upward I saw, as it were, the colour of amber with the appearance of fire all around within it; and from the appearance of His waist and downward I saw, as it were, the appearance of fire with brightness all around.

EZE.1:28 Like the appearance of a rainbow in a cloud on a rainy day, so was the appearance of the brightness all around it. This was the appearance of the likeness of the glory of the LORD. So when I saw it, I fell on my face, and I heard a voice of One speaking.

EZE.10:1 And I looked, and there in the firmament that was above the head of the cherubim, there appeared something like a sapphire stone, having the appearance of the likeness of a throne.

EZE.10:2 Then He spoke to the man clothed with linen, and said, «Go in among the wheels, under the cherub, fill your hands with coals of fire from among the cherubim, and scatter them over the city.» And he went in as I watched.

EZE.10:3 Now the cherubim were standing on the south side of the temple when the man went in, and the cloud filled the inner court.

EZE.10:4 Then the glory of the LORD went up from the cherub, and paused over the threshold of the temple; and the house was filled with the cloud, and the court was full of the brightness of the LORD>S glory.

EZE.10:5 And the sound of the wings of the cherubim was heard even in the outer court, like the voice of Almighty God when He speaks.

EZE.10:6 Then it happened, when He commanded the man clothed in linen, saying, « Take fire from among the wheels, from among the cherubim, » that he went in and stood beside the wheels.

EZE.10:7 And the cherub stretched out his hand from among the cherubim to the fire that was among the cherubim, and took some of it and put it into the hands of the man clothed with linen, who took it and went out.

EZE.10:8 The cherubim appeared to have the form of a man>s hand under their wings.

EZE.10:9 And when I looked, there were four wheels by the cherubim, one wheel by one cherub and another wheel by each other cherub; the wheels appeared to have the colour of a beryl stone.

EZE.10:10 As for their appearance, all four looked alike-as it were, a wheel in the middle of a wheel.

EZE.10:11 When they went, they went toward any of their four directions; they did not turn aside when they went, but followed in the direction the head was facing. They did not turn aside when they went.

EZE.10:12 And their whole body, with their back, their hands, their wings, and the wheels that the four had, were full of eyes all around.

EZE.10:13 As for the wheels, they were called in my hearing, «Wheel.»

EZE.10:14 Each one had four faces: the first face was the face of a cherub, the second face the face of a man, the third the face of a lion, and the fourth the face of an eagle.

EZE.10:15 And the cherubim were lifted up. This was the living creature I saw by the River Chebar.

EZE.10:16 When the cherubim went, the wheels went beside them; and when the cherubim lifted their wings to mount up from the earth, the same wheels also did not turn from beside them.

EZE.10:17 When the cherubim stood still, the wheels stood still, and when one was lifted up, the other lifted itself up, for the spirit of the living creature was in them.

EZE.10:18 Then the glory of the LORD departed from the threshold of the temple and stood over the cherubim.

EZE.10:19 And the cherubim lifted their wings and mounted up from the earth in my sight. When they went out, the wheels were beside them; and they stood at the door of the east gate of the LORD>S house, and the glory of the God of Israel was above them.

EZE.10:20 This is the living creature I saw under the God of Israel by the River Chebar, and I knew they were cherubim.

EZE.10:21 Each one had four faces and each one four wings, and the likeness of the hands of a man was under their wings.

EZE.10:22 And the likeness of their faces was the same as the faces which I had seen by the River Chebar, their appearance and their persons. They each went straight forward.

THE 4 BEASTS

In the final book of the Bible, Revelation, there's a description of 'Four Living Creatures'.

8.These amazing creatures have features in common with both the Seraphim, in having six wings and continually praising God; and like the Cherubim, that they number four, are covered in eyes and look like a lion, ox, man and eagle.

Whether these creatures are Seraphim, Cherubim or another sort of angelic/heavenly being, we simply don't know. But they are certainly amazing and very powerful.

REV.4:6 Before the throne there was a sea of glass, like crystal. And in the midst of the throne, and around the throne, were four living creatures full of eyes in front and in back.

REV.4:7 The first living creature was like a lion, the second living creature like a calf, the third living creature had a face like a man, and the fourth living creature was like a flying eagle.

REV.4:8 The four living creatures, each having six wings, were full of eyes around and within. And they do not rest day or night, saying: «Holy, holy, holy, Lord God Almighty, Who was and is and is to come!»

Source:- (http://www.whyangels.com/seraphim_cherubim_creatures.html)

Pictures:- (https://uk.images.search.yahoo.com/yhs/search?p=CHERUBIM+ART&hspart=bt&hsimp=yhs-

Please read 'When Heaven Calls' in this book.

CHAPTER 43

HALLOWEEN & THE PARANORMAL

Is It All A Pagan Festival? Or Are There Some Very Interesting Things To Take Note Of? Are There Some Good Aspects We Can Learn From Without Necessarily Compromising Our Christian Values

We all know that Halloween is mostly celebrated in the USA & the UK. For most people it is merely just another festival, where adults and teens and kids alike like to dress-up and be ghouls for a night or afternoon.

If so, many people are supposed to be Christians in both the USA & the UK, why such fascination with the so-called darkness of Halloween?

Sadly, I believe the answer lies in the fact that the organized official so-called Christian churches & other religions are mostly not giving any answers to such paranormal real activities, but as I stated in my Book "Out of the Bottomless Pit".

"Most Christians shy away from anything that smacks of the so-called negative side of the supernatural such as":

1) Ghosts

People genuinely seeing ghosts of their relatives when they died, as documented by doctors studying the phenomenon of Life After Death. (Over 8000,000 cases in the USA alone) as documented in my Book "Out of the Bottomless Pit" in chapter 45

2) Seeing *strange creatures*, that apparently not everyone can see.

These can range from people claiming to have seen 3 metre trolls, as documented on this website down in England last year, to the USA military have recently been involved in a ferocious fight against a very large 30 feet high cannibalistic Giant in Afghanistan, as first mentioned on Steve Quayle's website: www.stevequayle.com and also mentioned on my website under GIANTS. Steve Quayle also does a great job in mentioning the Wee People such as Leprechauns from Ireland to Trolls in Scandinavia. How is it even possible that so many people have seen, and often documented these creatures, all throughout history.

Are they all under the influence of drugs or mass hallucination? As tends to be the official explanation, or is there actually some underlying truth to the existence of these and many other creatures?

The study of hidden animals or creatures, is called Crypto-Zoology, whether physical or other worldly.

3) Encounters with people and beings from the spirit world both good and bad.

4) Bound spirits both in graveyards, and in haunted houses.

5) Encounters with the good angels of God

6) Encounters with the bad angels or fallen angels, in many different forms.

7) Being haunted by one's mistakes and sins, as was brought so well in the movie Flatliners.

8) Premonitions of knowing that a relative has died far away in another country, to have it confirmed hours or days later.

9) People hearing voices that they wish they didn't have to hear- in other words, not good voices which are dismissed by the psychiatric Department, as nothing more than Schizophrenic or in some cases mere hallucinations.

I mentioned in my book that during my life as a missionary that I have personally seen many supernatural happenings, both good and bad.

As far as I am concerned, they are not supposed to make us afraid, but on the contrary to strengthen our faith in God. I have personally met an angel when I was young, and in a very trying situation. I will give more details later

10) Many people seeing UFOS. What is the Link to the paranormal? As my wife and I have already testified we have seen UFOs on 3 different occasions, and all in the vicinity of where we live, or at least in our county over the past 6 years. For more exact info see: – UFO SIGHTINGS: http://www. outofthebottomlesspit.co.uk/418799994

11) **WITCHES & ZOMBIES**

Since there is so much evidence to support the supernatural and the fact that there are other dimensions all around us, it would behove us all to be flexible in our thinking, when it comes to what others claim that they have seen, and not automatically ridicule or dismiss out of hand what they are telling you, just because you didn't get to see it. Don't be like the farmer who when told about giraffes, for the first time, blurted out "there just ain't no such thing, because I never saw one!" Pretty narrow-minded and inflexible, don't you think?

Is God Really As Inflexible As He Is Generally Made Out To Be?

In my opinion having faith in God does not mean being an inflexible person, whose mind is closed to anything outside of their self-imposed religious MATRIX box. I see God as an Adventurer, who likes His children to be full of questions about how He created everything, and how the invisible dimension behind this physical realm works. It is not difficult to find out, if you but ask God. "Ask and you will receive, seek and you shall find, knock, and the door shall be opened unto you"

12) Salvation of the dead & damned or undecided? Can one pray for the

deceased? see below!

NB All of the above topics are mentioned in detail, in my book "Out of the Bottomless Pit Book I"

CHAPTER 44

HELL, GEHENNA, & SHEOL

THERE ARE THREE different words which are translated in our English Bibles as either Hell or the grave. The Hebrew word "Gehenna" is usually translated "Hell", meaning a fiery Hell, & the other word usually translated in the English as "grave" comes from two different words: The one in Hebrew "Sheol", & the other in Greek, "Hades". But neither one of the original words have the meaning of what we think of as a grave today a hole in the ground! What both of them mean is: "Sheol" the unseen state! "Hades" the unseen state! The Spirit World!

In other words, the dead are living spirits, existent & living in the spirit world, though unseen! Not buried in a hole in the ground! In other words, every place it says "grave" in the Old Testament is "Sheol", meaning "the unseen state", & every place it says "grave" in the New Testament it's "Hades", meaning the same thing! The Spirit World! Only the word "Gehenna" really means "Hellfire" in the Hebrew, real genuine Hellfire.

But today, to you & me, modern people of the 20th century, the word "grave" only means one thing, a hole in the ground that you bury a dead body in! But that is not at all what the original words mean! They mean "the unseen state", the invisible state of those spirits! Invisible to us except upon apparition or some manifestation. It means they're in the Spirit World! Not in a hole in the ground, neither all in Hellfire either, but they are in the Spirit World! They are very active, though invisible, usually unseen.

Too many of these translations & interpretations are coloured by the doctrine of their particular church, just as was the King James translation. Remember, it was translated, in a sense, by a bunch of Church men & by the Church, & they figured that the best way to keep their people in the church building was to scare them to death that any place outside was going to be Hellfire, & that if they died out of the Church they went straight to Hellfire, regardless, with no alternative, no in-between.

See how long the preachers & the churches have misled people in saying that that meant death & Hell & everybody in it were thrown into the lake of fire? When it isn't necessarily so! The Church has had to cling to those extreme doctrines about the building to support their own organisation: And about Hell being fire & eternal to scare people into the building! According to the Church, if they did not come to the building & go through the rites of the Church, they were going to go to Hell! What a travesty against the Truth! How horrible! My God, what the Churches are guilty of! Misleading the people & even offending people's sense of justice & grace & love & mercy of God by using words which are not true expressions of what the Lord really intended for it to mean. Because by their exclusive doctrine precluding any chance of anything between Heaven & Hell, they've ruled out anything that's outside of the Church! When here these words make it as clear as anything that there is an in-between! The spirits who are now in that in-between unseen state, their final fate is going to be decided at the Great White Throne Judgement.

In fact, those spirits of the dead who are now in the spirit world, they are again in a state of probation! They're going to be judged according to how they're behaving right now in the Spirit World, whether they're serving God or the Devil there! In other words, contrary to Church doctrine, their fate is not always completely sealed by death!

Those who were saved in this Age of Grace during this life, of course, their fate is settled! They are definitely saved & strictly going to Heaven, & have gone there, no doubt, & been sent back to help us. And it's possible that some of Satan's saints who have finally & forever rejected Jesus Christ & are still rejecting Him in the Spirit World & still serving the Devil, that their fate is pretty much settled as well, except for how bad & how much damage & evil they did, which they're still doing! Therefore, they can't get their final judgement until the Great White Throne Judgement when their cup of iniquity is full & they have finished all their God-damnable dirty work against us--including all the fiends of Hell & devils & evil spirits of the departed dead!

Therefore, Judgement cannot come until the end of the spirit world, of death & Hell & Sheol & Hades, the end of the unseen state because they're still operating in the unseen state! Ghosts are still haunting, spirits are still spiriting, our helpers are still helping, & the evil spirits are still cursing & damning & rebelling, so that all their dirty work isn't done until the Great White Throne Judgement. And all those who died unsaved & perhaps didn't know the Gospel, but maybe did the best they could with what they knew are now on probation or in the Spirit World & are going to be judged according to how well they operated in the Spirit World.

Maybe people are receiving Christ in the spirit world right now! Jesus went & preached to the spirits in prison who had died up till that time. (Mt.12:40;1Pe.3:19,4:6; Eph.4:9.) Could it be possible that some people are going to get saved now in the Spirit World, the Afterlife, when they see the realities of the real World of the Spirit?

Well, if you can get saved in the Millennium, if you can get saved in the

New Earth, why couldn't you get saved in the Spirit World right after death? In other words, there're going to be three classes of people in the Spirit World! The definitely Saved & bound for Heaven, their fate's settled. The unalterably reprobate incorrigible evil spirits of the departed dead who are still going to be just as rebellious & just as disobedient & just as loyal to the Devil in the Afterlife as they are now, their fate's settled too! And then there are people who are in-between & maybe are good but never heard the Gospel & never had a chance to get saved but were not really evil. That's why He has to wait until the Great White Throne Judgement to judge them as to whether they will be saved or not, whether they're written in the Book of Life or not. Look at the patience & mercy of God, that even the people who never heard will have a chance to receive the Lord in the next life in the spirit world--even between now & the great white throne judgement!

I always wondered what they had that Judgement for anyhow if everybody that came to that Judgement, all the unsaved dead, were being raised just to be cast into Hell? Then what's the point of the Judgement? But there are millions of people who die who are not that wicked & evil to go straight to Hellfire, but neither have they heard the Gospel in order to be saved, so therefore God gives them a chance in the Spirit World!

That explains all the strange verses in the Bible about Jesus preaching to spirits in prison & all that sort of thing! That's right now in the Spirit World! He went & preached to the spirits in prison the Gospel of salvation! To tell them that had not heard to believe on Him so they could live & be saved! "He that believeth on Me hath everlasting life!" (Jn.3:36) So there's a specific example of a concrete case of spirits being saved in the Spirit World! Why else is there this time of probation in the unseen World to watch their families & relatives & friends & what they're going through? My goodness, if anything would persuade somebody to get saved, that ought to be it--an after-death experience! God in His mercy is trying to persuade everybody to be saved that He possibly can, even after they die! The Bible says, "Thy mercy is from everlasting to everlasting"! (Ps.103:17)

Doesn't that give you a picture of a loving God & an everlastingly merciful Jesus Christ? That the people who never really had a fair chance here & now are going to get that chance? We're speaking of a different class of people, the departed dead being saved in the Spirit World, the Spirit Realm, the Unseen World, after death! Everybody's going to have a chance.

And this brings out another scripture: "This is the light which lights every man that cometh into the world!" (Jn.1:9) Whether dead or alive, they get the light! Sooner or later, they have a chance to be saved! Now doesn't that fit your picture of an all-loving all-merciful God Who will be not only merciful to the now-living, but also to the dead.

In other words, god's going to give everybody a chance, dead or alive, now or then--to hear the gospel, to even see & believe & receive Jesus Christ as their saviour! Boy, that sure fits the doctrine of Universal Reconciliation, that everybody's going to get a chance, either now or then, here or there, in this life or the next life, the Millennium or even Heaven on Earth! Soul-winning in the Spirit World! Hallelujah! Witnessing ghosts! Praise God?

God is all-loving, all-merciful, all-patient, "not willing that any should perish, but that all should come to the knowledge of salvation." "That all men might be saved." (2 Pe.3:9; 1 Ti.2:4) Hallelujah! TYL! So why not in the Spirit World as well as in the Millennium, if even on the New Earth? Hallelujah!

But only those saved now go straight to heaven when we die! Which way are you going? God help you to make your choice today! Tomorrow will be too late for Heaven now! "Choose ye this day whom ye will serve!" "Today is the day of salvation" for you! (Josh.24:15; 2Co.6:2) What'll it be? Do it now! God help you, in Jesus' name, amen!

CHAPTER 45

THE HAUNTED CASTLE

A Weird Personal Experience Whilst Visiting 'Glamis Castle' In Scotland

BACKGROUND: GLAMIS CASTLE is situated just north of Dundee in Eastern Scotland. It has been the castle of Royalty for perhaps 1000 years. So, it really does have some history. It is supposedly haunted. I am not normally one for visiting '*haunted castles*', but when my son and daughters were much younger, they insisted on visiting this 'tourist attraction'.

My wife and I took them to the 'Haunted Castle'. At the time, I had no idea of the 'deep history' of 'hauntings', that the Castle is actually very famous for, and for which many thousands of tourists come every year to visit this foreboding spooky castle.

The following is exactly what transpired some 10 years ago when my wife and I took our teens to visit this foreboding castle.

We entered the castle together with a tourist guide, and a whole host of tourists around us. The guide was very clever and knew his history, and even explained about many of the kings and queens who had lived there in the far past, as well as mentioning the Queen Mother who had also lived there some 30 years ago.

Some of those past kings and queens apparently had the misfortune of having been beheaded, like Mary Queen of Scots.

The tourist guides even 'larked about' warning the women when coming down a short flight of stairs. 'Watch out, as it is reported that an impish ghost likes to trip women up, as they go down the stairs.

Our reaction was at the time: *Ha, ha, ha – how funny, 'pull the other leg!'*

The guide also mentioned some of the '*ghostly apparitions*' that had been seen upon many occasions. He mentioned that 'The Queen Mother' (mother of the reigning Queen Elizabeth) had lived in that castle some of the time and died at the amazing old age of 102 years old.

We were being shown through the different rooms of the castle which did indeed feel 'deep with history' and had some sort of 'presence' in them.

One of my daughters quipped, 'Wow, this would be a great castle to hire for Halloween, with Michael Jackson's 'Thriller' playing in the background, especially with a full moon shing through one of the castle windows.

That was the sort of atmosphere there. Not evil, but most definitely 'very spooky' and a 'bit creepy' but not fore-boding.

Now, here is where I personally had a spiritual experience with what I will now call the 'Haunted Painting'.

Whilst my wife, son and daughters were all looking around at different interesting very old paintings and icons, I myself came across two very large paintings right next to each other, and I recognized them immediately. (See the LINK below to see the paintings)

One was King James I, who in 1611 had the Bible translated into English from Latin/Hebrew by 70 scholars. The other was his son Charles I, who unfortunately met an untimely death. I think he was beheaded by Oliver Cromwell.

Well, I was looking up at the painting of James the 1st and also simultaneously at the painting of Charles 1st, and I don't know, why but I personally have always thought that past paintings of hundreds of years ago, didn't do the Royal family any favours, as in the paintings I have seen from the past, most people seemed to be shall we say 'less than good-looking'.

On this occasion, it was no different, but I made the mistake of 'thinking out loud', as I looked up at the two paintings, 'Goodness, these royals certainly weren't very good looking, were they?'

Immediately, a strange thing happened, that I will never forget. I distinctly heard a voice come out of the painting of James 1st saying an expression that I had never heard before.

The voice simply spoke to me and said, 'Well, you're not the 'best slice of cake' yourself' either!

It was so real, and my immediate reaction was to be totally taken aback and startled by it all. Then, when I had collected my thoughts, I started laughing, thinking that it was very funny indeed. I thought, "The painting is actually talking with me". It sounded like something out of a Halloween movie, where paintings start talking with you before the horrors would begin. However, this experience was not so sinister or frightening and that was all there was to it.

I immediately went over to my wife and teens and told them that the painting was haunted. I was happy to see that those who have passed on – still have a sense of humour.

Many years later, I read on the website of <stevequayle.com> in the USA, that Glamis Castle in Scotland is known to be one of the most haunted castles in the whole UK.

We are not afraid of spirits, and I sincerely belief that they can appear upon occasion and speak to people in different ways. It is strange, as I don't for one moment think that King James 1st is a 'bound spirit' of Glamis Castle, but the painting is?!

He did a wonderful job for the Lord in translating the Bible into English and I am sure that he is in heaven. Well, he certainly visited the castle on the day that we visited it, and he really had a good sense of humour.

It was a happy experience which taught me that those who have passed on like to communicate with us on earth, upon occasion.

Spirit Helpers are a famous topic, and millions have testified throughout history to having been helped by the spirit of someone who had already passed on.

Many times, they visit people in very dangerous situations and instruct others exactly what to do in order to get out of the immediate dangers that they have found themselves in.

SEE THE HISTORY OF GLAMIS CASTLE:

https://www.thecastlesofscotland.co.uk/the-best-castles/grand-castles/glamis-castle/

CHAPTER 46

CHIMERAS: CHIMERAS
www.outofthebottomlesspit.co.uk

WHY DID GOD in speaking to His prophets, choose to use CHIMERAS as an illustration of future World Empires?

For example, in Daniel 7 and Revelations 13 mysterious Hybrid or Chimera **creatures** are mentioned, also mythological creatures such as a "7 headed *dragon*" in Revelations 12 (See Chapter 17 "Dragons & Dinosaurs" in my book "Out of the Bottomless Pit)

Why did the ancient Babylonians as well as the Egyptians, Assyrians, Greeks and Romans all mention Giants, Chimeras, and other strange creatures such as Trolls.

Why do we find richly fixed in nearly every culture on earth, all kinds of legends of small creatures as well as giants.

From Leprechauns in the Emerald Isle of Ireland to the Trolls of Scandinavia.

Everywhere one looks there is so much evidence that all of the above have been seen by human beings, and even in very recent times under special circumstances.

If evolution were true, then none of these creatures should in fact be possible; because according to evolution, and the "so-called survival of the fittest" these strange aberrations of nature would not have survived birth and yet apparently, they did survive very well! Why? How did they come into being?

GOD'S STRANGE CREATURES IN HEAVEN

In Revelations chapter 4 we see described 4 very strange beasts. Each Beast had 4 heads, and they are known as the Seraphim, around the throne of God Himself, which are also mentioned in other places in the bible upon occasion when God was visiting his prophets such as in Ezekiel, (Ezekiel1 and 10), and Isaiah.

The Seraphim have 4 heads in total, one head as a Lion, one as a Calf, one as a Man (Angel), and one as an Eagle. Their arms and legs are as those of a man. A very strange creature. Each one of the Seraphim also had 6 wings about them.

Just as so-called modern science largely denies the existence of giants & simply brushes all the evidence it finds under the carpet, that simply does not coincide with their erroneous doctrine of Evolution. (Romans 1, Hebrews

11); the same is true with mysterious creatures of mythology, which might in some cases have a basis in factual evidence; which again has been conveniently brushed under the carpet of evolutionary teaching that such things never happened and couldn't possibly happen.

However, the false doctrine of Evolution. cannot explain the many mysterious sightings of amazing creatures by so many people all through time, as documented by most cultures on earth at some time or other.

Sadly, most of the time, if anyone is brave enough, to even suggest that some of these creatures of mythology were probably real, they will be hooted down as a nutcase or delusional by the so-called scientific community which are not actually very scientific, as they refuse to see the evidence, even when it is right in front of them, just because it is outside of the Evolutionary paradigm.

ORIGIN OF BOTH THE GIANTS & THE CHIMERAS

Is it just possible that we can find the answers right there in the Bible itself?

Genesis chapter 6 is probably the best key to understanding how it all started.

Also, it is a good idea to be somewhat familiar with the non-canonical books such as, & especially The Book Of Enoch, The Book Of Jasher, The Book Of Jubilees.

They all agree with the bible, and sometimes give many more details concerning the same stories. All of them talk about Giants & Chimeras.

IF THE GIANTS & THE CHIMERAS CAME INTO BEING BEFORE THE GREAT FLOOD, WHAT ABOUT AFTER THE GREAT FLOOD.?

Did the same conditions happen again i.e., the Genesis 6 mating of the angels with the women on earth to create giants and the supernatural abilities of the fallen angels enabled them to tamper with the genetics of animals and birds and fish to form chimeras.

The following from the book of Jasher chapter 80 is about the 10 plagues of Egypt and the deliverance of the children of Israel by the hand of Moses. The subject of chimeras are in the 13-16th verses.

Jasher 80: 13-16 "And the lord sent all kinds of beasts of the field into Egypt, and they came and destroyed all Egypt, man and beast, and trees, and all things that were in Egypt" 14. And the lord sent fiery serpents, scorpions, mice, weasels, toads, together with others creeping in the dust.

15. Flies, hornets, fleas, bugs and gnats, each swarm according to its kind.

16. And all reptiles & "winged animals" according to their kind came into

Egypt and grieved the Egyptians exceedingly.

If that wasn't strange enough when we get down to the 19th verse, we read the following very strange account:

19. And when the Egyptians hid themselves on account of the swarm of animals, they locked their doors after them, and God ordered the Sulanuth, which was in the sea, to come up and go into Egypt.

20. And she had long arms, ten cubits in length of the cubits of a man (Egyptian cubit at the time was 25 inches) So each of her arms were around 20 feet long. She was apparently some sort of octopus-like creature or a small Kraken.

The next verse is almost impossible for modern man to even conceive.

21. And she went upon the roofs and uncovered the raftering and flooring and cut them and stretched forth her arm into the house and removed the lock and the bolt and opened the houses of Egypt.

22. Afterward came the swarm of animals into the houses of Egypt, and the swarm of animals destroyed the Egyptians, and it grieved them exceedingly.

There are many more interesting things happening in the 80th chapter of Jasher, which I highly recommend everyone to read.

For those who would naturally just dismiss the above account as a mere story or myth, I would like to remind everyone of the story of Jonah in the Bible, which also sounds totally impossible to our modern logic.

Imagine a man being swallowed by a very large fish of some kind, spending three days in its belly, and being still alive, after desperate prayer, God ordered the fish to vomit the prophet Jonah out on the dry land in the direction of Nineveh, the very city that God had told Jonah to preach to.

Jonah had originally refused and tried to run away from God by taking a ship to Tarshish (Southern Spain) across the Mediterranean Sea. A huge storm had arisen, and the sailors being afraid, asked all men on board, if any of them had committed a crime against any God. Jonah told them the storm had come because he had run away, from obeying his God.

So, in fear the sailors reluctantly threw Jonah (on his own insistence), into the sea, which immediately went completely calm, and a very large fish appeared alongside the ship and swallowed Jonah up whole. (Book of Jonah)

If God could cause a big fish to swallow up Jonah the prophet, and cause him to be vomited back onto dry land 3 days later, so that Jonah could repent and go on to do what God had originally commanded him to do, i.e. warn Nineveh of impending doom, then why couldn't God do the strange things mentioned in the Book of Jasher.

The Bible says that with God "Nothing is Impossible" (Luke 1.37)

We just have to have faith in the living God and that He can do absolutely anything if it suits His purpose. (Hebrews 11.6)

Pictures: -http://www.bibleexplained.com/prophets/daniel/da07.htm+

CHAPTER 47

ALIEN DISCLOSURE: THE BIG LIE – ALIENS ARE SAVIOURS AND NOT JESUS

FILMMAKER, ALIEN RESEARCHER and renowned radio host Steve Quayle says this is the year the truth is going to come out about aliens visiting earth. Quayle says, "The information is being released now by the same government that used to cover up every single UFO sighting, even when they started with 'Project Blue Book.' It wasn't to answer the alien question, it was to control all the information of all the different sightings. The number one goal of the world control, I call them the fallen angel puppet masters, is to spin everything in history to their advantage. They want to destroy everything that is good and what God created. Every barrier, natural barrier, supernatural barrier and all of the barriers are being broken."

Are we going to have the alien question answered this year? Quayle says, "Yes, and I think you are seeing it. I believe before 2019 is up, somebody and I don't know who, but there are two to three nations that are getting ready to release all of the artifacts and all of the film footage. They have been paid huge money to keep it under wraps. So, as Trump changes foreign policy and their money stops, this stuff is going to start to flow. I think 2019 is going to be the year of unparalleled revelation."

Quayle says dark powers are wanting humanity to believe a huge lie– that aliens created us. Quayle says, "They say the aliens created us. Ancient alien theory is that the aliens, through a process called panspermia basically dumped DNA in the primordial goo and out popped man and me and you. I categorically reject that. When people tell me we were created by aliens and Jesus was alien, I say I've got news for you. You say God was an alien, then why all of the recorded ancient records always talking about the aliens with male and female sexual reproduction? . . . The big lie is the ancient aliens created us. The reason why they want us to believe the aliens created us is because it takes away from the thought of hell, it takes away from the need for salvation and it absolutely minimizes the most important being in the universe, and that is Jesus. It teaches in the Bible that through Jesus and by Jesus all things exist. It is really hard for people to accept that. Now, the fallen angels are getting people to embrace Satan. What you are seeing is a post-Christian culture in America. The enemy, the Devil, is running wild with every form of perversion, every form of genetic mutation and every form of doing away with mankind. Look at sex robots. They are designed to do one thing and that is to displace human women."

Quayle says, "I want to give a warning. We are seeing the revelation that the aliens are finally real. This is the perfect storm, and they are going to bring the aliens on as a saviour. We rejected Jesus Christ as Saviour, but somehow 'digital nine' from the planet Neptune comes and says we created you. If they created us, who created them? This is a supernatural evil plan. The devil is going to use the aliens, and he's already preparing people to accept the fact that we can't save ourselves, and this planet is out of control and blah, blah, blah, blah, blah and here they come. The great deception is this: the God of the Bible isn't the one who created us. That's a lie. Jesus isn't the Saviour of the world and that's the lie."

THE FOLLOWING IS TAKEN FROM MY BOOK 'OUT OF THE BOTTOMLESS PIT' CHAPTERS 32 & 33

'In 1978 one writer proposed such a possibility saying, *"The Devil is going to really put on some phenomenal manifestations like that in the last days. In a lot of movies and TV that I have seen (over 30 years ago!), the enemy is preparing the world to receive the imitation saviour, the imitation messiah".* The Lord warned us of this deception, *that the delusion* would be *so strong,* if it were possible, even *the very elect* would be deceived. I realize a scenario such as this is a bit difficult to accept and believe. On the other hand, however, it would indeed deceive the whole world, and I personally don't see how anything short of this would accomplish that. It helps to remind ourselves that we are not at war with mere mortal men and earthly governments, but "against the rulers of the darkness of this world, against spiritual wickedness in high places", *i.e., the fallen angels and their demonic cousins.* The Antichrist himself may even be a hybrid. Why not? It's happened before! (Genesis 6) But maybe not again. It is hard to believe, I agree. We shall see. And we may find out *sooner,* rather than later.

An Invasion from outer space, what a way for the Antichrist to arrive! Just like the second coming of Christ! To arrive like he was coming from outer space, like he was a superior being, a higher intelligence arriving from some other planet to solve the world's problems.

Imitate the coming of Christ and make it all sound scientific so the people would believe him. People will believe anything that smacks of science or sounds scientific. if it smacks of religion or spiritually or anything like that, forget it; but if they can just make it sound and look scientific, then the people will receive him as a superior being who has come to help solve all these terrible problems we have, like a god.

He will be like a God to them, but his whole thing is to try to put it in a plausible scientific form that people will believe. the antichrist will be sort of a scientific god, if you want to put it that way.

So, I wouldn't be a bit surprised that the Antichrist, the Devil incarnate, is going to stage some kind of phoney invasion from outer space. well, in a way, since that's the devil and his demons, the fallen angels, they are from outer space."

'We are warned by Jesus, that even the elect would be deceived if that were possible (Matthew 24.24). I consider this a sobering and dire warning that what is coming is off the hook!

We must realize that the Satan has had millennia to construct his program of deception. He knows that his time grows short and yet he believes that he can defeat the Most High God. He is going to pull out all the stops when he manifests in full.

UFOs are real burgeoning and not going away! It would appear, from the rash of sightings and reports that are coming out, that we may be nearing some kind of partial disclosure of the so-called extra-terrestrial presence. The Fallen One has been at work, carefully crafting his deception. It links back to Darwinism that declares that there is no God and that man evolved. This of course raises the question; how and where did life begin?

I believe that we are on the doorstep to the last days. There are those who will disagree and that's fine. I really am not interested in debating it, as it goes nowhere. However, from my perspective, the signs are here. The writing is on the wall, for those who have eyes to see.'

CHAPTER 48

MULTI-DIMENSIONS/MULTIVERSE? ARE THERE REALLY ALIEN PLANETS

I PERSONALLY HAVE nothing against the idea of other types of beings living on other planets revolving around other star systems.

I do think that it is indeed time for us all to *expand our consciousness* into the fullness of the creation of God. God is a wonderful creator and is always creating new things for His and our pleasure.

REV.4:11 Thou art worthy, O Lord, to receive glory and honour and power: for thou hast *created all things*, and for thy pleasure they are and were created.

Dimensions: Scientists today are admitting that there are other dimensions than this physical plane. Apparently 95% of matter in space is invisible. What does that mean in real terms? It would mean that there must be another dimension or dimensions behind this physical realm which influence and control what goes on in our physical realm.

GOD'S PLAN FOR UNIVERSAL RECONCILIATION

Why did God create the physical universe in the 1st place? & * Satan's Rebellion (* I will add material over the coming days about these topics)

What if the 7000- year-Timeframe of our physical existence on earth will not be enough time for all of the souls who have lived in the spirit world to have been personally born on earth, in order to learn the things that God requires for each of us to learn?

Some things that are actually much harder to learn in the spirit world as they have to be learnt by 'Trial and error' and learning to 'Live by Faith' & to 'Trust God' even when you can't directly see Him in the flesh. Learning to totally trust God is very important to Him. I would go so far as to state that I think that it is paramount for all of His original creation to eventually learn this principle.

WHAT IS THE BEST METHOD FOR TEACHING GREAT MULITUDES?

Could our physical universe which according to the Bible and the Apocryphal books centres around the earth, actually be considered to some extent like a Cosmic Amphitheatre, where we on earth are the actors and players in the Cosmic Battle for God and Evil. Our physical realm is obviously surrounded by both good and evil dimensions and there are windows and doors through which the spirits appear and watch us daily.

MULTI-DIMENSIONS & THEIR PURPOSES

What if God has put many people on many planets that have the ability to actually observe our planet daily, but who are not allowed to interfere with our majesty of choice. I do not think that physical 'Aliens' are going to show up here from distant planets, as the distances are too great! They are allowed to observe and learn from our decisions and from our Faith and relationship with both God and His Holy spirit and Jesus as well as many spirit helpers and angels of God.

FAKE ALIEN GOSPEL & INVASION FROM OUTER SPACE

If there ever is an 'Invasion from outer Space', I predict that it will be faked! Faked by the Fallen Angels, their giant progenies (demons) and their human cronies, to deceive most of mankind into believing the insidious lie that man was 'seeded' on the planet earth millions of years ago. That the 'Aliens' are just coming back to see how we are doing and to rescue us from self-destruction. That argument simply does not make any sense because of the light years of distance involved; and is not backed-up by any real evidence.

THE ANTI-CHRIST COULD PUT ON A BIG SHOW in order to deceive the whole world, as he himself will be only part-human.

2TH.2:7 For the mystery of iniquity doth already work: only he who now letteth will let, until he be taken out of the way.

2TH.2:8 And then shall that Wicked be revealed, whom the Lord shall consume with the spirit of his mouth, and shall destroy with the brightness of his coming:

2TH.2:9 Even him, whose coming is after the working of Satan with all power and signs and lying wonders,

2TH.2:10 And with all deceivableness of unrighteousness in them that perish; because they received not the love of the truth, that they might be saved.

2TH.2:11 And for this cause God shall send them strong delusion, that they should believe a lie:

2TH.2:12 That they all might be damned who believed not the truth, but had pleasure in unrighteousness.

THE SPIRIT WORLD

Up until this point, I have always in my mind's eye imagined that all of the spirits in heaven stay in that dimension most of the time, except when they are sent on missions to the earth to help individuals with a myriad of needs and to enhance their abilities. I have envisioned the saints of all time who are already in heaven viewing our world directly from their celestial mansions on some sort of 3D TV screen.

However, what about those people or beings who have never had the privilege of having lived the earth life, at least not yet? (* It is appointed to men once to die and after that the Judgment)

Heb 9:27 And as it is appointed unto men once to die, but after this the judgment.

Could many of the planets out there in space be special assigned posts for some of those in heaven who have never been born on earth in the flesh. Places where it is very easy to observe and learn from our mistakes and to get more used to the physical life without necessarily going to earth, at least not quite yet?

LIMITATIONS PUT ON THE PHYSICAL REALM BY GOD HIMSELF

It is true as many have pointed out that physically speaking it is not logical for people to travel from one star-system to another at least not with these physical bodies.

If, however we think in terms of other higher and lower dimensions where Time & Space are not a factor in the sense that those people & beings there are not limited by Distance or Time. Being in a higher or lower dimensions to our physical plane would mean that those there, could probably very easily descent into our lowly dimension from above and into any part of our physical universe, simply because they are not earth bound or even bound to our physical universe's limitations or 'laws of physics'.

INTERNET CAPABILITIES

IMAGINE HOW MUCH THE WORLD HAS CHNGED IN THE PAST 25 YEARS+ SINCE THE INVENTION OF THE INTERNET

We today on planet earth can touch on our computer screens and instantly be whisked away to other places on the planet instantly. Perhaps those on other planets have a much better internet than we do, and thus can tune into our activities all the time just by getting on the exact right frequency?

HEB.12:1 Wherefore seeing we also are compassed about with so great a cloud of witnesses, let us lay aside every weight, and the sin which doth so easily beset us, and let us run with patience the race that is set before us,

Jesus Christ came to re-unite us all with God and to bring in everlasting redemption for all souls that would receive Jesus as their Saviour and Redeemer to God.

SATAN AND FALLEN ANGELS AND ENTITIES INCREASINGLY RESTRICTED

Is it just possible that the fallen angels and their ilk of evil entities are being more and more restricted and being pushed further and further downwards to eventually being in the big lock-up of Hell and the Bottomless Pit and then the Lake of Fire all within the earth. The negative world is sort of upside down and inside out and a 'shrinking in size world' as evidenced by 'Black-Hole Stars' are the exact opposite of bright shining stars, just as Satan is the exact opposite of God. God gives light like a star and Satan takes away and one is left with nothing but an in-gathering 'Black Hole'. Those who used to be so arrogant such as Satan and his band of roving Fallen Angels who count in the millions or even billions, and who boasted themselves to countless civilizations of their superior technology and powers are themselves being driven downwards and restricted more and more each and every day!

FORCES OF LIGHT SHOWING UP MORE AND MORE

Just a thought, but what if the forces of Light are starting to fill up some of the planets closest to the earth in preparation for the Battle of Armageddon which is not just a physical battle but a supernatural battle involving both man and angels and fallen angels and countless entities. Perhaps they are also practicing with the ideas of warfare. Something that they have never had to contend with before in the spirit realm from whence they came.

20 BILLION PEOPLE ON OUR PLANET THROUGHOUT 6000 YEARS OF OUR HISTORY AND EVERY DECISION THAT THEY EVER MADE!

If every person on earth has a guardian angel (or the potential to have one according to choices they make) not to mention countless guiding spirits or spirit helpers, just think how many quadrillions of actions done by humans that will eventually have to be corrected, in order to eventually restore God's entire creation to perfection again as it was in the very beginning. That will probably take at least another 1000+ years. There are many things that our heavenly counterparts can easily see us do in the Heavenly realm, but in preparation for God ushering in His Heavenly City closer to the earth during the soon-coming Millennium and to actually land the Heavenly City on the earth at the end of the Millennium; in a sense many people in heaven are going to have to learn how to interact on the physical plane, as the spirit plane is much more dreamy and infinite in possibilities as the spirit world is not limited by time or space. All of this would tend to imply that God needs places for millions of His people to practice with similar conditions to those on the earth in preparation for both the Millennium and the New Heaven and New Earth.

The physical planets would indeed make great places of practice and getting used to the physical dimension in preparation for the Millennium when millions of spirits and Saints will come to rule and reign over the whole earth's population whilst Satan and his Forces of Evil both physical and spiritual are in the in the 'lock-up' of the Bottomless Pit.

REV.20:1 And I saw an angel come down from heaven, having the key of the bottomless pit and a great chain in his hand.

REV.20:2 And he laid hold on the dragon, that old serpent, which is the Devil, and Satan, and bound him a thousand years,

REV.20:3 And cast him into the bottomless pit, and shut him up, and set a seal upon him, that he should deceive the nations no more, till the thousand years should be fulfilled: and after that he must be loosed a little season.

REV.20:4 And I saw thrones, and they sat upon them, and judgment was given unto them: and I saw the souls of them that were beheaded for the witness of Jesus, and for the word of God, and which had not worshipped the beast, neither his image, neither had received his mark upon their foreheads, or in their hands; and they lived and reigned with Christ a thousand years.

REV.20:5 But the rest of the dead lived not again until the thousand years were finished. This is the first resurrection.

REV.20:6 Blessed and holy is he that hath part in the first resurrection: on such the second death hath no power, but they shall be priests of God and of Christ and shall reign with him a thousand years.

REV.20:7 And when the thousand years are expired, Satan shall be loosed out of his prison,

REV.20:8 And shall go out to deceive the nations which are in the four quarters of the earth, Gog, and Magog, to gather them together to battle: the number of whom is as the sand of the sea.

REV.20:9 And they went up on the breadth of the earth, and compassed the camp of the saints about, and the beloved city: and fire came down from God out of heaven and devoured them.

REV.20:10 And the devil that deceived them was cast into the lake of fire and brimstone, where the beast and the false prophet are, and shall be tormented day and night for ever and ever.

CHAPTER 49

UFO'S

MANY PEOPLE QUOTE from EZEKIEL Chapter 1 & 10 concerning UFO'S or God's own flying chariot –'Chariots of the Gods' etc.

Are there other verses in both the Bible and Apocryphal books such as the Book of Enoch talking about UFO's. If so, what are UFO''s?

Are they good or evil or are they both? Is it just possible that there are in fact both spiritual and physical UFOS'. The physical ones being the imitation of the spiritual ones.

Lets' start our investigation by looking at the beautiful and mysterious Book of Zechariah in the Bible:

Zechariah Chapter 5

The first part of Zechariah Chapter 5 – I believe is talking about UFO's – prophesied 2500 years ago.

First of all, a few Bible verses from Zechariah 5.1-4

ZEC.5:1 Then I turned, and lifted up mine eyes, and looked, and behold a **flying roll.**

ZEC.5:2 And he said unto me, What seest thou? And I answered, I see a flying roll; the length thereof is **twenty cubits**, and the breadth thereof **ten cubits.**

[These dimensions are approximately 40 feet x 20 feet which could be similar to the size of some small UFO'S]

ZEC.5:3 Then said he unto me, This is the curse that goes forth over the face of the whole earth: for every one that steals shall be cut off as on this side according to it; and every one that swears shall be cut off as on that side according to it.

ZEC.5:4 I will bring it forth, saith the LORD of hosts, and it shall enter into the house of the thief, and into the house of him that swears falsely by my name: and it shall remain in the midst of his house, and shall consume it with the timber thereof and the stones thereof.

Now some verses from the 'Book of Enoch' also apparently talking about UFO's some 5000 years ago – taken from my book 'Enoch Insights'

ENOCH INSIGHTS – Chapter 108:

Book of Enoch: 3 And I saw there something like an invisible cloud; for by reason of its depth, I could not look over, and I saw a flame of fire blazing brightly, and things like shining mountains circling and sweeping to and fro.

"Invisible Cloud" is visible to some extent to Enoch but not visible to the rest of those in Enoch's time. I would venture to say that this is talking about what today is called "The Veil that Separates". It is the separation between the spiritual world and the physical world. Notice that Enoch is not able to see all that is hidden by the invisible cloud.

"*Shining mountains circling and sweeping to and fro*". This sounds like large pyramidical UFOs and their motions. Some UFOs have the appearance of a fiery flame within them, and look like an incandescent pulsating fire, or even like a beating heart.

BOOK OF ENOCH: 5.4 And I asked one of the holy angels who was with me and said unto him: "What is this shining thing? For it is not a heaven, but only the flame of a blazing fire, and the voice of weeping and crying, and lamentation and strong pain."

Talking about UFOs as, '*not a heaven, but only the flame of a blazing fire.*' Here it sounds like Enoch is explaining that the specific UFOs seen here, have nothing to do with heaven or goodness, but these ones are in fact very evil

In this life, the fallen angels have apparently shown off to mankind, throughout the entire history of the world, upon thousands of different occasions, as to how powerful and seemingly invincible they are, or appear to be. Including showing off their craft such as UFOs. One day all their powers will account for nothing, as they, with their UFOs descend into the Lake of Fire; and both they and all their supernatural powers will be destroyed for ever.

ZEC.5:1 Then I turned, and lifted up mine eyes, and looked, and behold a *flying roll*

ZEC.5:3 Then said he unto me, 'This is the *curse* that goes forth over the face of the whole earth: for every one that steals shall be cut off as on this side according to it; and every one that swears shall be cut off as on that side according to it.'

These verses in Zechariah are amazing & sound a lot like the movie "Aliens & Cowboys". In other words, UFOs in the future, will become much more frequently seen, and become a terrible curse to mankind in the End of Days. That is why the fallen angels who pretend to be aliens unto mankind will end up getting very severe judgement, as being Satan's emissaries, they will have practically destroyed all of God's original creation, and also mankind for a 2nd time, during the coming Great Tribulation or the last 3 and a half years of the Anti-Christ's 7-year Covenant.

BOOK OF ENOCH:108. 5 And he said unto me: "This place which you see; here are cast the spirits of sinners and blasphemers, and of those who work wickedness, and of those who pervert everything that the Lord hath spoken through the mouth of his prophets, even the things that shall be."

This chapter is one of the very strange chapters in the Bible.

I will be looking at some of the more supernatural and even paranormal chapters from the Bible that give 'Strange Truths'.

The first part of the chapter 5 of Zechariah – I already related about in one of my book: 'ENOCH INSIGHTS'.

The 2nd half of this short chapter also mentions something quite strange. It mentions some of the things mentioned concerning the location of the Tower of Babel which was built in the land of Shinar almost 4000 years ago and yet the story appears to be talking about modern times?

I thought it time someone did some investigating to get some answers concerning ancient biblical prophecies that no-one had found answers for – to the present time.

I do not claim to have all the answers and what I am stating could be just part of the picture, but I am writing this, as in my books, in the hope that people will show more interest in the stories in the Bible and also that they might do some research of their own to see if these things be so.

'Two tall women with wings like storks who carry the Ephah between the earth and Heaven and bring it down to give it its own house in the Land of Shinar.'

I have read this story many times before without realizing the immensity of its probable meaning.

I have been following a lead and doing research about this chapter and I think you will find what I found out to be very interesting.

The key words are Ephah and Shinar

CHAPTER 50

'WHEN HEAVEN CALLS'

My Wife's Serious Accident & Her Testimony – with my comments following.

MY STORY STARTS when I was 4 years old and my connection with God. Without that connection I would be dead right now. We go back to my childhood first, when it was close to Christmas and my mother brought me a fold-out manger scene. It was made of strong cardboard, but it was so pretty that it looked like it could have been made of painted wood and was painted in beautiful colours having Joseph and Mary and little baby Jesus lying in the manger. It had a sheep and a cow and a picture of a stable, where baby Jesus was born. My Dad bought me a large golden star to hold; in my window with a little light bulb inside which made a magical light appear through the holes in the star into my room. So, I was sitting there in front of my windowsill, with the beautiful star shining above the manger scene. The room was otherwise dark except for the manger scene and a little light coming through the door and my mother was working in the kitchen. So, as I sat there, I was thinking about the Bible Story and when Jesus was born, and I bonded with that little baby that was lying in the manger. I felt a beautiful peace come over me like the beautiful Spirit of God wrapping itself around me and giving me wonderful peace. And I felt so safe and cosy. So, for many nights up to Christmas I sat there all quiet. I like to be quiet, which later in life I have found to be a real blessing. I want to Fast forward to when I was 11 years old, and I was a girl scout, and I was sent out to buy ice-cream. We were having a scout meeting in a quit part of town where there were lots of nice houses there and we were having a meeting in one of the houses of the girls there. We had to cross a very busy road to reach an ice-cream shop. This was a long time ago when one bought ice-cream in an ice-cream shop and not in a supermarket as today. When we came back across the main road, I thought that I could just dodge the traffic and it went ok half the way and then a car stopped and let me pass but I had not seen the moped that was coming down the hill full speed and it drove right into me and knocked me over as I went head over heels onto the pavement and I got quite hurt. The man fell off his moped. While he was yelling lying on the ground, I ran away to go and get my daddy. It was very difficult. All the way back to my house it took about 20 minutes and I felt unwell all the time. I feel like I was going to faint. That same spirit of God that I mentioned earlier, kept me from fainting. My mother was crying when she saw what had happened to me as my face was bloody and I had lost some teeth in the front of my mouth. My father immediately went oof and sorted things out with the man on the fallen moped. Of course, it was the beginning of a long story of repeatedly going to the dentist. The doctors discovered that I had scoliosis, a curvature of the spine and that began a long story of going to the chiropractor as well. When I was 18 years old, I stopped going to the chiropractor as I didn't think that it was necessary anymore. I had some trouble with my back, but it didn't really bother me. Some years later I got married and had a family and I had children, and everything seemed to go just fine. When I got older, I had to go back to the chiropractor because I had pains in my spine and could not turn my head. I wanted to drive a car abut could not look behind me as it hurt too much. I started going to the chiropractor again and went for various sessions and she would move the vertebrates, she had scoliosis herself. She had a friend who also had scoliosis and they would fix each other's backs. The did not actually heal each other but just moved the bones in the spine around. Rather dangerous I would say considering that we have all the spinal nerves inside the spine and the whole nervous system and to the brain and the whole electrical system. It controls the body so that it is quite a dangerous practise. Anyway, the chiropractor moved the bones to the top of the spine and caused a bump which I still have to this day. I stopped going to the chiropractor as I no longer felt safe in doing it. Then I started having falling accidents. If I was working in the kitchen I would suddenly fall over, and I fly right into the cupboards and damaged my tailbone and my back again. Those kinds of accidents happened about three times. Then 2015 it was again getting close to Christmas and on 10th November. I wanted to make things for Christmas like crafts and things. One evening I decided in a big hurry by the way. Never, be in a hurry by the way as it can be very dangerous, I was walking outside of the Lord's protection I was not prayed up properly. I believe that it is extremely important to never leave your room in the morning without praying desperately from protection. And asking for help and protection. That particular day I did not have the Lord's protection. I have leaded that doing things without prayer and the Lord's protection can be very dangerous. We can suddenly rush out the door to work and |I have seen accidents with other people happen. When do we have the Lord's protection and when do we not have the Lord's protection? I have learned that going at a slower pace and avoid being late and praying a whole lot more before I leave my bedroom in the morning. Especially before drying a car ask for the Lord's protection. Of course, in my case there is the problem that my spine got damaged in the last visits to the chiropractor. Now I know that a lot of people get helped from going to the chiropractor and I also did initially but in the last visit something went wrong. There was nothing that I could do about it because when you initially go to the chiropractor one signs a paper stating that if anything goes wrong then the doctor chiropractor is not responsible. Anyway, it was 2015 before Christmas and I rushed up the ladder of the attic and I started throwing down things that I was going to use of Christmas materials. I was going back down the ladder but was holding onto the rail with one hand and throwing down things with the other. I lost my grip and suddenly and my body did not work, and I fell over backwards and hit my head in the top of the banister which had as wooden knob on the top. Which led down to the bottom of the stairs on the ground floor. It was a very serious fall, and I was lying there on the floor shaking. I could not stop shaking and my daughter came running. 'Hold on to my wrist' She did and the shaking subsided. She checked the back of my head and there was a big gash in my head, and I was bleeding everywhere. So, she said Dad call an ambulance. My husband was standing there and acting slow as is thinking 'that can't be my wife lying on the floor all injured'. It was as if he didn't seem to register what was going on and was in shock' as was my other daughter. We called the ambulance, and I was still lying on the floor, and I was shaking on the inside and I was not myself at all. He put me on a chair, and it felt good to have a professional around. He was so nice and calm and fun. He said 'Most of the so-called accidents that I am called to are not real, so it is nice to meet a real person and a genuine accident. He bandaged up my head and took me to the hospital. They fixed the wound in my head. My wrist was broken, and did they did all kinds of tests but they never told me that I could get a very serious concussion from my accident. Or they did not explain anything else that could go wrong. They were student doctors, but they did judge the situation and it really was. I went home and thought that everything was OK. It was my right hand that was broken and there it was difficult. I thought that every-thing was going to be fine. The next day my husband went to work, and I was putting away the dished from the dish washer. I found it difficult to bend over. I tried to feed my cats and it got more and more difficult. I got more and more ill. My heart started beating erratically and I went to lie down on the couch. While I was lying there, I didn't get any better. Then an angel appeared. A tall angel suddenly came through the glass doors to the garden, and he stood next to me. I was still shaking, and he put his hand on me and I stopped shaking and became calm. Then saints started streaming in along the wall. Some of them were people that I had known in this life that had passed on; and there were so many of them. There were streaming into the living room and up the stairs as though something very important was happening. I don't know how many there were It could have been a hundred saints maybe. The angel said to me 'Are you ready to come home to heaven with me. He did not take as human beings do but he talked to me in my mind. I beamed back to him 'I don't think that it can go right now because my husband is not that well and I ned to take care of him and also my two daughters have not grown up and left home yet. My youngest daughter was in a relationship with a shady character at the time and I could not face the fact that my children would come down and see me dead in the couch. The angel looked disappointed, but he did give me the choice. Then he left and all the saints streamed right back out of the house. I don't know if there was some sort of spiritual vehicle outside waiting for them or not. I don't know and I could not see it. But I was just lying there stunned. A little while later my husband came bursting in the front door. He said I was out there working in Edinburgh when the Lord spoke to me very clearly and said, 'What are you doing here when your wife is dangerously and gravely ill at home. Go home asap!' I told him my story of the angel and saints having visited me while he was gone to work. He decided to take me back to the hospital for further examinations and check-ups. In the hospital I had various tests on my brain and was given the option to stay in the hospital to do more tests or to go home.

(Steve: I have had a very hard time transcribing this testimony from my wife as I felt all the extreme trials of the last 7 years come up in my thoughts. I had to call on God's angels to rebuke Satan and all his accusations against me as all of my mistakes came to mind. It would appear that Satan is afraid of Lily's Testimony).

I felt quite in control and so I decided to go home and rest according to the doctor's instructions until I got better. I want to bed but it was the beginning of many spiritual battles. One minute I felt like I was going to pass away and go home to be with God and another minute I felt like I could stay and started singing psalms and songs to Jesus praising God and trying to stay alive. I had many visions in those days and one thing I could see very clearly in those days was a man kneeling or bent in prayer every day he was there on 'prayer vigil' for my life His name was Adoniram Judson. He used to be a missionary to Burma, and he had a very difficult life with his family being very sick and some member of his immediate family dies from sickness. He had a very hard life. He was a very determined person. It was a big comfort for me to have him there knowing that someone from beyond was so concerned for me and my well-being. I had a lot of pains if I would try to get up and go to the bathroom. Every time that I would step down to take a step as my heel hit the floor an electric shock would go up my spine to my brain. Every step it was very difficult. I had a computer I my room and I tried to go near to the computer to sign in and immediately I would get electric shocks just being near it. It affected my brain terribly. I had to quickly move away. That happened for a very long time and even unto this day I cannot use a computer. It is a bit better now 7 years later and I can stand near the computer, and I can watch a little bit like a few photos or something and then I have to go away. So, anyway it was a very spiritual experience lying in bed and not being able to get up. My husband was having a tremendous fight trying to be a mother and a father and doing his job and cooking and cleaning and do all the things that had to be down, and I was not able to do anything. It was very difficult for my husband emotionally also thinking that I could die at any moment. He was not always managing to behave in the early days. That is with the grace and kindness necessary in order to care for a very sick and incapacitated person suddenly. Some of our children would phone up and say 'Oh Mum is just pretending and needs to go and see a psychologist. That really affected him badly, and so he went to tell me what our daughters had said while I was lying there very ill, fighting for life. It was a battle for life and death I those days and it was a hard battle difficult battle. Hearing what my daughters had said and that he was having serious battles and that he could not really mange. I could not do anything about it apart from feeling incredibly sad. I felt kind of lost! I was feeling as if left in a dangerous situation. Not all the time, but when he came in and told me off or suggesting that the problem was mostly only in my head in reiterating what our adult daughters had said repeatedly. Being very sick and hearing these things was almost unbearable. My family did not understand my condition. That was harder than the pain. I felt like no-one on earth could help me not even the doctors. One day while I was lying in bed, I saw a vision of Jesus appearing in the door. Behind Him were spiritual beings some might have been human, and some seemed a little different than what we are used to. Jesus put his arms out and told them that they could not come in. They were allowed to watch but not get involved. They were like students, and they were learning things about me and about my situation. They probably know what was wrong with me and could probably see clearly into my body and brain and see the damages. Jesus was teaching them, but they were not allowed to come into the room. I could not understand why? Why are thy not allowed. I really wanted them to come in, but it was like we were all in a learning process. What really happened to my children I don't really know? I never really got to talk to them and ask them what had happened to them in those days. What went on in these minds and feelings. They did not act as if they were getting involved. The had their own set of problems land concerns. That just goes to show me that this life is a lot of learning. Before we can go to the next life. We must learn to make the right kind of decisions while we are yet on earth. If we get to the end of life without learning the many things necessary, then I suppose that the learning process continues in the place where each person goes to. Another day I was having a vision of this king and queen, and they were dressed in old-fashioned clothes like in the times of King Solomon. They were carrying gifts of gold and precious stones. Some kind of gifts of the spirit but pictured as things. Gifts of patience and mercy and learning and long-suffering. They came into my room and put these gifts down on the floor next to my bed. I think that the king smiled at me. The queen was very beautiful. Then they gracefully left and walked back down the stairs. Well, I sure needed those gits in those days I need them so much. I eventually got a little bit better, and I managed to go out into the garden. I still had to go very carefully and very slowly. Every step I had to concentrate if my brain was OK, even to this day some days are much more difficult than other days. In the mornings I originally after the accident could not walk down the stairs, I had to crawl. Later in time, I walked down the stairs but still I had to move very slowly, and it is now 7 years later since my serious accident and resultant concussion, and I still have to walk very slowly down the stairs. There are many activities that I can no longer do. I walked out in the garden, and I felt like I desperately needed oxygen. I was bending down and trying to breath in the grass in desperation. I said I ned to get into the hyperbaric oxygen centre as we had read about it. But my husband took his time loping along not really catching on. Finally, he managed to get a hold of those who ran the centre and in a city by us. And they said, 'Bring her in immediately,' and they gave me preference over may other potential patients to the MS Hyperbaric Oxygen centre. There was a long list of people trying to get into the centre. People with MS and ME and cancers. The supervisor was very understanding and gave me priority to go 2 x /week. it was making the different in the oxygen chamber. It was like the divers that go deep diving using a chamber to do experiments. We would sit in the chamber. There were about 6 persons in the chamber and the oxygen was turned on under pressure and the difference was amazing. Now I was not able to see very well at all since the concussion, but when I was in the oxygen chamber I could read. It was wonderful to be able to read and study about some of the things that I like to study like gardening and many other topics. I was so thankful to be able to do that. As soon as I got home, I would feel really sick. I could not walk. I had to go straight to bed, and it was extremely difficult for my family as my children no longer had a mother and it felt like my husband did not have a wife anymore. So, it was very hard for everyone. That went on for about 5 years of so. I can't remember about the exact details. I would say 7 years later that I am definitely better than I used to be, but I am still sick and am in a wheelchair most of the time. I can walk a little bit. I have to have two sticks wherever I walk, and my husband takes me out for a walk frequently. I can only walk ad few steps at a time, and I use a mobility scooter. I have been able to some acupuncture with a chines doctor, and it did help some, but it became expensive. She discovered that I had damage to the nerves at the back of the head. I still have nerve damage to this day to my neck and spine and up the back of the head where I got hit during the accident. The areas of the brain hit were the sight, hearing. I should be thankful that I can see. My eyesight is normally blurry, and I can see better when I am lying down. I can't have glasses, I had two check-ups, but they told me that I could not focus, and the brain was not healing well in the area of sight. I should be thankful that I can still see to some degree, and it is a lot better than it was 7 years ago when I had the accident. Even though it difficult being handy-capped. What I miss the most is being able to read. To study ad I can't. it depends on my husband who is my full-time carer. I depend on him when he has time as he is always very busy working. When he has time, I dictate my e-mails for him to send to our children and to friends and others. If I want to study anything he needs to find it and I can only learn using audios. This year however it has been better as I have been able on a few occasions to lie down on the couch and watch most of a move like Top Gun. I had to close my eyes quite a few times. I finally got to enjoy part of a movie after all this time and that was nice.so I just have to be really thankful for everything that I can still do and not get depressed about all the things that I can no longer do. It is a very different kind of life being crippled and handy-capped. Again, I thank God that I have Jesus and my angels. Remember this if you are already saved. Think about asking Jesus to save your soul. I say do it! Praying to Him every day gives wonderful miracles and support in some many ways. Do it. Just reach out to Jesus to save your soul. I know that you Jesus died for my sins and that I will go to the eternal life when I die. I know that you suffered on the cross for me. Once you have made the decision to pray that simple prayer then you are saved so pray it. In finishing this Testimony. I asked God why could this accident have happened? He showed me that I was walking outside of His protection. But He also showed me a vision of these two beings who stood where the accident happened. When I was a child to used to make balls out of rubber bands. We would take some silver foil and crumple it up to a ball and then attach rubber bands and around the silver ball and tighten them and attach many more. Eventually, we had a ball that was slightly smaller than tennis ball and that was powerful and could really hurt someone. These dark spiritual entities that were on the scene of my almost fatal accident were made of material like that. They were made of elastic bands. It was actually muscle. They were incredibly strong. I believe that they could kill someone with just one blow. Their job is to cause accidents. Now some reason why you really want to know Jesus, and to be saved and you really need to learn to pray every day before you go anywhere to avoid accidents. You don't want to meet these guys. They are vicious, they are fierce they are evil. They cause a lot of accidents. Be warned. If anyone reading this book has anyone who is very ill do not give up on them but be a career and be a help and a strength and do everything to be a help and understanding. Don't leave and think that you can't handle the situation stay by the sick and injured. There is a very great reward in Heaven for those who do the unselfish thing and sacrifice all to care for others. You wait and see.

Steve: My side of the story. This very serious and almost fatal accident initially seemed like a fatal blow to everything that we were doing and involved in as my wife going from a fairly healthy woman to being an almost total invalid so suddenly was definitely a great shock to me. Initially it was a very heavy burden for me in so many ways and I kept thinking that my wife could die any day because of her serious injurious in her head and because of the brain damage due to a very serious concussion.

I suppose initially, as my wife stated when she had the accident, I just stood there in unbelief as to what had happened well, that is for a few seconds until I reacted and called the ambulance.

What I want to mention is what we have gained from this situation and experience as I know for many people who have faith in Jesus, they will not understand why my wife had not gotten well again in the past 7 years and why is she still incapacitated? The truth be known on many other occasions my wife and I have seen many miracles of healings and protection and miraculous deliverances from all kinds of difficult and dangerous situations as we were missionaries in foreign countries for many years. Why has God chosen not to totally heal my wife? Well, that is a very good question, but it is not because we don't believe that God can. Of course, he could still miraculously heal her at any time. After all we have had a lot of people praying for her over the years. So, what is the difference you may ask? The truth be said, I think that God likes to test His people and those who work for him. I would agree with my wife that perhaps one reason is for us to comfort others who are in the same situation when they have been ill or incapacitated or handicapped for many years.

I must again give Glory to the Lord in stating that I have seen far too many outright miracles of healing, protection, supply, deliverance, change and much more that I am 100% certain God could still raise up my wife today if it serves His purpose. I would like my wife to be able to enjoy doing all the things that she used to do and enjoy. As a husband, I believe it is essential when you truly love your wife to stick by her side through thick and thin, no matter what until God takes us Home to heaven. I am in love with my wife and although our relationship is now more on a spiritual plain, I don't feel lonely or lost anymore, because of the physical no longer working. I have gotten accustomed to that although sometimes it stills hurts, but the fact that she truly loves me enables me to wait until God heals her. It is however important to maintain unity and harmony when many things are not working as they used to. I am her carer, and I am here until God either heals her or takes her home to heaven. It is so important to be thankful to God for everything that we have already enjoyed in this life. Whatever we suffer or have to go through in this life, it is just for a moment compared with eternity and our heavenly life when all things will be made right and perfect. I believe heaven is where all your dreams do come true and are more fully realized than in this physical life which is somewhat limited. Love is supreme in Heaven.

The good side of our situation is that at least we are not all alone like so many older people. I am 70 now. We can still care for each other in so many ways. Our great Joy is Jesus and reading the Bible and singing Psalms and spiritual songs unto the Lord. My wife being very ill over the past 7 years has, as an offshoot, caused me to have written 8 books and 7 since her accident in 2015. I decided a long time ago to get my mind of myself and our totally altered situation. All my life I was a people person, and I was always out of the house doing something or talking with others or visiting churches and helping others. When my wife's accident happened, she was suddenly totally helpless, and I found myself mostly at home and trying to be mother and father and do all the work that needed to be done. It was very tough initially, as I myself am not well some of the time, as I have various health conditions myself.

I decided early on after her serious accident, to get up earlier each morning and to start to write books before I had to start caring for my wife. This was good as it took my mind of myself and what we could no longer do together and that many things we could no longer enjoy. It got me to focus on Jesus and asked Him what I should write about, and He told me to work on the Apocryphal books. This we have done, I say that because my wife has become an integral part in helping me and encouraging me with the books, and our motive is to encourage as many people as possible out there with God's stand of Faith and Trust.

Until 2015 and my wife's accident, I could not have seen myself as a writer writing a lot of books, as I like being out teaching others about God and the deeper lessons of life.

When my wife's accident happened, it was as though God Himself wanted me to change gears, and slow down my life. Now, today in 2022, I can see God's wisdom in what he has allowed. I have had to learn that we can't just expect God to always do what we say, and when we insist, we want it done.

Scriptures do indicate that 'Nothing is impossible for God' and there is nothing that God can't heal, and we have seen God answer countless times, but occasionally God has a greater purpose to what He allows to happen in our lies that we initially find so painful and difficult and seemingly restrictive.

Romans 8.28 'For all things work together for good to those who love the Lord, to those who called according to His purpose.'

We must not treat the Lord as if He is some sort of Magician who is our 'Presto Chango' superman to do miracles when we so want!

The most important quality to develop in this life, is Firstly: The ability to listen carefully to God's instructions; 2ndly to carry out those instructions; 3rdly to do it when God tells you to. 4thly Don't delay when God tells you to do something. If you can learn those 4 things, then you will become very useful to God Himself.

All of us can do our 'two cents' for God using the talents that He has given us for His Glory.

Finally, I like this quote that I once read 'You have got to keep serving God even if He never sees fit to heal you in this life'. Keep going for God.

What is serving God? It is listening to Him on a regular basis -every day and asking Him to bless our endeavours for each day, and to bless others and to ask Him for His direct council. If you get used to doing these basic spiritual things, then your life will come into proper focus and purpose.

You do not need a church or religious organization to know Jesus and God. You just need to ask Jesus into your heart and believe in Him and read His word as in the Bible. I started as a young man with the Gospel of John, as it has so many Bible verses on Salvation.

John 3.36 'He that believes on the Son has everlasting life'.

Once you believe it is permanent because the Salvation is a gift of God and not of self-works. Once you believe and receive Jesus into your heart in a simple prayer, then you are saved 'no matter what', as it is a gift of God.

SALVATION

HOW TO GET SAVED?

Finally, I challenge you, that if you have not already prayed to receive Jesus into your heart, so that you can have eternal life, & be guaranteed an eternal place in Heaven, then please do so immediately, to keep you safe from what is soon coming upon the earth!

If we confess our sins, God will save us from our sins and mistakes.

1 John 1:9 If we confess our sins, He is faithful and just to forgive us our sins and to cleanse us from all unrighteousness.

Revelations 3.20 "Behold, I stand at the door and knock, if any man hear my voice, and open the door, I will come in to him and live with him and him with me".

"He who believes on the Son of God has eternal life." John 3.36. That means right now!

Once saved, you are eternally saved, and here is a very simple prayer to help you to get saved:

"*Dear Jesus,*

Please come into my heart, forgive me all of my sins, give me eternal life, and fill me with your Holy Spirit. Please help me to love others and to read the Word of God in Jesus name, Amen.

Once you've prayed that little prayer sincerely, then you are guaranteed a wonderful future in Heaven for eternity with your creator and loved ones.

As I mentioned earlier in this book, your Salvation does not depend on you going to church, and your good works.

Titus 3.5 states "Not by works of righteousness which we have done, but according to His mercy he saved us".

Your salvation only depends on receiving Christ as your Saviour, not on church or religion!

(If I could get saved having been an atheist and an evolutionist whilst at university, then anyone can get saved! Just challenge God to prove He exists & ask Him into your heart! He will show up in your life & teach you the truth!)

"He that comes unto me I will in no wise cast out"- Jesus

Jesus explained that unless you become as a child you won't even understand the kingdom of heaven. (John 3.3)

"About the Author" from my 1st book 'Out of the Bottomless Pit I'- how I personally got saved when i was 20 years old.

http://www.outofthebottomlesspit.co.uk/413469553] SALVATION – www.outofthebottomlesspit.co.uk

Please read the chapter about the Seraphim in this book as it was the Holy Spirit encouraging my wife Lisa, when she was very seriously ill.

CHAPTER 51

FAIRIES, 'WILL OF THE WISP'?

MY WIFE AND I have seen what might have been what is called 'Will of the Wisp' or small fairies upon occasion, including inside our houses. Well, in doing research, I am surprised to find that most of the mention of fairies and 'Will of the Wisps' tend to mention the word 'mischievous'. The truth is that my wife and I have both seen something described as a 'Will of the Wisp' but in our case what we saw was a small 'encouraging' and 'happy spirit' – like a small fairy of light dancing along the wall in our house.

I first noticed it when I was by myself one of the houses that we lived in around the year 2000. My wife and I also saw the same type of fairy of light 10 days after her accident and she was very ill in bed. This fairy danced along the wall happily and then shot at a right angle into our bathroom in the bedroom. Jesus said, 'Wherefore by their fruits you shall know them'. The affect that the fairies of light of dancing 'Will of the Wisps' had upon us was to encourage us at the time. My wife just told me that her angel has told her that he allowed the fairy to come and be an encouragement to my wife when she was very sick. It was amazing as we both saw it. I tried to locate a source of light from a car headlamp or some other light source in our darkened bedroom to try and explain it away at the time, and then the 'happy little dancing light' disappeared at a right angel very quickly into our bathroom. I followed it but it was gone. I have discovered that the house that we lived in the year 2000 was exactly to the north of us on the other side of the hills and therefore also on the same Ley-Lines. Maybe that has nothing to do with the fact I saw that 'Will of the Wisp in outhouse', but then who knows? It was a fun experience, and it is the first time that I have heard of people seeing small fairies dance around inside their houses. I think that in doing research most things about fairies are sort of relegated to 'Myth' and 'Folklore' but that does not mean that fairies don't exist. They do exist because my wife and I have both seen them in broad day-light, on several occasions, and no they were not bad spirits or demons, but they were sweet comforting spirits at the time when my wife was deathly ill.

Why is it that so many people dismiss what they simply can't understand.

This dimension in which we live is surrounded by other dimensions and peoples and beings and creatures, some know and others unknown. This explains so much of so-called Myth and Folklore. Someone somewhere has seen the fairies and pixies and 'Will of the Wisps' and hundreds of different creatures. I would say however as having studied the Book of Enoch at length, (see my book Enoch Insights), that it is possible that some of the negative creatures mentioned by others as either being 'mischievous' or even very 'dangerous' could be traced back to the Fallen Angels and the Giants and their progeny. The most dangerous trait of the Fallen angels is that they are shapeshifters. Another thing is that they created other creatures by mingling with the DNA of all kinds of animals, birds and fish and even insects. This being the case, there could be thousands of different hybrids like creatures somewhere. Whether in this dimension on in lower dimensions where the Giants were trapped at the time of the Flood or some in the sea or in the deep caverns of the earth. There are so many possibilities when you realize what happened before the Great Flood. The interesting thing is that there are also good protective spirits and beings that can also come in many forms. I think that both C.S. Lewis and R.R.Tolkien got the right ideas in their books of The Chronicles of Narnia & Lord of The Rings respectively. You know Centaurs and Dryads, mermaids and giants, nymphs, and Minotaurs, Harpies, and many others as well as fairies and pixies and trolls. Also, Sirens which are very dangerous type of mermaid creature which are mentioned in the Book of Enoch.

CHAPTER 52

PLAGUE?

Our own experience with Covid-19 – 02/07/2021

BACKGROUND: AROUND 7 weeks ago or in the 2nd week of July, my daughter›s boyfriend who is in the military was forced to take a covid vaccine against his own will.

Within days he himself was sick with covid-19 and this was confirmed by the military in doing a covid test. He tested positive. Then my daughter was required to take a test and the nurses came around to our house. The test proved that our daughter was positive.

Then we put ourselves into quarantine for two weeks. Our other daughter who lives with us tested negative.

Both our daughters work in care-homes.

The daughter who tested positive recovered quickly within days and the other never got sick.

Only my wife and I who are in our late sixties got very sick. A third adult daughter who also lives with us never got sick.

Symptoms Of Our Sickness: 13/06/2021 to13/07/2021

I reckon that I personally have had the so-called COVID-19 VIRUS sickness twice in the past 16 months.

Symptoms: Starts with a sore throat which gets worse and worse and is very annoying.

Hot and cold flashes. Headache(slight) runny nose (slight) constant weaknesses. Then eventually a really nasty cough that simply won't go away!

In my case infection in the throat. Eventually I had breathing problems and was afraid to fall asleep lest I would suffocate. Even in the daytime sitting in a chair for a few days I was afraid of suffocating, as my lungs were not working properly. Lack of sense of smell and taste. Forget the coffee, as it tastes like tar!

In the beginning of the sickness, it was almost impossible to sleep, but as time went by sleeping has no longer been a problem. Now after 19 days of being sick, I feel pretty much as normal except for this persistent and annoying cough and catarrh.

My wife on the other hand, became sick one week later than I did. She has the same symptoms plus she feels nauseous. I have had problems with my lungs on and off throughout my life including pneumonia a few times.

Conclusions: Would I conclude that these symptoms were nothing more than a cold or flu? No, somehow not! It behaves differently than a cold or a flu. It would seem that whatever it is it in particular targets the lungs and one›s ability to breath. Incidentally, I had not been sick at all in well over a year as we live as naturally as possible in our diet and in general, we don't get flu's and colds.

Part II 02/07/2021

We have been very fortunate as both my wife and have been having problems with breathing, but we happen to have a supply of oxygen tanks in our house due to my wife having M.E.

My wife rescued my health about a week ago by telling me to take three drops of Peppermint Essential Oils in some boiling water and to breath it into my lungs.

That has indeed been a lifesaver for me! I can now breath much better! Thank God for that mercy. No joke!

Last night, unfortunately, my wife had trouble with breathing, something that she never normally has! Just when I think I am getting better, I suddenly get strangely very tired, at right now at 10.00 a.m. I have only been up since 7 a.m. I guess that I have to go and lie down -again. Lots of rest needed with his sickness!

What on earth is going on with this Covid targeted weapon?

Part III 04/07/2021 Unfortunately, my wife in particular has been in a bad shape the past 3 days. It has now been exactly 21 days since I got Covid, but I am much better except for a persistent cough on and off.

Current Condition: My wife has pains in her head and in her eyeballs. She is having a problem walking and can do next to nothing at present. She also feels nauseous.

In talking with her, when possible, over the past couple of days, we both feel that Covid-19 is not a virus but is some sort of targeted weapon.

The Russian government stated recently that there is no evidence that this devilish sickness is a normal virus, but that it is in fact a bacterium which is triggered by 5-G.

Well, that is one possibility, I suppose, as it is very difficult to know the full truth of this covid-19 situation as so much has been deliberately covered -up by the governments of the planet for whatever nefarious reasons.

I have heard that the new World Order Powers that be – who control the covid-vaccine through big pharma: They have stated that if the peoples of the world refuse the Covid vaccines then they will simply drop it out from the sky through Chemtrails.

Is this true? I suggest everyone else starts to do their own research, if you are not already doing so – about these serious matters, as it could save someone's life! Maybe yours!

I have plenty of material on my website on the following page from the beginning of the Covid Crisis: WHAT IS GOING ON V? – www.outofthe-bottomlesspit.co.uk

There is an overwhelming amount of evidence from thousands of honest doctors and nurses who have stated that more dangerous than the covid-19 is to take multiple covid vaccines which have the ‹spike protein› in them which happens itself to be poisonous to the human cells.

Read the articles on this website from many sources to make your own well-rounded conclusions.

As I said before, we ourselves certainly won't be getting the COVID vaccine. Hell no, – Never, as it is potentially dangerous! Look it up the Covid-vaccine is not a vaccine!

Part IV day 26

The truth is I don't like what I am observing with this covid-19 sickness or whatever it is! I have been getting better except for the persistent cough. There have been new symptoms for both my wife and I. 'Sudden sharp pains in the head' and in my case slight headaches. Today I went cycling for the first time in more than 3 weeks to try to improve my circulation and keep me from the difficulty with feeling 'hot and cold', My cycling was much slower than normal.

This is what I observed about my health today that shocked me. I was walking up a steep hill with my bike and I found that after only 30 yards I was 'out of breath' and when I checked my heartbeat, I was shocked to see it was beating 120 -150 beats/minute. This is most definitely not normal for me. My wife has also complained of irregular heartbeat during the past weeks. Sudden tiredness and weakness are now common and unpredictable for us. Just when I think the nasty cough has all but gone it returns. It is not as bad as it was a week ago Thank God! How are we treating ourselves? We learned from Mike Adams that it has been discovered that dandy-lion leaves destroy the spike protein associated with covid-19. I also take garlic water and ginger as well as lemon and organic honey. In studying covid it is infamous for infecting the lungs and even causing pneumonia in the worst cases.

Part V 13/07/2021

This story is getting stranger as time goes by, and in conclusion for having had covid for a month as a family ourselves – we would all say that something is 'out of place'. That is our summary of the topic. Now for the details:

It is now one month and 1 day since I got sick with Covid 19 or whatever it is.

Many have stated that they don't think COVID-19 actually exists. I think they are 'dead wrong' on that one as my wife and I, and daughters have already experienced it, some a little, and some much more.

Every day recently, I have been thinking that I am now almost back to normal, then something happens out of the blue. I still have attacks of sudden 'extreme tiredness' which is unpredictable.

Right now, it is pains in my ears and the irritating cough is still there *at times*. My wife is also finally getting better and the 3 adult daughters who live with us have not gotten sick in the past 3 weeks. My wife just told me that she does still have a cold and extreme tiredness and cough at times.

Behavioural Changes: What I am about to tell you is just our family's observations.

Please see if you notice the same things happening where you are.

Behavioural change after taking the vaccine? my daughter stated the following about her recent experience with covid about 5 weeks ago now.

She caught covid-19 from her boyfriend, who had just taken a vaccine the very same day, that she last saw him, as the military had forced him to do so, even though he had been against taking the vaccine.

Strangely, after taking the vaccine he became totally pro-vaccine and has since broken off his relationship with our daughter.

He has totally changed from being a positive person to being depressed all the time, says our daughter.

Our daughter also expressed how so many people are becoming intolerant and vocal against those who don't believe in the vaccine, and often act angrily! The issue is separating people. Why? Is this just a co-incidence?

Part VI 16/07/21 Getting much better TKS for all of your prayers for us and all the comments which have been very helpful: https://www.outofthe-bottomlesspit.co.uk/449969050

Part VII added 24/07/21 My wife and I, are much better, but I still have a slight cough. My wife still has some exaggerated symptoms of older ailments. Thanks again for everyone's prayers for us, for the which, we are very grateful!

Part VIII Added 28/07/2021 Do we still have any covid symptoms after 46 days of having contracted covid-19? My cough is now only slight. Well, for myself I have a 'new strange condition' which I never had before. At night-time I sweat very badly, but only through my head, so that my pillow gets very wet and my hair the same. We think that my body is trying to get rid of poisons, – for this I am taking natural detox tablets from the Chinese doctor. My wife has a 'little breathing problem' that she did not have before we got covid. She also states that she is weaker than before having covid. My wife suggests that people take 'dandelion leaf' tea 3 x's/ day to help against the 'spike protein' in covid vaccines in particular.

Part IX added 01/08/2021

I am still experiencing 'side-effects' for having had the covid-19 since June 13. Today, I am experiencing pains in my lungs, which were not there before. I have also been having swellings or bloating in the intestine in the past 48 hours. I still have a slight cough. I am now mostly concerned about my lungs, as I have had pneumonia 3 times in my life in the far past. Yesterday, I found it very difficult to go cycling, and had to turn back home after only 300 yards, with weakness problems. This is definitely not normal for me. I am hoping the pains are just a coincidence after the end of having had covid. Assessment: as stated before, it would appear that covid attacks 'already weakened areas' in your body and even 'old' injuries.

If you have experienced something similar with those around you, please write to us at the address: strangetruths@btinternet.co.uk

Please stay away from the covid vaccines. Here is a report from an world expert in pharmaceuticals: scientific proof that the covid-vaccines are mass poisoning: the actual contents inside pfizer vials exposed! – forbidden knowledge tv

Reactions to Covid-19 updated 19/07/21

Dear Stephen, So sorry to hear about your bad bout with Covid 19.

Back about 1 year and 4 months ago I watched a series of videos on Covid 19 by Chis Martenson on the Peak Prosperity site, and I started then to take the supplements that he recommended and then about 4 months ago I started taking Ivermectin:

Doctors Raise Awareness on Ivermectin Treatment for C. Doctors Raise Awareness on Ivermectin Treatment for COVID-19 (theepochtimes.com)

Once a month on top of those supplements. It turns out that what I have been taking is exactly what the FLCCC (Front Line Covid-19 Critical Care Alliance) recommends (except I haven't been taking Melatonin) for prophylaxis and early treatment. What I took daily was Vitamin D3, Vitamin C, Quercetin and Zinc. Vitamin D was found to be deficient in most people that died of Covid. Zinc prevents the virus from multiplying in the cells and Quercetin makes it possible for the Zinc to enter the cells. Ivermectin coats the spike proteins so they can't bind to the ace-2 receptor cells.

Best Wishes,
J. Sharp

The following was sent into us on the 04/07/2021 by Cathy Gehr from N.Z about how to detox from heavy metals and poisons: those with covid-19 need to detox their bodies:

"Heavy Metal Detox Diet: Symptoms and Recommended Foods":

https://www.healthline.com/health/heavy-metal-detox

"Heavy metal detox foods to eat include":

- cilantro (Aka coriander – I use regularly in cooking in ground form; have it growing in my garden.)
- garlic (ALWAYS!! In hummus, pesto, any egg breakfasts and dinners.)
- wild blueberries
- lemon water
- Atlantic dulse
- curry (We use curry powder in scrambled eggs, soups, on cheese toasties – it's almost as always as garlic!)
- green tea (We drink one pot of green tea every day with breakfast. Don't buy Chinese [chemicals] or Japanese [radiation] green tea, or any food from those 2 countries! Our loose-leaf green tea is from Sri Lanka.)
- tomatoes (Even though pricier in the winter – like now – we still purchase. We grow some in the summer. We augment with store-bought organic passata sauce.)
- probiotics (We have some low-fat natural yoghurt every other day, if not every day. I also make my own pickles – daikon pickles. I'll send you the recipe, if you'd like.)

"Horsetail tea, too, because it helps purify your blood." We oftentimes do a blend of green tea, peppermint tea, rosemary, and horsetail tea in our tea pot.

Here's another article, highlighting cilantro / coriander (one in the same):

"How Cilantro Can Remove Most Heavy Metals From Your Body In Less Than 2 Months!":

https://timesofindia.indiatimes.com/life-style/food-news/cilantro-can-remove-most-of-heavy-metals-from-your-body-in-less-than-2-months/photostory/68285600.cms

"15 Best Foods for Detoxing Your Body – EcoWatch":

https://www.ecowatch.com/15-best-foods-for-detoxing-your-body-1882157131.html

– a lot of these I've posted info about in my ‹Celebrating Wellbeing› Facebook page:

1. Apples. We strive to eat one a day.

2. Avocados. Pretty much purchase 2 a week. Have some slices on our rice cracker with hummus and pickle snack.

3. Beets. We're growing these. Use grated in soups, baked, steam and this whizz in food processed when making hummus.

4. Blueberries. 10ish years ago we bought a blueberry bush which we doted over whilst apartment living in Auckland. When we moved in 2019 to our home, we planted it and it didn't miss a beat! Last summer it gave us 7 kilos of berries!

5. Cabbage. Always! A MUST! It's cheap, TTL!

6. Celery and Celery Seeds. Another always! I normally buy a large 1/2 a celery per week. Helps keep blood pressure down.

7. Cranberries. In our homemade granola we have dried cranberries.

8. Flaxseeds and Flaxseed Oil. In our homemade granola we have ground flaxseed (aka linseed).

9. Garlic.

10. Grapefruit. We're more into lemons; the reasons the article gives sound good!

11. Kale. We grow it year around. Super yum; use in soups, stir-fries, Peter makes kale chips.

12. Legumes. Always as well. I use red lentils to thicken soups. I make a brown-lentil loaf which, when baked, I divide up in portions and freeze and use as needed. My hummus recipes include a variety of beans (chickpeas, black "turtle" beans, black-eyed beans). We make faux "meatballs" and falafels out of lentils. Legumes are a great source of slow-release protein.

13. Lemons. We consume these in the lemon water mix I mentioned earlier.

14. Seaweed. When we lived in Auckland we made homemade brown-rice sushi (store-bought sushi contains sugar and a lot of salt in the rice – one of our homestays worked at a sushi shop and gave us the lowdown on how they make the sushi rice!) and used Korean-sourced seaweed. Need to get back into that!

15. Watercress. Haven't gotten into watercress, I should give it a go!

[The following was sent in on the 06/07/2021]

Dear Stephen, I would recommend vitamin D, which is one of the main sources from sun's rays and is very important to fight and prevent Covid, also Turmeric and Ginger root, which are natural anti-inflammatory fight against the swelling part of this disease, and that Covid virus doesn't kill people, but can leave your body weak, and if you don't take good care of body like taking multivitamins, especially the whole vitamin B complex Vitamin B12 as well and Vitamin D3, because if not in this weak period you can catch pneumonia which should be treated with antibiotics, before it becomes worse.

Also, between the Godly doctors that have been fighting this disease not following the mainstream, there is one that has a very effective treatment.

I personally know people that have used her treatment, DR Maria Eugenia Barrientos, She belongs to the Spanish speaking world, she has been saving lives since last year, in Central America, she breaks down the disease from the swelling part, that covid does, till the part when the swelling isn't treated to the pneumonia phase explaining to take ibuprofen which is an anti-inflammatory during the swelling phase which is between 7 to 10 days .

Anyway, soup made of chicken specially from chickens that are raised as in times of old is full of antibiotics.

One thing I know is that the WHO has been demonizing the Ibuprofen and praising the paracetamol, the WHO can't be trusted at all since they promote the vaccine, also I forgot to speak about the minerals this is mostly now that we know that Zinc is as important to fight all type of flu virus and also this I learned too that areas towns and cities the mineral copper was in abundance people did not get infected with covid but now the people of this area are becoming sick due to the vaccine enforcement,

Also I forgot to speak about lemon and onions besides eating them or drinking the lemon juice which is very good which is part of daily diet PTL,

Also when there is any type of flu, corona virus or whatever, cutting a couple of onions in half each and putting them in the room absorbs most of the flu, or covid germs, bacteria and virus in the air but you have to throw all these onions after a day because they absorbed all this. And on last but not least drinking Eucalyptus leaf with black tea, and burning the eucalyptus leaves to clean the area where someone with covid had been, this was done by some friends and other people we witnessed before this pandemic, when we had a chance to get in touch with them again they told us this was a very good remedy against covid and one of them that did this treatment was a lady that got sick in the beginning of the pandemic, and went to the hospital and was denied a bed sent home she had the Eucalyptus leaves and black tea so she made tea with it since she couldn't get out because of the restriction imposed on her, and healed too.

Here is excellent advice about how to get rid of all types of inflammation in the body whether it be from covid or otherwise: Top 8 Herbs Proven To Cure Inflammation (positivehealthwellness.com)

Natural Treatments

- Indulge in yoga and exercise. Treat the swelling in fingers and hands or any other body part by indulging in some simple...
- Benefits of yoga and exercise. Practicing yoga or some other simple workout optimizes the functioning of your...
- Epsom salt bath. Epsom salt bath is one of the most effective ways to reduce swelling. Try an Epsom salt bath to get rid...
- Benefits of soaking in Epsom salt Bath. Epsom salt contains magnesium sulphate which effectively works to reduce swelling.

Hear the 'Nightlight' international radio program where we talk about what it was like having Covid for 6 weeks?

Stream 278.NIGHTLIGHT ("Our Own Experience With Covid" – with Steven Strutt) by NIGHTLIGHT | Listen online for free on SoundCloud

CHAPTER 53

GMO'S

Three types of genetically engineered potatoes have been approved by the U.S.

I WROTE IN great detail about this subject on 03/08/16.

Last year I wrote about how I believed that genetically altered potatoes, had given me internal bleeding in the past which had caused very severe anaemia and kidney problems. (See below for full original articles)

Since I became aware of this, I have started only using organic potatoes, and other vegetables and fruits, and I have stopped being anaemic, and my kidneys are recovering.

This latest article proves that they have already been introducing genetically altered potatoes for a very long time, and probably since 2001, according to research done by a famous doctor in Edinburgh, Scotland, with whom I have had direct communication.

You can read about it all here below, and how *dangerous genetically altered potatoes are & why?* It is apparently because of their very design, that *genetically altered potatoes*, are in fact *much more dangerous than other vegetables*.

Please read below and see for yourselves!

13/03/17

According to federal officials, these three types of genetically engineered potatoes are able to resist the pathogen that caused the Irish potato famine. Officials say that they are safe for the environment and safe to eat, yet there has not been enough testing for this claim to be proven.

The U.S. Environmental Protection Agency and Food and Drug Administration gave Idaho-based J.R. Simplot Co. permission to plant the potatoes this spring and sell them in the fall.

The company claims that the potatoes contain only potato genes and that the resistance to late blight, the disease that caused the Irish potato famine, comes from an Argentine variety of potato that naturally produced a defence.

Changing the genetic code of foods presents ethical and health issues for many people, farmers, and companies alike.

These three new varieties of potato – the Russet Burbank, Ranger Russet, and Atlantic – have been approved by the U.S. Department of Agriculture. According to Simplot spokesman Doug Cole, the potatoes have the same taste, texture, and nutritional qualities as conventional potatoes.

The company said these GMO potatoes will have reduced bruising and black spots, enhanced storage capacity and a lower amount of the chemical that is a potential carcinogen.

Potatoes are the fourth staple crop in the world behind corn, rice, and wheat.

The Non-GMO Project, which opposes GMOs and verifies non-GMO food and products, said the new potatoes don't qualify as non-GMO.

"There is a growing attempt on the part of biotechnology companies to distance themselves from the consumer rejection of GMOs by claiming that new types of genetic engineering ... are not actually genetic engineering," the Washington state-based group said in a statement.

Ariana Marisol is a contributing staff writer for REAL farmacy.com. She is an avid nature enthusiast, gardener, photographer, writer, hiker, dreamer, and lover of all things sustainable, wild, and free. Ariana strives to bring people closer to their true source, Mother Nature. She graduated The Evergreen State College with an undergraduate degree focusing on Sustainable Design and Environmental Science.

GMO'S

Has my own health been affected directly by GMO vegetables

About 4 years ago, I was suddenly admitted to hospital with very severe anaemia, from which I almost died.

I received 4 blood transfusions and stayed one week in hospital.

Many tests were done on me, including internal cameras looking at my stomach wall and intestines.

The doctors were trying to understand why I had severe anaemia (not usual for men), and I was told that I had lesions in my stomach.

The consultant doctor of the hospital told me that I was haemorrhaging internally, but that he did not know what was causing it.

To Those Who Are Still Listening Concerning GMO Potatoes, And Other Crops:-

I Don't Like What I Am Discovering About Modern Potatoes, Tomatoes & Other Vegetables, (Which We Think Are Ok), But Are Actually GMO!

That Is A Real Shame, Because I Have Always Just Loved Potatoes & Tomatoes!

I Will Now Have To Scrap Most Of The Potatoes That We Planted This Year As Evidence Is Now Proving That Contrary To Most Official Stories, Many Of The Potato Plants Are In Fact Genetically Altered, And In Particular The Ones Whose Flowers Don't Fall Off So Easily!

These lilac & yellow potato flowers in this photo, are identical to some of those in our garden, & most likely are genetically engineered, without farmers or individual growers, even knowing about it. I am getting rid of ours!

Please read the following revealing report by the soil association in the UK & especially points 5-7 about the dangers of GMO vegetables & the damage they do to the gut!

Briefing: Summary of the risks of GM potatoes

Soil Association (UK) briefing on GM potatoes

Fuente: http://www.soilassociation.org

Below is information on the risks of GM potatoes. This includes a summary from the report by the National Pollen Research Unit and other information on the risks of GM contamination of normal non-GM crops. Also evidence of health problems.

SUMMARY

There would be no market for GM potatoes in the UK ·the major food retailers rejected GM potatoes in the US in 2002, including McDonalds, Burger King, McCain's and Pringles. The British Retail Consortium has said UK supermarkets won't be stocking GM potatoes.

Given that potatoes are a staple food, consumed fresh, and considered wholesome, there would be little or no desire to eat them ·any contamination would be much more serious as it would result in whole potatoes being GMOs, as opposed to some GM presence in a quantity of grain

- with potatoes, there is less direct risk of contamination of non-GM crops via cross-pollination than with GM grain and oilseed crops, as potatoes are tubers, not seeds

- however, there is still a risk of contamination from cross-pollination in later years via potato volunteers

- cross-pollination seems to be much greater when the GM and non-GM varieties are different and when the main pollinator is the pollen beetle, which travels far

- a study found the cross-pollination level was 31% at 1km from the GM crop

- blight resistant GM potato varieties pose much more of a risk of contamination as the flowering tops are less likely to be removed

- the NPRU has recommended a separation distance of 500m

- there are major health concerns, as two animal feeding trials, one funded by the UK Government, found GM potatoes cause lesions in the gut of animals

1. General

Potatoes are a staple food in the UK, and the fourth largest staple food in the world. Originally from South America, they have been grown in the UK for 300 years. Each person eats about 100kg per year, equivalent to 820 medium-sized potatoes. Potatoes are also used for industrial purposes, as a source of starch. The total area of potato production in the UK was 137,000t in 2005, of which 1,805t were organic (1.3% of the total area). Many varieties are grown in the UK.

2. Scientific evidence on the risks of contamination

The NPRU report on pollen dispersal reviewed the scientific literature on pollen transfer ("Pollen dispersal in the crops maize, oil seed rape, sugar beet and wheat", by Dr Treu and Prof. Emberlin, January 2000, commissioned by the Soil Association):

- the NPRU recommended a separation distance of 500m (in contrast with the proposal by Defra in August 2006 of no separation, their 'co-existence' paper)
- potatoes are an annual plant. The commercial crop is produced from 'seed' tubers, not true seeds. There are no sizeable seed producing areas in the UK.
- potatoes both self- and cross-pollinate. Cross-pollination rates are estimated to range from 0-20%
- cross-pollination is mainly by insects, mainly bumblebees – which tend to travel short distances, but can be by pollen beetles – which can fly far. The pollen beetle is "very common" in England
- ·potatoes pose a relatively low risk of cross-pollination because (i) potatoes are not grown from seeds but from tubers, which are clones of individuals of the desired variety, and (ii) the harvested crop is the tuber which is not affected by any cross-pollination
- however, potatoes produce volunteers, called 'ground keepers', and these pose a risk of GM contamination of non-GM crops in following years.
- importantly, the risk of cross-fertilisation is increased if (i) the GM and non-GM varieties are different but flower at the same time; (ii) if the varieties are blight resistant as the GM crop is more likely to be left flowering; or (iii) when the main pollinator is the pollen beetle, not bumblebees
- many varieties rarely produce berries as they are male sterile, but several modern varieties can produce very large numbers, each containing 400 seeds
- seed can survive seven years in southern England. When seeds grow, they mature into full potato plants, producing normal tubers, in the second year
- one study (Skogsmyr, 1994) found very high rates of cross-pollination between a GM variety (a version of Desiree) and a different non-GM variety

(Stina), of 36% at 100m and 31% at 1km. This indicates that still considerable rates of cross-pollination would be occurring at greater distances. These high rates were attributed to the fact that higher levels of cross-pollination often occur between different varieties in outbreeding plants, and because the main pollinator in this case was probably the pollen beetle.

- two other studies found low levels of cross-pollination. It was assumed that this was partially because the main pollinator was bumblebees. In one study (McPartlan and Dale, 1994), the rates were 2% at 3m and 0.017% at 10m; the low rate was probably also because the GM and non-GM varieties were the same (Desiree). In the other (Tynan et al, 1990), the rate was 0.05% at 4.5m; a 'wild type' variety was used; the low rate of cross- pollination was probably also because the GM and non-GM varieties appeared to have a different flowering time.

- but these rates are probably considerable underestimates as these three studies were all only on a research plot scale, not using agricultural scale fields which would normally produce much higher rates of cross-pollination

- 'relic' potato plants from earlier crops can be found and persist on tips, waste grounds and fields

- potatoes are not interfertile with other crop or wild species

Defra has also considered the contamination risks from GM potato crops[1]:

- the main risk of GM potatoes is from cross-pollination of non-GM crops and GM volunteers appearing in later seasons: "the recipient plant will ... produce GM hybrids, which means that GM volunteers may be created. It is possible that over time there could be some limited GM transfer between farms via the development and persistence of GM volunteers."

The NPRU says "the role of the pollen beetle in long distance distribution of potato pollen is in need of further research". Further research into the significance of wind pollination in long range dispersal is also suggested.

3. Agricultural practices affecting the risk of GM contamination

- many different potato varieties are grown in the UK

- potatoes flower at similar times to the time when the tubers are being produced

- to prevent fungal 'blight' damage to the plant from affecting the growth of the potato tubers, farmers usually defoliate the plants, removing the flowering heads and green leaves (done with acids or, among organic farmers, mechanically or with flame-weeders). This is done at flowering or soon after. So, flowering is common, even if not present in most fields and generally only for short periods.

- after the defoliation, the crop is left for a few weeks to let the potato skins 'set'

- however, the defoliation itself affects tuber growth, so farmers prefer to leave the green tops if they can. They are therefore more likely to leave the flowers if the varieties are blight resistant. This means that blight resistant GM varieties pose a higher risk of flowering presence, cross-pollinating and producing seed volunteers are usually controlled with herbicides but, according to Defra, "it is not possible to guarantee the complete elimination of volunteers"

- also, not every potato tuber will be removed from the ground

4. Organic potato production techniques

Organic farmers primarily control crop pests and disease with natural processes, including healthy soils, crop rotations and by encouraging natural predators. Blight in potatoes is one of the very few crop diseases where such management techniques are not wholly effective, and instead late blight in organic farming is controlled by copper sprays. Copper is a naturally occurring element and many soils are deficient in it. The amounts used are limited to 6kg/ha per year and it does not build up in the soil, due to the crop rotations. The copper is sprayed onto the plant's leaves and does not end up in the potatoes, unlike the pesticides used in non-organic farming which are found in a quarter of potatoes and may pose a risk to human health.

5. Development of GM potato varieties

The German chemicals group BASF has developed a blight resistant GM potato. It is currently trialling them in Germany, Netherlands and Sweden and has applied to Defra for approval to carry out two 1ha trials in the England in spring 2007 (one in Derbyshire and one in Cambridgeshire). After 3-4 years, they intend to seek permission to grow and sell the potatoes in Britain. The potatoes contain two genes from a wild Mexican potato.

According to BASF, the GM variety would reduce the number of fungicide sprays from about 15 per season to just a couple. These would be the first GM trials in the UK since the end of the farm-scale trails in 2003. BASF has also applied for EU approval for a potato that is rich in a type of starch used in the paper industry; it hopes for approval later this year.

GM potatoes are unnecessary and are unlikely to deliver significant environmental benefits. Only 1,300t of the 12,000t of pesticide used on potatoes in the UK are fungicides, so it seems that at most they could reduce pesticide use by 10%.

Conventional breeding of existing varieties is making progress in developing blight resistant varieties. These are being developed and trialled for use in organic farming. Using old Hungarian varieties, Sarpo Mirea and Axona, potato grower Dr David Shaw has developed blight resistant red varieties with a high dry content, suitable for chips and baking, and he is looking into a variety suitable for salads.

6. Commercial experience of GM potatoes

In the US, attempts at selling GM potatoes failed after being rejected by major food companies, including McDonald's, Burger King, McCain's and Pringles [2]. There are no GM potatoes sold in the US now. On the radio programme, Farming Today, on 24 August 2005, Andrew Opie of the British Retail Consortium, representing supermarkets, said, "We won't be stocking GM potatoes for the conceivable future ... The fact is people remain suspicious of GM". (Comment by Steve 05/08/16 Well a lot has changed since 2005 and GMO's are now extensively used and promoted in agriculture)

7. Health problems with GM potatoes

There is a major concern that GM potatoes pose a risk to human health. There are many serious concerns about GMOs in general, most of which would apply to GM potatoes. However, there is a particular concern with GM potatoes as for several years there has been evidence indicating that they could cause haemorrhages.

Feeding trials by two scientific teams found that GM potatoes cause lesions in the gut wall of rats and mice[3]. Both studies were published in scientific journals. One was a controlled UK Government funded study, peer reviewed and published in the Lancet, the most respectable medical journal, in October 1999 (Ewen and Pusztai, 1999). The editor said the paper "deserved further scientific attention."

Author: Has my own health been affected directly by GMO vegetables?

About 4 years ago, I was suddenly admitted to hospital with very severe anaemia, from which i almost died.

I received 4 blood transfusions and stayed one week in hospital.

Many tests were done on me, including internal cameras looking at my stomach wall and intestines.

The doctors were trying to understand why I had severe anaemia (not usual for men), and I was told that I had lesions in my stomach.

The consultant doctor of the hospital told me that I was haemorrhaging internally, but that he did not know what was causing it.

He stated that over time, it would cause severe blood loss and sever anaemia- cause unknown.

Well, I have been treating my anaemia naturally with natural iron pills daily, but I know that the root cause of my problem has not yet been fixed.

I get anaemia if I don't take a lot of iron pretty quickly.

After reading about GM vegetables, and my personal liking potatoes so much, I am wondering if it has been GMO potatoes and tomatoes which have caused my internal bleeding and resultant anaemia?!

The only way to find out for sure, is if I stop eating all non-organic potatoes and tomatoes and only eat organic for 6 months and see if the anaemia totally disappears.

The biotechnology industry reacted very aggressively and tried to mobilise the scientific community to undermine the credibility of the work.

However, no further work has been undertaken since which could in any way suggest that the finding was wrong. Moreover, the credibility of the findings is supported by the fact that similar effects have been found with GM tomatoes in two US feeding trials, which found that GM tomatoes cause lesions in the gut wall of rats.[4]

GA, 24.8.2006, GM briefing 23

[1] "Consultation on proposals for managing the co-existence of GM, conventional and organic crops", July 2006

[2] "GE crops – increasingly isolated awareness and rejection grow", Greenpeace International, briefing, March 2002

[3] Ewen and Pusztai, "Effects of diets containing genetically modified potatoes expressing Galanthus nivalis lectin on rat small intestine", The Lancet, 354, 1353-1354, 1999; A. Pusztai, "Can science give us the tools for recognizing possible health risks of GM food?" Nutr. Health, 16, 73-84; Fares, N.H. and El-Sayed, A.K., "Fine structural changes in the ileum of mice fed on endotoxin-treated potatoes and transgenic potatoes." Natural Toxins, 6, 219-233, 1998.

[4] Unpublished studies carried out for Calgene and at the request of the FDA respectively, in early 1990s, in reviewed "Food safety – contaminants and toxins", CABI Publishing, 2003.

WEB SOURCE:- (http://webs.chasque.net/~rapaluy1/transgenicos/Papa/GM_potatoes.html) The origin of the article was:- http://www.soilassociation.org

(**COMMENT** by Steve 03/08/16.) When I tried to contact this website:-http://www.soilassociation.org it was no longer available. I have no exact date for when the above article was written, but I suspect that it was written before 2009. From what I can gather so far, prior to 2013 there was a lot more information available about the dangers of GMO's

It would definitely seem that those in favour of GMO's are burying the information, like the above article.

You would almost think that it is being covered-up deliberately!

What is the real agenda behind all this GMO cover-up?

(Steve: My e-mail is: strangetruths@outofthebottomlesspit.co.uk)

Official position concerning GMO›s?

Source: (https://en.wikipedia.org/wiki/Genetically_modified_food)

Genetically modified foods or GM foods, also genetically engineered foods, are foods produced from organisms that have had changes introduced into their DNA using the methods of genetic engineering. Genetic engineering techniques allow for the introduction of new traits as well as greater control over traits than previous methods such as selective breeding and mutation breeding.[1]

Commercial sale of genetically modified foods began in 1994, when Calgene first marketed its unsuccessful Flavr Savr delayed-ripening tomato. [2][3] Most food modifications have primarily focused on cash crops in high demand by farmers such as soybean, corn, canola, and cotton seed oil. Genetically modified crops have been engineered for resistance to pathogens and herbicides and for better nutrient profiles. GM livestock have been developed, although as of November 2013 none were on the market.

There is a scientific consensus that currently available food derived from GM crops poses no greater risk to human health than conventional food, but that each GM food needs to be tested on a case-by-case basis before introduction. Nonetheless, members of the public are much less likely than scientists to perceive GM foods as safe.

From my observations in our own garden with so-called "Potato Fruits" which are so rare that one famer stated that her & her husband had not seen the phenomenon in 40 years of farming potatoes and tomatoes!!?

The so-called potato fruits in out garden are only growing on the non-organic potatoes, which we bought in the supermarket.

One person stated that when he tasted a "potato fruit" that it tasted of a tomato, but that it was very bitter, which one would expect now, knowing that it is in fact poisonous.

Why did it taste like a tomato, if it is only a so-called "potato fruit"?

Here are their exact words & the source of the information: -

"One other thing... In case anyone is curious... I did taste them. I knew that the potato is a nightshade, so I only took a small bite. Moderation is the key, right? I found them to be quite similar in texture to a tomato, but they are VERY bitter. From now on, I think I'll stick with the tomato!"- **SOURCE:-** **(http://tinyfarmblog.com/potato-fruit/)**

OBSERVATION 01/08/16

Today in taking a photo of the following cluster of 7 "potato fruits" on one potato plant in our garden, 3 of them easily fell off without any resistance. Obviously, these "potato fruits are being rejected by nature because they are poisonous.

It has been stated that even just grafting a tomato with a potato is not a good idea, as the inherent poisons, sometimes associated with potatoes, when they are found green, could easily be transmitted to the tomatoes.

Those for grafting the tomato with the potato, are stating that the genetics of the tomato and potato are almost the same, and that the flowers are the same.

I beg to differ. The flowers are actually totally different from each other in shape, size and colour!

The purple flower is from the potato. The yellow flower from a tomato. They are clearly not the same!

One gardener stated: "Usually, potato flowers just drop off"

Wow! See the purple flower from the potato in our garden in the photo above? Well, it isn't rare anymore as very single potato plant next to it is covered in purple flowers.

I will add a photo of this later, as it very unusual, as the flowers are flourishing, and if pollinated, it will mean a lot more dangerous "potato fruits" in our small garden. Yikes! Our granddaughter is coming for a stay next month, so we had better be careful about those so-called "potato fruits".

CONCLUSIONS about the so-called "Potato Fruit" and the experimental TOMATO. This tomato, which was largely advertised in 2013 in the UK, but has since disappeared.

The information officially given about the very rare "potato fruit" being quite normal and caused by certain rare climatic conditions, and when the potato flower gets pollinated on a rare occasion, simply does not face the light of investigation.

The pollination of potato plants, like any other plants should produce more of the same i.e., potatoes, and not some strange "potato fruits" or bitter and poisonous tomatoes!

I could be wrong, but it sounds more like a GMO experiment gone wrong!

I will write more about this. I received a letter from a professor in genetics, to whom I reported the strange so-called "potato fruits", & who has encouraged me to tell the public about the fact & that in the USA today 70% of all of our food is now GMO.

You can see the professor's letter to me from yesterday, if you scroll-down on this page.

Genetic tampering has obviously been involved, & those behind it are simply trying to cover their tracks, & the result is probably that we permanently have poisonous so-called "potato fruits" which are dangerous enough to kill someone!

Watch out if you have kids, that they don't play with, or eat the so-called "potato fruits" they can kill you!

I wonder what happened to those people who grew the tomato back in 2013. Please let me know!

Please pass on the following information to everyone who can handle it!

TomTato, Tomato-Potato Plant, Now Available (VIDEO) 27/09/2013

We're all about combining potatoes and tomatoes together when cooking — but the development of a new plant, the TomTato, has us a little weirded out. The TomTato, now available in the U.K., is a tomato and potato plant in one. Both the tomatoes and potatoes ripen at the same time.

Thompson & Morgan, the horticulture company behind the TomTato, says the the tomatoes are sweeter than most supermarket varieties. The TomTato is not genetically modified — it is a grafted plant, meaning that tissue from one plant is attached to tissue from another.

A different version called the Potato Tom, made by another company, is available in New Zealand starting in October.

The TomTato lasts only one season.

Correction: An earlier version of this article referred to the plant as a hybrid. It is technically a grafted plant, not a hybrid. SOURCE:- (http://www.huffingtonpost.com/2013/09/27/tomtato_n_4003791.html)

That video was from 2013.

But what has hatched from their hybrid experiments, since 2013?

I will investigate more, as if I am not mistaken, mixing a tomato plant with a potato plant, might have already caused some serious problems, and side effects by 2016.

Here is one comment by a fellow gardener from 2013:- "do not graft tomato to potato because the alkaloid poison transfers and you will get sick if not dead! Look it up." source: – (http://tinyfarmblog.com/potato-fruit/)

Important And Potentially Dangerous Matter.

Watch Out About Potato Fruits Developing In Your Gardens!

Especially Keep Children Away From Those So-Called "Potato Fruits", Which Are Probably A Very New Development, As They Can Kill, And Are Deadly Poisonous!

Direct link:-http://www.outofthebottomlesspit.co.uk/421556550

UPDATE 28/07/16

Steve: My wife and I, have planted potatoes for many years, and this is the first time that we have encountered what look like tomatoes growing on a potato plant, but we have been told today 28/07/16, by a friend, that these "tomatoes" seemingly growing on the potatoes, are in fact called a "potato fruit".

They are classified as being a rare phenomenon, and the fruits are in fact poisonous.

My question would now be why does a potato have to produce a poisonous potato fruit,(which look like tomatoes) and only happen on a rare occasion, unless there is something wrong with the soil, rain, air or climate?

Perhaps plants try to get rid of poisons when there are too much of them in their immediate environment. I notice that the organic potatoes are not growing "potato fruits" only the ones from the supermarket.

Warning: – "Potato fruits or berries, are a member of the poisonous night-shade family. Potato berries should not be eaten. All green parts of the potato plant contain toxic glycoalkaloid compounds that can cause headaches, diarrhoea, cramps, and in severe cases, coma and death.

Potato fruit

Here's something I haven't seen before in my, uh, six years of growing potatoes: green, tomato-like, walnut-sized potato fruit. Bob hadn't seen 'em either, in 40 plus years of farming. I hit the web for education.

These are genuine fruit, but not that common. Usually, potato flowers just drop off. When fruit do form, they're more likely found on certain varieties, like Yukon Gold. This year, there were fruit on just about every Chieftain plant, here and there on the Kennebec, and none that I noticed on the Yukon Gold...

Each fruit contains 300-500 seeds that don't come true: planting them doesn't result in the same potatoes as the parent plant, there's lots of genetic variation. Potato breeders plant out thousands of seeds, check out the results, then keep replanting the most desirable potatoes for many years or so to get new commercial varieties—apparently, this is the way new potatoes are bred.

Meanwhile, it apparently only takes only two seasons and one generation to breed genetically stable new potatoes, so for the small farm or home garden, as opposed to the big potato breeder, this seems like a viable way to go. Harvest seed one season—you can hand-pollinate to cross two varieties—plant out the next and select your favourites. Those tubers should be stable and ready to go, you just have to build up a quantity, which takes another season, unless you need hardly any at all!

And, the fruit are poisonous, rich in solanine, not for eating (potatoes, tomatoes, peppers, eggplant and tobacco are all members of the "deadly nightshade" family, all prone to having toxic parts). Interesting!

Since they suddenly appeared this year on two varieties, I'd guess it was about the weather!

source: – (http://tinyfarmblog.com/potato-fruit/)

Comment Send To Me By A Member Of The Public In The UK: – (28/07/16)

"About 3 years ago they released a cross spliced potato/tomato plant - spuds below ground tomatoes above and they were released for global public sale, the 2 plants as solanum species so splicing one to other wasn't hard or requiring GM tech.

Having said that in the case that you are reporting: You might have managed the progeny doing what they didn't expect.

Screwing with mother nature can cause very unexpected outcomes!"

How can a potato that we planted 6 weeks ago, now be giving tomatoes on its stem?

You tell me?

Genetically Engineered Foods
Genetically Engineered Potatoes
25/07/16

Arpad Pusztai, a genetic scientist working at the Rowett Research Institute in Scotland was very pro GE. In 1998, he set up a 3-year $1.6 million study to test the effects of genetically altered foods on rats, His study included rats feeding on three different types of potatoes as follows:

1) Regular non-GE potatoes

2) Genetically altered potatoes (the potatoes were spliced with a snowdrop lectin) the lectin was believed to make the plant toxic to insects.

3) The third group of potatoes were regular potatoes mixed with the same lectin – but not genetically engineered lectin

Out of the three groups of rats, only the group feeding on GE potatoes suffered ill effects. In ten days all their organs reduced in weight, signalling a compromised immune system. Also, they suffered from viral infections of the stomach lining.

Prior to his own research Dr. Pusztai was a proponent of GE; he fully expected his research to give GE a clean bill of health. After evaluating ten days of the much longer study, he went on a TV show and told of his research and misgivings. Within 48 hours, Dr. Pusztai was relieved of his long-standing post at the Rowett Research Institute, denied access to his research and put under a gag order. You may well ask, what could keep him from talking – why was he successfully gagged? Because the Institute also threatened to fire his research team. Now, of course, the Dr. has retrieved his research documents and is talking through lectures all over the world. This is only one of too few "independent research" studies that have been conducted and which suggest that GE food is dangerous to human health.

It is very difficult to get the truth out when the very institution that authorizes the research, because of not liking the results, tries to suppress it.

One of the facts of life in our times is that many Institutions which are supposed to conduct "independent research" are really beholden to the private industries which fund them. This has happened in our landgrant universities where these universities have contracted partnerships with private industry. How can we rely on research data to be made public when and if the results of that research may go against what the private industry partners are promoting? Honesty, integrity and transparency seem to get lost in these kinds of arrangements.

You can read more about Arpad Pusztai by putting his name into a Google search. There is also more information on my website: www.rawfoodinfo.com both in the Articles section under Biotechnology and in the links section under Genetic Engineering.

In 1989 a genetically engineered batch of L-tryptophan* sold in the US by a Japanese company, Showa Denko, caused the death of dozens of people, and the permanent disability of 1500. 5000 people were affected. This only occurred with the genetically modified version, yet all L-tryptophan was taken off the market. The genetic engineering of L-tryptophan produced a toxin – an unexpected occurrence. Had there been testing done prior to this occurrence, the deaths and disabilities could have been avoided.

* L-tryptophan is a naturally occurring amino acid.

A very strong thread throughout your letter is the conviction that somehow people will starve around the world if GE is not allowed to proceed. Research available on yield, quite the opposite, shows that the yield is decreased in GE plants. A 2-year study out of the University of Nebraska on Round Up Ready soybeans, showed conclusively that yield was reduced. High yielding conventional soybeans produced 57.7 bushels per acre, while GE soybeans produced 52 bushels per acre, a substantial reduction. At the same time herbicide usage was increased. Genetically engineered Round Up Ready soybeans are engineered to resist herbicides. Specifically, the Round Up Ready Herbicide is also sold by Monsanto, the same company that is selling the GE seed. When these herbicides are applied, all surrounding plant life (weeds) and the attendant life that lives and feeds on these plants is killed. Only the target plant is allowed to live. In this sense GE is a culture of death and destruction. True organic agriculture understands and works with surrounding plant life (weeds). Weeds in cohabitation with target plants assist them in many beneficial ways; breaking up hardpans with their stronger root systems; bringing moisture up to the surface and recycling nutrients when applied as mulch, and also as a mulch, reducing water needs.

Researchers say that yield is reduced in GE plants because the alteration of the genome in a plant or organism causes a destabilization of the entire organism. The plant is not functioning at its optimum level, and yield is reduced. The same destabilization also causes a reduction of nutrient values.

So far, all independent research substantiates this reduction in yield and nutrient values.

The biotechnology industry has launched a 250 million advertising campaign to convince the American people of the {dubious} benefits of GE. Probably your belief that we need these foods to feed the starving people in the world were garnered from PR input. Not all the money is spent on ads – some of it is spent in strategically placed propaganda which looks like science.

One thing that you can be sure of is that within the scientific community there is no agreement or consensus as to the safety of GE foods.

Two more points I will mention before I end. For those who choose to be a vegetarian, how can their choice be respected if we allow the splicing of animal and insect genes into plants and then do not tell them about it through labelling?

And lastly, in Nature's wondrous system, pollen goes forth through wind, insects and bees to fertilize and even spontaneously hybridize new plants with a plant's close relatives in the weedy community. This has been a form of evolution for plants. But in all the eons of our earth, Nature never, ever crossed a fish gene with a tomato or a rat gene into a broccolini plant because Nature has placed barriers, natural constraints, that do not allow this to happen. Now, all of a sudden, in what is surely an affront to the integrity of Nature, we are allowing the crossing of all kinds of organisms.

You finished your letter with the question of choice. You said that we have the same choice as the farmers who plant GE.

I choose to be an organic farmer. If my neighbour plants GE across the way from me, and our plants come to flower at the same time, my organic plants will be contaminated with his GE organisms. How does that give me the choice that I need to be organic? This has happened already and many organic farmers in the Midwest can no longer call themselves organic through no fault of their own. GE technology is a form of trespass onto another's property and essentially denies them the right to harvest the plant of their choice. In the upside-down world that we live in – farmers are being sued because they are growing GE plants (that they never planted) because of this contamination process. The Monsanto's and other biotech corporations are suing the farmers because they say the farmers stole their patented technology, when in reality the biotech corporation's GE technology has been the trespasser and stolen the farmer's land and denied him the right to grow the plant of his choice on his own land. An unhappy state of affairs.

I note that you are a gardener, so perhaps you understand the unfairness of this. GE plants, if they are to be grown at all, should be grown in contained environments – biospheres and such – so that their pollen cannot contaminate the entire countryside.

I hope that I have been able to give you at least some food for further thought and deliberation.

Respectfully,

Rhio

Rhio's Raw Energy

www.rawfoodinfo.com

Letter sent by S.N.Strutt 25/07/16

To Rhio

Rhio's Raw Energy

www.rawfoodinfo.com

I just read the following very interesting article on your website:- http://www.all-creatures.org/cb/a-gefood-potato.html

I wanted to ask you about genetically altered potatoes.

Why? Well today something odd happened in our garden.

Maybe it is nothing, but I would like to have a professional opinion, as to what we are dealing with, as I have never heard of such a thing before!

For years my wife and I, have planted tomatoes and potatoes and other vegetables like nearly every other gardener.

This year something is just not right!

In June we planted some potatoes that were bought at the organic farm here in the UK. However, we also planted some of the naturally sprouting bags of potatoes that we had bought at LIDL.

Here is the strange thing: -

Today when looking at the large coverage of potato plants, I noticed to my great surprise, that what looked like tomatoes were growing on the stems of the some of the potato plants. This is not something that I have ever heard of; and there is nothing on the web, that directly talks about such a possibility.

I have photographed the tomatoes which are growing of the potato plant and put a real home-grown tomato alongside it. They are not similar. The "tomato" growing on the potato plant has no seeds in it and is darker in colour.

I have not yet checked whether the same potato plant that is growing tomatoes, is also growing potatoes underground, as it is too early normally for that, but I could check if it becomes necessary.

What are we dealing with here?

It makes me want to only buy organic vegetables both for planting and eating.

It would seem that GMO's have totally screwed up the vegetables and crops all around us here in Scotland and elsewhere.

It would be good to hear what you think on this matter.

Best Wishes,

Looking forward to hearing from you.

S.N.Strutt

E-mail: strangetruths@outoffthebottomlesspit.co.uk

ANSWER from Rhio's Raw Energy

www.rawfoodinfo.com 30/07/16

Hi, Stephen:

Thanks for writing AND I certainly do hope you start writing about the dangers of these untested, unlabelled GMOs that are now in over 2/3rds of the foods on America's grocery store shelves.

Though some time ago, you might find info on our web site of interest: http://www.all-creatures.org/cb/a-grandmoms.html

Gerry

I had the pleasure of speaking at a World Vegetarian Congress held at Edinburgh University several years ago.

Background Information about: Gerry Coffey, CAJA: Court Appointed Juvenile Advocate

Health Educator/Councilor/Global Media Liaison, IVU

M.O.W.W. Deputy Director: YOUTH LEADERSHIP CONFERENCE

Coffey Break: A Healthy Alternative: www.all-creatures.org/cb/

Recipient: Int'l. Vegetarian-of-the-Year-Award, Bangkok, Thailand,

http://www.all-creatures.org/cb/images/Resume-GerryCoffey08-15-2012.pdf

"The day we stop learning we stop living."

I left the following comment on another website today:- **(http://iceagenow. info/huge-huge-girder-placement-machine-video/#comment-352719)** about strange hybrids: 27/07/16

GENETICALLY ALTERED CROPS

"Dear Robert,

Again on this occasion, what I am going to tell you, is not about Global Cooling, but it is definitely to do with Genetically Altered Crops.

Something very strange has just happened in our garden, which I have put on my website. I have already sent the information to a genetics expert here in Scotland, as what we are seeing in our garden *should be impossible!*

What is it? See on my website how those potatoes that we planted in our garden 6 weeks ago, are growing some sort of strange tomatoes, on stems hanging down on the stalks of the of the potatoes. I have never seen anything like this, and I know that many scientific people go on your website. If anyone can explain this strange phenomenon, how a planted potato can yield tomatoes, my wife and I would very much appreciate it.

Here is the LINK on my website: – **http://www.outofthebottomlesspit. co.uk/421556550**

E-mail: **strangetruths@outofthebottomlesspit.co.uk**

I will also post more photos of this strange phenomenon shortly.

If potatoes planted in the ground can yield tomatoes, what is next?

I bought those potatoes in LIDL, and would normally have eaten them, but they were budding, so I put them in the ground, and 6 weeks later they have produced tomatoes of a strange kind!?

Has to be some sort of GMO aberration.

The Ultimate Hybrid Will Involve Man Himself (08/08/16)

Related: 24 Genetically Modified Seedless Fruits You Hardly Knew About – Nutrineat

CHAPTER 54

OXYGEN IS DISAPPEARING FROM THE PLANET

Is IT TRUE that we used to have a lot more oxygen in our atmosphere in the past, and that "lack of oxygen" could possibly be the cause of many modern sicknesses or at the very least exacerbating the conditions?

Well, I certainly found plenty of shocking evidence, that the oxygen levels on our planet are decreasing at an alarming & dangerous rate, whilst foolish global warmists worry about insignificant CO2 (0.02% of the atmospheric gases, compared to 19+% oxygen, which you will see is dangerously low!) See for yourselves in the following comprehensive article on the topic by expert Dr. Mae-Wan Ho

O_2 Dropping Faster than CO_2 Rising Implications for Climate Change Policies

New research shows oxygen depletion in the atmosphere accelerating since 2003, coinciding with the biofuels boom; climate policies that focus exclusively on carbon sequestration could be disastrous for all oxygen-breathing organisms including humans

Dr. Mae-Wan Ho

Threat of oxygen depletion

Mention climate change and everyone thinks of CO_2 increasing in the atmosphere, the greenhouse effect heating the earth, glaciers melting, rising sea levels, floods, hurricanes, droughts, and a host of other environmental catastrophes. Climate mitigating policies are almost all aimed at reducing CO_2, by whatever means.

Within the past several years, however, scientists have *found that oxygen (O_2) in the atmosphere has been dropping,* and at higher rates than just the amount that goes into the increase of CO_2 from burning fossil fuels, some 2 to 4-times as much, and accelerating since 2002-2003 [1-3]. Simultaneously, oxygen levels in the world's oceans have also been falling [4] (see Warming Oceans Starved of Oxygen, *SiS* 44).

It is becoming clear that getting rid of CO_2 is not enough.

Oxygen has its own dynamic and the rapid decline in atmospheric O_2 must also be addressed. Although there is much more O_2 than CO_2 in the atmosphere – 20.95 percent or 209 460 ppm of O_2 compared with around 380 ppm of CO_2 – humans, all mammals, birds, frogs, butterfly, bees, and other air-breathing life-forms depend on this high level of oxygen for their wellbeing [5] Living with Oxygen (*SiS* 43).

In humans, failure of oxygen energy metabolism is the single most important risk factor for chronic diseases including cancer and death.

'Oxygen deficiency' is currently set at 19.5 percent in enclosed spaces for health and safety [6], below that, *fainting and death may result.*

The simultaneous decrease in ocean oxygen not only threatens the survival of aerobic marine organisms, but is symptomatic of the slow-down in the ocean's thermohaline 'conveyor belt' circulation system that transports heat from the tropics to the poles,(this itself could trigger an ice-age) overturns surface layers of into the deep and *vice versa*, redistributing nutrients and gases for the ocean biosphere, and regulating rainfall and temperatures on the landmasses.

This dynamical system is highly nonlinear, and small changes could make it fail altogether, with disastrous runaway effects on the climate [7] (Global Warming & then the Big Freeze, *SiS* 20). More importantly, it could wipe out the ocean's phytoplankton that's ultimately responsible for splitting water to regenerate oxygen for the entire biosphere, on land and in the sea [4]. Global CO_2 records go back more than 50 years [8], but O_2 measurement in combination with CO_2 goes back barely two decades [9] and is already giving important information on the size of the carbon sink in the ocean relative to the land. For one thing, O_2 and CO_2 have very different solubility in seawater; while 99 percent of the O_2 remains in the atmosphere, 98 percent of the CO_2 is in seawater.

Decrease in atmospheric O_2 has been detected in stations around the world for the past decade, a consistent downward trend that has accelerated in recent years.

The largest fall in O_2 was observed in the study of Swiss research team led by Francesco Valentino at University of Bern, for data collected at high altitude research stations in Switzerland and France

The researchers speculated that the large decrease in atmospheric oxygen since 2003 could have been the result of oxygen being taken up by the ocean, either due to a cooling of water in the North Atlantic, or water moving northwards from the tropic cooling, both of which would increase the water's ability to take up more oxygen. However, it would require unrealistic cooling to account for the change in O_2 concentration. And all the indications are that the ocean waters have warmed since records began

O_2 is decreasing faster than can be accounted for by the rise in CO_2. Furthermore, the decrease is not uniform throughout the entire period; instead, it is much steeper between 2002 and 2005 at both stations and is not accompanied by any change in the trend of CO_2 increase. This sharp acceleration in the downward trend of atmospheric O_2 from 2002-2003 onwards in Ireland and The Netherlands is in accord with the findings in Switzerland and France [1]. And this cannot be explained by a realistic increase in fossil fuel use, or oxygen uptake by cooler ocean waters; if anything, oxygen level in the oceans has also been falling [4]. So, where and what is this oxygen sink that is soaking up oxygen?

Thus, the expansion of agriculture and grazing during the 20th century has probably caused a decrease in the oxidative ratio of the plant biomass within these disturbed ecosystems. Using several simple models, the researchers showed that, indeed, small changes in R_{ab} could lead to substantial decreases in atmospheric O_2.

Another research team has raised the possibility that reactive nitrogen produced in making artificial fertilizers for agriculture could also be tying up more oxygen in plant tissue, soil organic matter and oceans in the form of nitrates [13].

This includes wide-spread deforestation and replacement of woody vegetation with pastures and crops in the tropics, an increase in fire activity and tree mortality and increasing the abundance of deciduous tree species and herbaceous plants in the boreal (northern) regions. Globally, this includes an increase in invasive species and increased disturbance of agricultural soils by ploughing and grazing during the 20th century.

Change in land use, and increased oxidation of nitrogen could explain the long-term steady decline in atmospheric O_2 and may well also account for the sharp acceleration of the downward trend since 2002 and 2003.

These years happen to coincide with record rates of deforestation. In Brazil, 10 000 square miles were lost mainly to pastureland, soybean plantations and illegal logging, a 40 percent rise over the previous year [14]. Massive deforestation has continued in the Amazon and elsewhere, spurred by the biofuels boom [15]; it is estimated that nearly 40 000 ha of the world's forests are vanishing every day.

The crucial role of forests and phytoplankton [4] in oxygenating the earth shows how urgent it is to take oxygen accounting seriously in climate policies. Reductionist accounting for CO_2 alone is insufficient, and even grossly misleading and dangerous.

A case in point is the proposal of the International Biochar Initiative (IBI). 'Biochar' is charcoal produced to be buried in the soil that IBI has been promoting worldwide over the past several years [16] as a means of sequestering carbon from the atmosphere to save the climate and enhance soil fertility. It involves planting fast growing tree and various other crops on hundreds of millions of hectares of 'spare land' mostly in developing countries, to be harvested and turned into charcoal in a process that could produce crude oil and gases as low-grade fuels. There are many excellent arguments against this initiative [17], but the most decisive is that it will certainly further accelerate deforestation and destruction of other natural ecosystems (identified as 'spare land'). In the process, it could precipitate an oxygen crisis from which we would never recover [18] (Beware the Biochar Initiative, SiS 44).

References

1. Valentino FL, Leuenberger M, Uglietti C and Staburm P. Measurements and trend analysis of O_2, CO_2 and $D^{13}C$ of CO_2 from high altitude research station Junfgraujoch, Switzerlnd – a comparison with the observations from the remote site Puy de Dôme, France. Science of the Total Environment 2008, 203-10.

2. Sirignano C, Neubert REM, Jeijer HAJ and Rödenbeck C. Atmospheric oxygen and carbon dioxide observations from two European coastal stations 2000-2005: continental influence trend changes and APO climatology. Atmos Chem Phy Discuss 2008, 8, 20113-54.

3. Tohjima Y, Muai H, Machida T, Nojiri Y. Gas-chromatographic measurements of the atmospheric oxygen/nitrogen ratio at haterumna island and Cape Ochi-ishi, Japan. *Geophys Res Lett* 2003, 30, 1653, doi:10.1029/2003FLO17282

4. Joos F. Trends in Marine Dissolved Oxygen: Implications for Ocean Circulation Changes and the Carbon Budget. *EOS* 2003, 84, 197-204.

5. Stramma L, Johnson GC, Sprintal J and Mohrholz V. Expanding oxygen-minimum zones in the tropical oceans. *Science* 2008, 320, 655-8.

6. Ho MW. Living with oxygen. Science in Society 43 (in press).

7. Oxygen deficiency hazards (ODH) Manual 5064, Fermilab, Revised 05/2009, http://www-esh.fnal.gov/FESHM/5000/5064.pdf

8. Ho MW. Global warming & then the big freeze. Science in Society 20, 28-29, 2003.

9. 50th anniversary of the global carbon dioxide record symposium and celebration, Kona, Hawaii, 28-30 November 2007, http://www.esrl.noaa.gov/gmd/co2conference/background.html

10. Manning AC, Keelilng RF, Paplawsky WJ, Katz LE, McEvoy EM and Atwood CG. Atmospheric oxygen in the 1990s from a global flask sampling network: trends and variability pertaining to the carbon cycle. Draft 29

January 2003, http://bluemoon.ucsd.edu/publications/mip/manning.pdf

11. Battle M, Fletcher SM, Bender ML, Keeling RF, et al. Atmospheric potential oxygen: new observations and their implications for some atmospheric and oceanic models. *Global Biogeochemical Cycles* 2006, GB1010.

12. Randerson J T, Masiello C A, Still C J, Rahn T, Poorter H and Field C B. Is carbon within the global terrestrial biosphere becoming more oxidized? Implications for trends in atmospheric O_2, *Glob Change Biol* 2006. 12, 260–71.

13. Ciais P, Manning A C, Reichstein M, Zaehle S, and Bopp L. Nitrification amplifies the decreasing trends of atmospheric oxygen and implies a larger land carbon uptake, Global Biogeochem Cy 2007, 21, GB2030, doi:10.1029/2006GB002799, 2007.

14. Rain Forest is losing ground faster in Amazon, photos show", Tony Smith, The New York Times, 27 June 2003, http://www.mongabay.com/external/record_amazon_deforestation_2002.htm#1

15. "Environment: Biofuels boom spurring deforestation", Stephen Leahy, IPS, 21 May 2007, http://ipsnews.net/news.asp?idnews=37035

16. IBI Programs and Projects, International Biochar Initiative, accessed 3 August 2009, http://www.biochar-international.org/

17. Ernsting A and Rughani D. Climate geo-engineering with 'carbon negative' bioenergy, climate saviour or climate endgame? Biofuelwatch, November 2008, http://www.biofuelwatch.org.uk/docs/cnbe/cnbe.html

18. Ho MW. Beware the Biochar Initiative. Science in Society 44 (to appear).

SOURCE: – (http://www.i-sis.org.uk/O2DroppingFasterThanCO2Rising.php?comment=1)

RELATED:

According to the data Keeling has meticulously collected since 1989 the world is running out of breathable air—and the rate that its losing oxygen is now on the verge of accelerating

Scientists have painted a scenario that could account for mass extinctions from terrestrial oxygen depletion which would certainly lay the foundation for a rapid acceleration of oxygen depletion and the resulting mass death to follow—mass death on a planetary scale.(http://survivalacres.com/blog/oxygen-levels-are-dropping/)

CHAPTER 55

THE PRE-FLOOD ATMOSPHERE

PRE-FLOOD- 50% More Oxygen In Our Atmosphere In Pre-Flood Times

THERE IS EVIDENCE that the atmosphere enveloping the early earth was very different than it is today. At one time the entire earth enjoyed a warm tropical environment and there was enhanced oxygen in the atmosphere. Organisms grew larger and lived longer as a result.

Many creationists have attributed this to a water vapor canopy that was created by God on the second day, the "waters above the firmament" (Genesis 1:7). This theory holds that a "vast blanket of invisible water vapor, translucent to the light of the stars but productive of a marvellous greenhouse effect which maintained mild temperatures from pole to pole, thus preventing air-mass circulation and the resultant rainfall (Genesis 2:5). It would certainly have had the further effect of efficiently filtering harmful radiation from space, markedly reducing the rate of somatic mutations in living cells, and, as a consequence, drastically decreasing the rate of aging and death." (Morris, Henry, *Scientific Creationism,* 1984, p. 211.) Citing evidence of denser atmosphere in the past, Morris postulated that this vapor layer could have dramatically increased the atmospheric pressure on the surface of the early earth, again contributing to a healthier environment (like a natural hyperbaric chamber). Later the canopy would have collapsed in the form of rain (the "windows of heaven" in Genesis 7:11), contributing to the Flood water, and resulting in the dramatic drop-off in longevity after the deluge.

Genesis 9 tells how Noah planted a vineyard after the flood and became drunk from the fruit of it. This is an aberration in the life of this godly man. Some have suggested that Noah did not know his grape juice would ferment so quickly or so extensively in the post-flood atmosphere. Or perhaps the reduced atmospheric pressure made it harder for him to "hold his drink." While this is only speculation, the removal of the vapor canopy could help explain this curious situation.

Some creationists emphasize other factors that may have caused the worldwide temperate conditions that existed before the Flood. They stress the evidence of far greater concentrations of carbon dioxide levels in the past and point out that the earth's magnetic field was far stronger than today. This could have acted as the shield for cosmic radiation and produced the healthier environment. (Humphreys, Russel D., *Starlight and Time,* 1995,

p. 63.) John Baumgardner of Los Alamos has suggested that the atmosphere surrounding the original earth was far thicker than it is today and that the exploding of the fountains of the great deep during the initial stages of the Genesis Flood stripped some of this atmosphere away. Certain Bible scholars cite the language of the Psalm 148:4 as evidence against a vapor canopy. If the canopy had collapsed during the flood, they reason, why does the Psalmist still reference the waters above the firmament? But this poetic allusion could hark back to the original creation, or it could make reference to waters God expanded out into deep space as part of creation, or it could refer to some of the original water vapor (left over from the canopy) still in the outer reaches of our atmosphere.

It is interesting that scientists who would not subscribe to the water vapor canopy theory described above, have published articles that lend credence to portions of that theory. "Using evidence collected in South America and New Zealand, an international team of researchers has determined that climate changes – both warming and cooling patterns – during the late Pleistocene occurred rapidly and were global in scale. As giant iceberg armadas flooded the North Atlantic, alpine glaciers were simultaneously advancing across the Chilean Andes and Southern Alps of New Zealand. Thomas Lowell, associate professor of geology at the University of Cincinnati, and his colleagues published their findings in the September 15, 1995, issues of *Science*. ...So, what did cause the climate changes? Lowell admits that he and his colleagues have no quick and easy answers. Possibly water vapours played a role. 'A lot of water vapor in the atmosphere leads to a warmer climate,' he states. 'If there's less vapor, temperatures become colder. Amounts of water vapor can change quickly, and the geological record indicates that climate changes could be very fast.'" (Anonymous, "Were Climate Changes Global During Ice Ages," *Geotimes*, vol. 41, 1996, p.7, as cited in Morris, 1997, p. 305.) Additionally, some scientists have been quite surprised to find water vapor in the freezing atmospheres of Jupiter, Uranus, Neptune and Saturn. (*Dayton Daily News*, April 8, 1998, p. 12A)

The water vapor canopy hypothesis would neatly explain yet another observed anomaly...too much water in Earth's upper atmosphere. NASA satellites have confirmed far more hydroxyl in the hydrosphere than current models predict. The parent molecule of hydroxyl (OH) is water (H2O). Because ultraviolet radiation from the sun breaks down water in Earth's upper atmosphere into hydroxyl and hydrogen, a large amount of water must have previously existed. Some have proposed a constant influx of mini comets as a source for the mysterious water, but that theory has been strongly criticized as unworkable. (Matthews, Robert, *New Scientist*, July 1997, pp. 26-27.)

Another interesting feature of the early earth atmosphere was enhanced oxygen. The analysis of microscopic air bubbles trapped in fossilized tree resin gave Robert Berner of Yale and Gary Landis of the U.S. Geological Survey a glimpse into the ancient past. "The researchers clamped the amber into a vacuum chamber of a quadrupole mass spectrometer, a device that identifies the chemical composition of a substance. As the machine slowly crushed the sample, the microscopic bubbles were released, exhaling up to 100 billion molecules. These breaths disclosed some surprising evidence: the ancient air contained 50 percent more oxygen than the air today." Landis believes that the reduction in oxygen could have led to the dinosaur's demise. (*Discover*, February 1988, p. 12.)

Other studies of air bubbles in amber have found increased pressure as well as greater oxygen levels. "One implication is that the atmospheric pressure of the Earth would have been much greater during the Cretaceous era, when the bubbles formed in the resin. A dense atmosphere could also explain how the ungainly pterosaur, with its stubby body and wingspan of up to 11 meters, could have stayed airborne, he said. The spread of angiosperms, flowering plants, during the Cretaceous era could have caused the high oxygen levels reported by Berner and Landis, scientists said last week." (Anderson, Ian, "Dinosaurs Breathed Air Rich in Oxygen," *New Scientist*, vol. 116, 1987, p. 25.) A Yale study published in the March 3, 2000; issue of *Science* independently confirmed the high levels of oxygen present in the earth's distant past. Some have even suggested that without such an atmosphere the relatively small lung capacity in certain dinosaurs could not have supplied their massive tissue with the needed oxygen.

In October 2006 *Science Daily* publicized a study led by Arizona State University staff entitled "Giant Insects Might Reign If Only There Was More Oxygen In The Air." The article claims, "The delicate lady bug in your garden could be frighteningly large if only there was a greater concentration of oxygen in the air, a new study concludes. The study adds support to the theory that some insects were much larger during the late Palaeozoic period because they had a much richer oxygen supply, said the study's lead author Alexander Kaiser. The Palaeozoic period...was a time of huge and abundant plant life and rather large insects — dragonflies had two-and-a-half-foot wing spans, for example. The air's oxygen content was 35% during this period, compared to the 21% we breathe now, Kaiser said." This research concurs with the biblical model of the early earth. In 2010 researchers at Arizona State University presented the results of experiments raising insects in various levels of atmospheric oxygen. Ten out of twelve varieties of insects studied decreased in size with lower oxygen. Some, like dragonflies, grew faster and became bigger in an enriched oxygen atmosphere (*Science Daily*, October 30, 2010.).

Some object strongly to using the scriptures to gain scientific insight into the natural world. While the Bible is not a science text, there are several clear lines of evidence that the Bible is God's Word. If God's word is truly inspired, it speaks accurately to all areas of knowledge: historical, political/economic, sociological, and scientific.

Source: – (http://www.genesispark.com/exhibits/early-earth/atmosphere/)

I will be adding a lot of material to this shortly, after my wife has finished her hyperbaric oxygen treatment at the MS centre.

Here is the website for MS oxygen treatment in the UK. It is a very interesting website and well worth visiting.

(https://www.hyperbaricoxygentherapy.org.uk/find-chamber)

Steve:-I intend in to investigate more, but I suspect that even the Oxygen content in our atmosphere, used to be a lot higher, and thus I think that in the past we would have had less problems with certain modern medical conditions such as skin afflictions, asthma and host of modern sicknesses and ailments.

I have been reading the amazing book called "Oxygen & The Brain" By Dr. Philip B James whilst going to the MS Oxygen Treatment Centre,

One MS patient stated: "I personally believe that the real root cause of MS is sugar!"

Here is a definition by a doctor who is an expert on cancer: "If I was to define cancer it would be 'when the oxygen absorbing ability of a cell is removed, and replaced with sugar, which has fermented'- "that is cancer!" We all know that cancer feeds on sugar!

Getting rid of the sugar, and the resultant acidosis, which causes cancer, and alkalizing the body through eating 70% organic fruit & vegetables, can stabilize and even eventually totally get rid of cancer, as happened to our 24-year-old daughter last year (2015) who was diagnosed as having aggressive breast cancer.

She got totally healed by prayer & juicing.

(Recommended A bestselling book: Juicing, Fasting, & Detoxing For Life, by Cherie Calbom, MS)

The following is a very interesting dissertation about **sugar** from: -

Food or Poison?

"Doctors have come to the conclusion that too much sweet in the diet is the most common cause of illness amongst Europeans. Now when they talk about sweets they're not talking about natural sweets like figs, raisins, honey, blackstrap molasses and raw sugar. They're talking about refined sugar sweets, desserts, candies, soft drinks and so on.

They claim that most of the diseases Europeans have can be traced to sugar as the main culprit and fat as the next. Now I think that's what the Bible means where it says, "lest your hearts be overcharged with surfeiting". (Luke 21:34.) They have traced a lot of heart failure and heart trouble straight back to too much fat and too much sugar.

Most diabetics, for example, suffer heart trouble. So, in this note I said, 'This Obsession For Sugar I Believe Is An Absolute Demonic Perversion!'

I think it is just as diabolical and demon inspired as a craving for liquor or drugs or gambling or what have you! I believe it! It›s an obsession with some people, it is something that they haven›t got the will power to withstand if it›s within reach.

Most Americans have grown up with that perverted sweet tooth, so in order to stop the habit, just like me, you just have to keep it out of reach. If you don't have it in the house, I won't eat it. I don't go to the store and buy myself some sugar.

It's just like a drunk or an alcoholic or a drug addict, you've got to keep it out of reach if he hasn't got the will power to resist it. If it's where he can get at it then you'll have to take it away from him."

CHAPTER 56

A HEAVENLY GIFT

A HEAVENLY GIFT

GOD'S SPIRIT IS THE 'SPIRIT OF LOVE' FIRST AND FOREMOST

'**GAL.5:22** But the fruit of the Spirit is love, joy, peace, longsuffering, gentleness, goodness, faith,

GAL.5:23 Meekness, temperance: against such there is no law'.

THE GIFT OF TONGUES:

God's Love is what is the most important in our lives in one form or the other. giving love and receiving love. god has given us, his saved children, many gifts, not least of which is the gift of tongues. The gift of tongues is an intimate gift given by God himself to help us be intimately much closer to him even as the bride with her husband Jesus. How to get the gift of tongues?

You just have to ask for it – once you are saved and – have received god's holy spirit through prayer. (See prayer:

SALVATION: http://www.outofthebottomlesspit.co.uk/418605189

2CO.11:2 For I am jealous over you with godly jealousy: for I have espoused you to one husband, that I may present you as a chaste virgin to Christ.

Jesus wants His Bride to be very happy – and has given her the beautiful 'GIFT of TONGUES' to communicate directly with HIM in 'total freedom of Spirit' and total abandonment.

There should be a lot of passion between a husband and wife who truly love each other.

The gift of tongues is indeed one of the intimate gifts. There are others also.

This gift by-passes the human carnal mind and is in fact the Spirit of Love Herself speaking through us in a sort of 'baby language'.

Well, that's what it sounds like to others. We actually are able to more fully 'express ourselves' to God in this way in a much quicker time.

As one who has practiced this gift upon many occasions – what the scriptures below say are true. Speaking in tongues mostly edifies the person who is speaking in tongues, but that it can also be a witness to others of the spiritual side of our natural. One where God and His Spirit have full control and not us.

It is very beautiful and liberating to be set-free in spirit by speaking in tongues even if to us it all sounds like mere gibberish. God understands it, even if we don't have a clue what we are saying. It matters not. The whole purpose for tongues is to edify our spirits before God and to sort of refresh us in spirit, mind and body so to speak.

The following Bible verses apply to the wonderful gift of speaking in tongues. The gift of tongues is very useful to use when you want to praise the Lord, but don't know what to say. It is also useful to use when you feel confused and need an immediate pick-up from heaven. It works every time to lift your spirit. Speaking in tongues quickly makes you totally positive in your outlook.

'When the day of Pentecost came, they were all together in one place. Suddenly a sound like the blowing of a violent wind came from heaven and filled the whole house where they were sitting. They saw what seemed to be tongues of fire that separated and came to rest on each of them. All of them were filled with the Holy Spirit and began to speak in other tongues as the Spirit enabled them.'

- Acts 2:1-4

'And when Paul had laid his hands on them, the Holy Spirit came on them, and they began speaking in tongues and prophesying.'

- Acts 19:6

'So, my brothers, earnestly desire to prophesy, and do not forbid speaking in tongues'.

- 1Cor 14:39

'Pursue love, and earnestly desire the spiritual gifts, especially that you may prophesy. For one who speaks in a tongue speaks not to men but to God; for no one understands him, but he utters mysteries in the Spirit. On the other hand, the one who prophesies speaks to people for their upbuilding and encouragement and consolation. The one who speaks in a tongue builds up himself, but the one who prophesies builds up the church. Now I want you all to speak in tongues, but even more to prophesy. The one who prophesies is greater than the one who speaks in tongues, unless someone interprets, so that the church may be built up'.

- 1Cor 14:1-5

'Therefore, my brothers and sisters, be eager to prophesy, and do not forbid speaking in tongues. But everything should be done in a fitting and orderly way'.

- 1Cor 14:39-40

'When the Spirit of truth comes, he will guide you into all the truth, for he will not speak on his own authority, but whatever he hears he will speak, and he will declare to you the things that are to come. He will glorify me, for he will take what is mine and declare it to you. All that the Father has is mine; therefore, I said that he will take what is mine and declare it to you'.

- John 16:13-15

CHRISMANEWS 18/07/19

Medical Study Proves Validity of Speaking in Tongues

In 2008, the University of Pennsylvania released findings from a medical study proving that the practice of speaking in tongues is sourced by the Holy Spirit. In the study, participants› brain activity was monitored while they spoke in tongues, giving the medical researchers scientific insight into the parts of the brain active while speaking in these «heavenly tongues»—and the results were astounding.

Much of the study is outlined in the below piece by ABC News, findings that are well worth the watch.

Speaking in tongues, as ABC News accurately states, "is an ancient practice mentioned in the Bible. [Apostle] Paul called it 'speaking in the tongues of angels.' Jesus' apostles were first said to do it at Pentecost."

It is this spiritual phenomenon that Dr. Andrew Newberg, while at the University of Pennsylvania, set out to find an explanation "for what most regard as unexplainable." While trying to discover the relationship between faith and science, his study quickly ascertained that speaking in tongues is absolutely not regular language. Newberg states to ABC News: "It's not language—it's not regular language at least that would normally activate the frontal lobe [of the brain]."

So, what did Newberg's medical study show happens to the brain during one's deepest moments of faith then?

Newberg shares the heart of his study: "If we're really going to look at this very, very powerful force in human history of religion and spirituality, I think we really have to take a look at how that affects our brain, what's changing or turning on or turning off in our brain" during those extremely deep and powerful moments of faith.

And "remarkably he discovered that what's happening to [the test subjects when they pray in tongues] neurologically looks a lot like what they say is happening to them spiritually."

When test subjects prayed in their native language, their brain activity indicated normal behaviour for speech in the frontal lobe. However, when the same test subjects prayed in tongues, their brain activity showed something extremely different. "[The test subject's] scan showed that the frontal lobe, the part of the brain that controls language, was active when he prayed in English. But for the most part, it fell quiet when he prayed in tongues."

Dr. Newberg confirmed this finding saying, "When they are actually engaged in this whole very intense spiritual practice for them, their frontal lobes tend to go down in activity, but I think it's very consistent with the kind of experience that they have because they say that they are not in charge—it's the voice of God, the Spirit of God that's moving through them."

The study found many other fascinating findings that affirm that speaking in tongues is truly a spiritual gift and not a mental practice. We encourage you to watch the full ABC News piece to learn more.

THE LOVE CHAPTER: 1 CORINTHIANS CHAPTER 13:

1CO.13:1 Though I speak with the **tongues of men** and **of angels**, and have not **LOVE**, I am become as sounding brass, or a tinkling cymbal.

1CO.13:2 And though I have the gift of prophecy, and understand all mysteries, and all knowledge; and though I have all faith, so that I could remove mountains, and have not **LOVE**, I am nothing.

1CO.13:3 And though I bestow all my goods to feed the poor, and though I give my body to be burned, and have not **LOVE**, it profits me nothing.

1CO.13:4 LOVE suffers long, and is kind; **LOVE** envies not; **LOVE** vaunts not itself, is not puffed up,

1CO.13:5 Doth not behave itself unseemly, seeketh not her own, is not easily provoked, thinketh no evil;

1CO.13:6 Rejoices not in iniquity, but rejoices in the **truth;**

1CO.13:7 Bears all things, believeth all things, hopes all things, endures all things.

1CO.13:8 LOVE never fails but whether there be prophecies, they shall fail; whether there be tongues, they shall cease; whether there be knowledge, it shall vanish away.

1CO.13:9 For we know in part, and we prophesy in part.

1CO.13:10 But when that which is perfect is come, then that which is in part shall be done away.

1CO.13:11 When I was a child, I spake as a child, I understood as a child, I thought as a child: but when I became a man, I put away childish things.

1CO.13:12 For now we see through a glass, darkly; but then face to face: now I know in part; but then shall I know even as also I am known.

1CO.13:13 And now abides faith, hope, **LOVE**, these three; but the greatest of these is **LOVE.**

SPIRITUAL GIFTS

1CO.12:1 Now concerning **spiritual gifts**, brethren, I would not have you ignorant.

1CO.12:4 Now there are **diversities of gifts**, but the same Spirit.

1CO.12:10 To another the working of miracles; to another prophecy; to another discerning of spirits; to another diverse kinds of **tongues**; to another the **interpretation of tongues**:

1CO.12:11 But all these worketh that one and the self-same Spirit, dividing to every man severally as he will.

1CO.12:12 For as the body is one, and hath many members, and all the members of that one body, being many, are one body: so also is Christ.

You can contact me at: Steve: strangetruths@outofthebottomlesspit. co.uk

BRAIN DECAY

Scientists Have Found That Our Bodies And Our Minds Have Both Deteriorated Significantly Compared To Our Ancestors.

In fact, just this week a very prominent professor at Cambridge University said that "our most highly trained athletes pale in comparison to these ancestors of ours".

The biggest reason for this, of course, is the degradation of the human genome. Ground-breaking research by Dr. John Sanford of Cornell University and others has shown that our genes contain tens of thousands of mistakes (mutations), and with each passing generation even more errors are added and passed on. So, it should be no surprise that our ancestors were bigger, stronger, faster and smarter. The truth is that they had better genes.

This kind of information comes as a shock to many people. It is widely assumed by the general public that humanity is "progressing" and that we are better both physically and mentally than our predecessors were. But that is not the case at all. In fact, research conducted at Cambridge University shows that we are "weaker than we used to be" and that the most highly trained athletes of today "pale in comparison" to those that lived thousands of years ago.

'Even our most highly trained athletes pale in comparison to these ancestors of ours,' Dr Colin Shaw told Outside Magazine. 'We're certainly weaker than we used to be. The study looked at skeletons dating back to around 5,300 BC with the most recent to 850 AD – a time span of 6,150 years. It then compared the bones to that of Cambridge University students and found the leg bones of male farmers 5,300 BC were just as good as those of highly trained cross-country runners. In addition, earlier research at Cambridge University showed that our bodies are "significantly smaller" than they were thousands of years ago and that our brains are also smaller...Wow. Most movies and television shows portray our ancestors as short, stupid, hunched-over people that could barely survive in a cold, cruel world. But the hard science is revealing a very different picture to us. As I mentioned above, the primary reason for our decline as a species is the systematic deterioration of our genes. According to Dr. John Sanford of Cornell University, the author of Genetic Entropy & The Mystery of the Genome, each one of us already carries tens of thousands of harmful mutations, and each one of us will pass on at least 100 new mutations to future generations. Many scientists believe that this will ultimately lead to something called "mutational meltdown". The following is an excerpt from a paper This is incredible stuff with absolutely staggering implications. For much more on all of this, check out the video interview with Dr. Sanford that I have posted below.

Not only are our brains getting smaller, but humanity is also getting dumber.

This sounds strange to many people, especially considering the technological boom that we have seen in modern times, but it is actually true. In fact, a Stanford University biology professor recently published two papers in which he expressed his conclusion that humans have been getting dumber for thousands of years.

Professor Crabtree, like Dr. Sanford, is convinced that this loss of mental capacity is due to the accumulation of errors in our genes.

And to be honest, we can see the loss of mental capacity all around us.

Just check out the following video in which average Americans are asked really basic questions that appear on the U.S. citizenship test.

Source:- **(http://www.infowars.com/scientists-discover-proof-that-humanity-is-getting-dumber-smaller-and-weaker/)**

http://endtimeinfo.com/2014/08/ archoninvasion-the-return-of-the-nephilim/)

141 Gene Disintegration: http://endtimeinfo.com/2014/05/scientists-discover proof-that-humanity-is-getting-dumber-smaller-and-weaker

CHAPTER 58

'MESSIAH' – AS PREDICTED BY THE PROPHETS OF THE OLD TESTAMENT.

Introduction: Christ and Christmas:

It is stunning to see the prophets of God writing about the Messiah hundreds and even thousands of years before Jesus the Christ and Saviour was even born.

At Christmas we are all familiar with Bible verses such as:

ISAIAH 9.6

⁶ For unto us a Child is born, unto us a Son is given; and the government shall be upon His shoulder. And His name shall be called Wonderful, Counsellor, The Mighty God, The Everlasting Father, The Prince of Peace

MICAH 5.2

² "But thou, Bethlehem Ephrathah, though thou be little among the thousands of Judah, yet out of thee shall come forth unto Me He that is to be ruler in Israel, whose goings forth have been from of old, from everlasting.".

These are indeed very beautiful verses about the birth of Christ Jesus.

There are at least **300 Bible verses** in **the Old Testament** that prophesied about **Jesus as the Messiah** and **Saviour.**

I thought it might be a good idea to delve into two of my 'INSIGHTS' books which are based on 1) The Book of Enoch and 2) The Book of 2ⁿᵈ Ezdras, both of which have been part of the canon of scripture.

Out of my '7' INSIGHTS books – these two have something very special in common, in that they directly talked about the coming Messiah on different occasions throughout the books.

With my 'INSIGHTS' books, I am trying to get people to give more attention to the less known Apocryphal, books which have been part of the official canon until just over a century ago.

Let's now examine the following excerpts from two of my 5 'INSIGHTS' books to see if they are an enlightenment to you about scriptures that used to be in the KJV of the Bible until 1885.

Why were the scriptures removed from the Protestant Bibles and not the Catholic Bible? The argument that it was because the apocryphal books such as 2ⁿᵈ Ezdras had not been written in Hebrew back in 1885 was proven with the discovery of the Dead Sea Scrolls in 1947 to be incorrect – as both the Book of Enoch and 2ⁿᵈ Ezdras were found in the Hebrew text as well as many of the other 14 Apocryphal books that had been removed from the Protestant

Bible without a justifiable reason.

Why would beautiful books that prophesied about Jesus be removed from the Bible back in 1885? That is a very good question, which I have tried to answer in my 'INSIGHTS' books – both 'Enoch Insights' and 'Ezdras Insights' in particular.

SUMMARY

The Messiah is mentioned in the Book of Enoch in chapters 46, 55 & also chapter 70 and is referred to as the Son of Man walking together with the Head of Days. He is also mentioned as God's Son who will rule over all nations and throw out the kings of the earth and the demon princes that rule from 'behind the scenes'.

He is mentioned as the King of Kings in chapter 84, just as in the Book of Revelations 19. We see God the Father and God the Son in chapter 105 walking together in the book of Enoch similar to in the Book of Daniel chapter 7.

Jesus is also called the Elect One in the Book of Enoch in chapters 49 and 55.

Similarly, in the Apocryphal Book of 2nd Ezdras originally written 400-500 BCE we see direct references to the Messiah as the 'Son of God.'

2nd Ezdras Chapters 7 and 13 describe **Jesus** very well indeed as well as His awesome power.

The Actual Text From My Books 'Enoch Insights' And 'Ezdras Insights' – with both biblical cross-references and my commentaries.

EZDRAS INSIGHTS 7.13 'For my son, the Messiah, shall be revealed with those who are with him, and those who remain shall rejoice (in) four hundred years: and after these years my son the Messiah shall die, (for) all who draw human breath'.

This Chapter 7. Verse 13 – is probably the most important verse in the entire Book of II Ezdras. Why? Because God is directly telling Ezra, who lived around 400+ years before Christ, that *God was sending His only son the Messiah to the earth in 400 years, from Ezra's time*. God also predicted that His Son, the Messiah, would die (for) all humanity. Somehow the expression "rejoice (in) four hundred years" has been altered to omit the (in), which could change the whole meaning. However, whoever tried to obfuscate the truth of this verse, made a big mistake, because God Himself goes on to state in this same verse, that the Messiah, God's Son shall die, so obviously looking at history we find that Jesus Christ fulfilled this exact prophecy given to Ezra, and that he did die some 400 years after the time of Ezra! What an amazing prophecy about Jesus! '*after these years my Son the Messiah shall die, (and) all who draw human breath*'.

Why does it say here that '*all who draw human breath shall die*', which seems totally out of context? In the original text it probably didn't. The text would appear to have been deliberately altered, in order to change the meaning.

In verse 13, where I put a bracket around the word (for), the modern text gives the word (and). Well, it is true that all of us humans will die sooner or later, but I think that the real meaning here was that God's only Begotten Son, the Messiah would die (for) all humanity, otherwise we would all be destined to spiritual, as well as physical death.

'EZDRAS INSIGHTS'- Chapter 13

2ND EZDRAS CHAPTER 13 verse 1 'After seven days, I dreamed a dream in the night: and behold, a wind arose from the sea and stirred up all its waves. And I looked, and behold, this wind made something like the figure of a man come up out of the heart of the sea. And I looked, and behold, that man flew with the 'clouds of heaven'; and wherever he turned his face to look, everything under his gaze trembled. And whenever his voice issued from his mouth, all who heard his voice melted as wax melts when it feels the fire'.

This is clearly talking about Jesus coming with the 'clouds of heaven.'

DAN.7:13 "I was watching in the night visions, and behold, one like the Son of Man, 'Coming with the clouds of heaven'! He came to the Ancient of Days, and they brought Him near before Him.

DAN.7:2 Daniel spoke, saying, "I saw in my vision by night, and behold, the four winds of heaven were stirring up the Great Sea.

REV.19:15 And 'Out of His mouth' goes a sharp sword, that with it He should strike the nations. And He Himself will rule them with a rod of iron. He Himself treads the winepress of the fierceness and wrath of Almighty God.

2nd EZDRAS 13.2 And after this I looked, and behold, and 'innumerable multitude of men were gathered together' from the four winds of the heaven to make war against the man who came up out of the sea.

And I looked, and behold, and he carved out for himself a great mountain and flew upon it, and I tried to see the region or place from which the mountain was carved, but I could not.

At the end of this world all the armies of the world shall gather together in Israel at Armageddon, to fight against Jesus who returns with the clouds of heaven on a powerful white horse together with the armies of heaven.

The Anti-Christ ruler of the earth of the near future, will probably have persuaded the world that Jesus and his armies are invaders from another galaxy, and that he is the enemy.

Well, this time Satan is going to lose big time. All Satan's lies and deceptions, through his stooge, the Anti-Christ, will soon be coming to an abrupt end, at the battle of Armageddon!

REV.16:16 And they gathered them together to the place called in Hebrew, Armageddon.

REV.19:19 And I saw the beast, the kings of the earth, and their armies, gathered together to make war against Him who sat on the horse and against His army.

The Beast is The Anti-Christ.

Daniel 2 is a very important Bible prophecy chapter which describes a giant Image, which King Nebuchadnezzar of Babylon saw in a dream. I won't go into all the details right now, except to state that the Image had a head of Gold, arms and chest of Silver, belly of Bronze, legs of Iron and feet and toes part of Iron and part of clay.

Daniel, God's prophet, interpreted the Kings dream, without even knowing the dream, and explained how that Babylon was the Head of Gold, the next empire of Silver would be Medio-Persia, followed by the Greek empire of Bronze, and the legs of Iron was Rome, and the feet and toes partly of Iron and Clay was the type of governments that are around in the world today.

Iron governments being strong dictatorships. Clay being weak Democracies. In the Vision of the Image, a rock came from the heavens and smashed the entire image to pieces and then became a mountain which filled the whole world. That mountain is the Kingdom of God.

DAN.2:34 "You watched while a stone was cut out without hands, which struck the image on its feet of iron and clay and broke them in pieces.

DAN.2:35 "Then the iron, the clay, the bronze, the silver, and the gold were crushed together, and became like chaff from the summer threshing floors; the wind carried them away so that no trace of them was found. And the stone that struck the image and became a great mountain that filled the whole earth.

DAN.2:44 "And in the days of these kings the God of heaven will set up a kingdom which shall never be destroyed; and the kingdom shall not be left to other people; it shall break in pieces and consume all these kingdoms, and it shall stand forever.

2ND EZDRAS 13.3 'After this I looked, and behold, all who had gathered together against him, to wage war with him were much afraid, yet dared to fight. And behold, when he saw the onrush of the approaching multitude, he neither lifted his hand nor held a spear or any weapon of war; but I only saw how he sent forth 'from his lips a flaming breath as it were a stream of fire', and from his lips a flaming breath, and from his tongue he shot forth a storm of sparks'.

ENOCH INSIGHTS

Book of Enoch 46.1 'And there I saw One who had a head of days, and his head was white like wool. With Him was another being whose countenance had the appearance of a man, His face was full of graciousness, like one of the holy angels'.

DAN.7:9 I beheld till the thrones were cast down, and the Ancient of days did sit, whose garment was white as snow, and the *hair of his head like the pure wool*: his throne was like the fiery flame, and his wheels as burning fire.

DAN.7:13 I saw in the night visions, and, behold, one like the *Son of man* came with the *clouds of heaven*, and came to the *Ancient of days*, and they brought him near before him.

2 CO.8:9 For ye know the *grace of our Lord Jesus Christ*, that, though he was rich, yet for your sakes he became poor, that ye through his poverty might be rich.

Enoch 46.2 'And I asked the angel who went with me and showed me all the hidden things, concerning that Son of Man, who he was, and whence he was, and why he went with the Head of Days? He answered me and said unto me:

Enoch 46.3 This is the Son of Man, who hath righteousness, with whom dwelleth righteousness, and who reveals all the treasures of that which is hidden, because the Lord of Spirits hath chosen him, and whose lot hath the pre-eminence before the Lord of spirits in uprightness for ever.

PRO.2:4 If thou seek her (Wisdom) as silver, and search for her as for *hidden treasures*.

PRO.2:5 Then shalt thou understand the fear of the LORD and find the knowledge of God.

Enoch 46.4 And this Son of Man whom thou hast seen shall raise up the kings and the mighty from their seats, and the strong from their throne. He shall loosen the reins of the strong and break the teeth of the sinners.

PSA.3:7 Arise, O LORD; save me, O my God: for thou hast smitten all mine enemies upon the cheek bone; thou hast *broken the teeth* of the ungodly.

Enoch 46.5 He shall put down the kings from their thrones and kingdoms, because they do not extol and praise Him, nor humbly acknowledge whence the kingdom was bestowed upon them.

REV.6:15 And *the kings* of the earth, and the *great men*, and the *rich men*, and the chief captains, and the mighty men, and every bondman, and every free man, hid themselves in the dens and in the rocks of the mountains.

REV.6:16 And said to the mountains and rocks, 'Fall on us, and hide us from the face of him that sits on the throne, and from the *wrath of the Lamb*':

REV.6:17 For *the great day of his wrath is come; and who shall be able to stand?*

Enoch 46.6 'He shall put down the countenance of the strong and shall fill them with shame. Darkness shall be their dwelling, and worms shall be their bed, and they shall have no hope of rising from their beds, because they do not extol the name of the Lord of Spirits'.

ISA.65:13 Therefore thus says the Lord GOD, Behold, my servants shall eat, but ye shall be hungry: behold, my servants shall drink, but ye shall be thirsty: behold, my servants shall rejoice, but ye shall be *ashamed:*

MAR.9:44 Where their *worm dies not*, and the fire is not quenched.

PSA.107:10 Such as sit in *darkness* and in the *shadow of death*, being bound in affliction and iron;

PSA.107:11 Because they *rebelled against the words of God*, and contemned the counsel of the most High:

Enoch 46.7 'And these are they who judge the stars of heaven, and raise their hands against the Most High, and tread upon the earth and dwell upon it. All their deeds shall manifest unrighteousness, and their power rests upon their riches, and their faith is in the gods which they have made with their hands, and they deny the name of the Lord of Spirits'.

The above verse 7 is describing the coming Anti-Christ and his empire or the 7th and last World Empire of Mankind. The coming one world government will have 10 leaders who 'have horns' or are demon possessed and shall rule the earth together with Satan through the Anti-Christ.

REV.17:12 And the ten horns which you saw are ten kings, which have received no kingdom as yet; but receive power as kings one hour with the beast.

REV.17:13 These have one mind and shall give their power and strength unto the beast.

REV.17:14 These shall make war with the Lamb, and the Lamb shall overcome them: for he is Lord of lords, and King of kings: and they that are with him are called, and chosen, and faithful.

DAN.7:25 And he shall *speak great words* against the Most High and shall wear out the saints of the most High, and think to change times and laws:

and they shall be given into his hand until a time and times and the dividing of time.

REV.13:6 And he opened his mouth in blasphemy against God, to *blaspheme his name*, and his tabernacle, and *them that dwell in heaven*.

Enoch 46.8 'They persecute the houses of His congregations, and the faithful who hang upon the name of the Lord of Spirits'.

REV.12:17 And the dragon was wroth with the woman and went to make war with the remnant of her seed, which keep the commandments of God, and have the testimony of Jesus Christ.

MAT.5:10 Blessed are they which are *persecuted* for righteousness> sake: for theirs is the kingdom of heaven.

MAT.5:11 Blessed are ye, when men shall revile you, and *persecute you*, and shall say all manner of evil against you falsely, for my sake.

MAT.5:12 Rejoice, and be exceeding glad: for great is your reward in heaven: for so *persecuted* they the *prophets* which were before you.

You can find the rest of the verses mentioned above in my books 'EZDRAS INSIGHTS' and 'ENOCH INSIGHTS'

More Biblical Prophecies About Christ

Son Of Man: Son of God: The Messiah: The Saviour

Why Does Jesus Frequently Refer to Himself In The Gospels Of The New Testament As "The Son Of Man

He called Himself the Son of Man because He was human, He was born of a woman just like the rest of us. He had the same kind of body that we have, He had the same feelings that we have, the same human limitations we have, He felt the same kind of weariness and pain.

The Creator of all things willingly stripped Himself of His unlimited power and became a tiny helpless infant. The Source of all wisdom and knowledge had to study and learn to read and write. He left His throne in Heaven where innumerable angels worshipped Him, where all the forces of the Universe were at His command, and He took the place of a servant--scoffed at, ridiculed, persecuted and ultimately killed by the very ones He came to save.

The Bible tells us that Jesus is "a High Priest Who is touched with the feeling of our weaknesses, for He was in all points tempted the same way WE are, yet without sin."- Hebrews 4:15.

Imagine! The Son of God literally became a citizen of this World, a member of humanity, a man of flesh, in order to reach us with His Love, prove to us His compassion and concern, and help us to understand His Truth in simple childlike terms that we could grasp.

Isaiah 53:3 "He was a man of sorrows and acquainted with grief."

He wept over the grief of His friends, over the suffering of humanity, and even over Jerusalem, a city that rejected its Saviour and was therefore doomed to destruction.

Jesus was so merciful, so kind and kind-hearted. There were times when He was wearied, worn and virtually exhausted from constantly ministering to the crowds that thronged Him.

On one occasion He tried to retire from the busy scene for a little rest and recuperation, but the Bible tells us that when He saw the multitudes who needed His help, He had compassion upon them. He felt so sorry for them that despite the weariness and pain He felt, He went out and healed all that came to Him and taught them all the wonderful Words of God's Kingdom of Love. – Matthew 9:36; Mark 6:31-34.

There were also times when God's anger blazed through Jesus, the Living Word, against pretence and hypocrisy. He told the self-righteous leaders of the ruling religious hierarchy of His day, "If I had not come and spoken unto you, you would not be guilty of sin, but now I have come and exposed you, so you have no covering for your sin!"-John 15:22.

Actually, most of the time He had very little to do with the lofty, rich-robed, powerful and wealthy religious leaders, the Scribes and the Pharisees. --Except when they insisted on annoying Him and raising critical questions, doubts and accusations among those He was teaching. Then He unleashed scathing rebukes against them, publicly exposing them as the "blind leaders of the blind" that they were "whitewashed sepulchres, tombs, which, although they appeared beautiful, clean and holy outwardly, were full of rottenness, corruption and stinking dead men's bones within!"- Matthew 23:27,28.

These religious leaders considered themselves to be the most "righteous and holy" people in town, but Jesus exposed them for the hypocrites, liars, robbers and cheaters of the poor that they were, which of course infuriated them.

But most of the time Jesus avoided the self-satisfied religionists, and spent His time helping and loving the poor, the common man, speaking to them, healing them, feeding them and most importantly, giving them the spiritual answers, Love, forgiveness and Truth that they longed for.

The Bible says that He mingled with and preached to the fishermen, drunks, prostitutes, tax collectors and sinners, and "the common people heard him gladly."-Mark 12:37.

But when He went into the temple and gave His message to the religious leaders, they mobbed Him, threw Him out and finally crucified Him!

Son Of God

He not only claimed to be the Son of God, God manifest in human flesh, but He convinced a great portion of the World that He in fact IS God's Son.

Jesus said, "I and my Father are One."-John 10:30.

Before being born to Mary and living in a fleshly human body, He and His Heavenly Father were together in very close personal Heavenly fellowship, something He had to forsake while He was down here on Earth.

The Bible tells us, "In the beginning was the Word (Jesus) and the Word was with God and the Word was God. All things were made by Him, and without Him was not anything made that was made...And the Word (Jesus) was made flesh and lived among us, and we beheld His glory, the glory as of the one and only Son of the Father."-John 1:1,2,14.

Just before He was arrested and crucified, knowing that He would soon be reunited with His Heavenly Father, Jesus prayed:

"And now, Father, glorify Me along with Yourself and restore Me to such majesty and honour in Your presence as I had with You before the world was made...for you loved me before the foundation of the World."- **John 17:5,24.**

The Messiah – The Saviour

If any adjective were to describe Jesus, it would be "unique"! His message was unique. the claims he made regarding himself were unique. his miracles were unique. And the influence he has had on the world is unsurpassed by any other. One very outstanding and undeniably unique aspect of Jesus' life is that literally hundreds of detailed predictions and prophecies were made by ancient prophets and seers, many centuries before He was born. Specific details regarding His birth, life and death, that no mere mortal man could possibly have fulfilled!

In the first books of the Bible, known as the "Old Testament," over 300 such predictions about the "Messiah" or "Saviour" can be found. The discovery of hundreds of ancient Old Testament manuscripts by archaeologists during this century has proven without a doubt that these prophecies were indeed written centuries before this man called Jesus was born.

How could anyone manipulate their bitter enemies to pay a specific price for their betrayal, mock and revile them as they are dying, much less cause a band of soldiers to gamble for their clothing and pierce their side after they've died, & cause a rich man to bury their body in his own personal tomb? yet Jesus of Nazareth fulfilled not only these, but over 300 more specific predictions regarding his birth, life, ministry, death and resurrection!-truly he was and is "unique" in every sense of the word!

II In the first books of the Bible, known as the "Old Testament," over 300 such predictions about the "Messiah" or "Saviour" can be found. The discovery of hundreds of ancient Old Testament manuscripts by archaeologists during this century has proven without a doubt that these prophecies were indeed written centuries before this man called Jesus was born.

Here is a small sampling of the kind of specific predictions we're talking about: In 750 B.C., the prophet Isaiah made the astounding prediction that:

"The Lord Himself Shall Give You A Sign; Behold, A Virgin Shall Conceive And Bear A Son, And Shall Call His Name Emmanuel."--**Isaiah 7:14.**

7-1/2 centuries later, a young virgin girl in Israel named Mary was visited by the Arch-angel Gabriel, who announced to her that she would bear a Son Who would be called Emmanuel, which means "God with us." The books of the Bible which were written after Jesus came to Earth, the "New Testament," tell us that, "Mary said to the angel, 'How can this be, seeing I have not lain with any man?' and the angel answered, 'the spirit of god shall come upon you, and the power of the almighty shall overshadow you! therefore that holy one which shall be born of you shall be called the Son of God!'"-Luke 1:26-35.

So even the very beginning of his life on earth-his conception and birth-were not only unique, but miraculous, in that the simple and humble young girl who became His mother had never slept with a man!

In fact, the Bible tells us that the news of her pregnancy was so shocking to the young man to whom she was engaged to be married, Joseph, that when he learned about it, he promptly decided to break off the engagement and call off the wedding! -

Until the angel of the Lord appeared to him also and instructed him to stay with her and rear and protect the very special child that she was carrying.

A full 800 years before Jesus was born, the prophet Micah foretold the exact village where the Messiah would be born:

"You, Bethlehem, though you are small among the clans of Judah, yet out of you shall he come forth unto me who is to be ruler over Israel; whose goings forth have been of old, from days of eternity."-Micah 5:2

Although His earthly parents lived in the town of Nazareth, 100 miles to the north of Bethlehem, a decree from Rome demanded that all families return to their ancestral homes to register for a worldwide census. The decree came just as Mary's child was due to be born. -Thus, God used a Roman emperor, Caesar Augustus, to help bring about the fulfilment of Micah's prophecy.

Joseph and Mary journeyed to Bethlehem, and upon their arrival, Mary went into labour, and as the Gospels inform us, "Jesus was born in Bethlehem of Judea" (Matthew 2:1), just as the prophet Micah predicted.

Micah's prophecy also tells us that the messiah "Has been of old, from days of eternity." Jesus himself said, "before Abraham was (around 2000 BC), I am."-John 8:58.

Abraham was the forefather of the Jews and Arabs, who lived about 2,000 years before Jesus was born to Mary. So, Jesus was referring here to His pre-existence with God before His life on Earth in the form of a man.

Though born in Bethlehem, Jesus grew up in Nazareth. In His first recorded public address there, He openly declared that He indeed was the fulfilment of the Old Testament prophecies regarding the Messiah.

While attending the local house of worship, He stood up before the crowd and read a prophecy from the book of the prophet Isaiah. In the passage, Isaiah predicted that the Messiah would be anointed with the Spirit of God to "preach Good News to the poor, to heal the broken hearted, to give freedom to the captives, recovering of sight to the blind and to set at liberty those who are oppressed, to proclaim the acceptable year of the Lord."-Isaiah 61:1,2. The New Testament tells us that after He read this prophecy aloud to the congregation, Jesus told them,

"Today is this scripture fulfilled in your ears!"-**Luke 4:18-21.**

Another outstanding prophecy regarding the Messiah was made by Israel's King David around the year 1000 B.C., or over 10 centuries before Jesus was born. In his prophecy, David gave details of a cruel and agonising death which he himself never suffered:

"I am poured out like water, and all my bones are out of joint. My heart is like wax, it has melted within me...Like a pack of dogs, they have surrounded me; a company of evil doers has encircled me. They have pierced my hands and my feet. They divide my clothing among them and cast lots for my garment."-Psalm 22:14-18.

King David died a peaceful, natural death, so we know he was not talking about himself in this passage of Scripture. But being a prophet, he predicted with unerring accuracy the circumstances surrounding the cruel death on the cross of the Messiah, the Christ that was to come. Let's examine some of the details outlined in the above prophecy:

"I am poured out like water...my heart is melted within me." Jesus not only poured out His life for us spiritually, but the New Testament tells us that shortly after He died, while He was still hanging on the cross, "one of the soldiers pierced His side with a spear, and immediately blood and water flowed out." John 19:34. Modern medical authorities have affirmed that in the case of heart rupture--when a human heart literally bursts open under extreme stress and trauma-the blood collects in the pericardium, the membranous sac that encloses the heart and the roots of the main blood vessels. This blood then separates into a sort of bloody clot and a watery serum, thus when the soldier pierced His side, His life was literally, "poured forth like water." (Unwittingly, this Roman soldier fulfilled another prophecy, "They will look upon Me whom they have pierced," a prophecy given by the Prophet Zechariah around 500 B.C.-Zechariah 12:10.)

"All my bones are out of joint."-This is one of the horrors of death by crucifixion; the weight of the victim's body literally pulls his arms out of their sockets.

"Like a pack of dogs...a company of evil doers has encircled me." The New Testament tells us that Jesus' wicked and vengeful religious enemies, the Scribes and the Pharisees, gathered around Him as He was nailed on the cross, mocking and reviling Him. Matthew 27:39-44

"They have pierced my hands and my feet." This is probably the most astounding prediction within this prophecy. Crucifixion was not practiced by the Jews of David's time.

Their religious laws demanded that criminals be executed by stoning. but God showed his prophet, David, how the Messiah would die 10 centuries later, executed at the hands of an empire that did not even exist in David's day, Rome, whose principal means of executing criminals was crucifixion!

"They divide my clothing among them and cast lots for my garment." In the Gospels of the New Testament, we find the almost incredible fulfilment of this prophecy: "When the soldiers had crucified Jesus, they took His clothes, and divided them into four shares, one for each of them, with the undergarment (a long robe-like tunic) remaining. This garment was seamless, woven in one piece from top to bottom. So, they said one to another, 'Let us not tear it, but let us cast lots to decide whose it shall be.'"- John 19:23,24.

In 487 B.C., the Prophet Zechariah predicted: "And I said unto them, if you think well, give me my price; and if not, keep it. So, they paid me 30 pieces of silver."- Zechariah 11:12.

On the night that Jesus was arrested by His enemies, the New Testament tells us that, "One of the twelve Apostles, Judas Iscariot, went to the chief priests and said to them,

'What will you give me if I deliver Him to you?', and they counted out for him 30 pieces of silver."- **Matthew 26:14,15.**

Imagine! Over five hundred years before the event took place, god's prophet, Zechariah, predicted the exact "price" that Jesus' enemies would pay to his traitorous disciple, Judas! in the next verse of Zechariah's prophecy, he goes into even more astounding details:

"And the Lord said, 'cast it unto the Potter, the handsome price at which they priced me!' so the 30 pieces of silver were taken and cast to the potter in the house of the lord."- Zechariah 11:13.

The New Testament tells us that, "when judas saw that Jesus was condemned, he repented, and returned the 30 pieces of silver to the chief priests of the Jews, and he cast down the pieces of silver in the temple.

Then the chief priests picked up the silver pieces and said, 'It is against our law to put it into our treasury because it is blood-money.' So, they used the money to buy a potter's field, to bury foreigners in."-**Matthew 27:3-6.**

The 30 pieces of silver were literally "cast to the potter in the house of the lord"! --just as Zechariah predicted 500 years earlier!

In 712 BC, the prophet Isaiah predicted that the Son of God would "be given a grave with the wicked, and with the rich in his death."-**Isaiah 53:9.**

Jesus' bitter religious enemies condemned him as a criminal, as a wicked man, thus as he died, the bible tells us "There were two robbers crucified with Him."-**Matthew 27:38.**

After His body was removed from the cross, "a rich man named joseph of Arimathea went to Pilate and pleaded for the body of Jesus, and when joseph had taken the body, he laid it in his own new tomb."-**Matthew 27:57-60.**-a "grave with the rich!"

1,000 years before Jesus was born, the spirit of God prophesied through king David that the saviour would be resurrected from the dead: "God will not leave his soul in the grave, neither will he suffer his holy one to see corruption or decay."-Psa.16:10.

King David died and was buried in a grave, and his flesh saw corruption and decay. but Jesus was raised from the grave three days after his death! As the angel said to the mourners who came to Jesus' tomb, "He is not here, but is risen! Why do you seek the living among the dead?"-**Lk.24:5,6.**

CHAPTER 59

'LIFE AFTER DEATH'

In Beyond Science, Epoch Times explores research and accounts related to phenomena and theories that challenge our current knowledge. We delve into ideas that stimulate the imagination and open up new possibilities. Share your thoughts with us on these sometimes-controversial topics in the comments section below.

If the mind is just a function of the brain, it stands to reason that the worse the brain is injured, the worse the mind would function. While this is what much of current brain research is finding, a body of evidence exists suggesting otherwise: under extreme circumstances, such as close to death, the mind may function well—or even better than usual—when the brain is impaired.

This suggests the mind may function independently of the brain.

One of the researchers who has been studying such cases is Dr. Alexander Bethany, a professor of theoretical psychology and the philosophy of psychology in Liechtenstein and at the cognitive science department at the University of Vienna.

In his most recent study, published this month in the Journal of Near-Death Studies, Bethany and his colleagues reviewed thousands of accounts of near-death experiences (NDEs) to determine the quality of vision and cognition.

He reported: "The more severe the physiological crisis, the more likely NDEers are to report having experienced clear and complex cognitive and sensory functioning."

Part of Bethany's goal was to replicate earlier studies, few as they are, that have looked at the quality of vision and cognition during NDEs.

In a 2007 study by researchers at the University of Virginia, titled "Unusual Experiences: Near Death and Related Phenomena," 52.2 percent of NDEers reported clearer vision. Jeffrey Long, M.D., founder of the Near-Death Experiences Research Foundation (NDERF), found in a survey of 1,122 NDEers, that about 74 percent reported "more consciousness and alertness."

"I felt extremely aware, totally present, sharp, and focused. In hindsight, it's like being half asleep when I was alive, and totally awake after I was pronounced dead," said one experiencer, as noted in Bethany's study.

"My mind felt cleared, and my thoughts seemed quick and decisive. I felt a great sense of freedom and was quite content to be rid of my body. I felt a connection with everything around me in a way that I cannot describe. I felt as if I was thinking faster or that time had slowed down considerably," said another.

While Bethany's study confirmed, to a certain extent, the results of the previous studies that had shown an increase in cognitive and sensory functioning during NDEs, his methodology had some limitations. He said these limitations may have led to lower estimates for the percentage of NDEers who have heightened cognition.

Methodology Limitations

He compiled thousands of written accounts from online repositories of experiences, such as the NDERF website, and ran them through a computer program, which identified words related to vision or cognition (such as "saw" or "thought").

He and his colleagues then rated the quality of vision or cognition described in this smaller sample on a scale from -2 to +2. They further narrowed their study to experiences that included detailed explanations of the medical conditions that accompanied the NDEs. Only patients with cardiac and/or respiratory arrest were included in this study.

Previous studies had asked NDEers directly about the quality of their vision and cognition. Bethany's study, however, could only analyse the information given in general NDE accounts. So, for example, when he decided that there was "no change" in cognition or vision in some accounts, it may have been that there was indeed a change but that the NDEer hadn't described it specifically enough to be counted.

Of the NDEers who mentioned visual perception, about 47 percent said they had enhanced vision. And 41 percent had unchanged vision, "which in itself is quite remarkable, given that these patients were in a severe medical crisis, and often unconscious," Bethany said in an email to Epoch Times.

Of the NDEers who made explicit references to awareness and mentation, about 35 percent said they had increased awareness and mentation. And about 61 percent reported normal everyday awareness during cardiac and respiratory arrest.

Given the implications of his study, Bethany was careful to note other shortcomings in his methodology, including the fact that online NDE descriptions may include some fraudulent reports. But he also noted reasons that these methodological shortcomings do not likely impact his overall finding that NDEs, by and large, include improved vision and cognition.

For example, concerning the risk of including fraudulent accounts, he wrote: "On NDERF, the largest contributor of NDEs studied here, less than 1 percent of posted NDEs have been removed due to concerns about their validity. Additionally, given the sheer number of accounts, it is unlikely that fake reports have significantly biased our results in one or the other direction. One would expect fake accounts ... to be prototypical of the popular NDE narrative."

In addition to these NDE studies, studies on the phenomena of terminal lucidity and mindsight also support the conclusion that the mind may engage in complex conscious activity even as brain functioning severely deteriorates, Bethany said.

Terminal Lucidity, Mindsight

He has studied terminal lucidity in Alzheimer's patients. This is a phenomenon in which patients who have been completely incoherent for many years seem to suddenly return to their senses shortly before death.

When the brain is at the furthest stage of degeneration, the expectation would be that the ability to make coherent connections between memories and various thoughts and emotions would be so far gone that a "whole" person could no longer emerge. Yet at this time, the whole mind seems to flash through, with all its connections intact.

"Mindsight" refers to the phenomenon in which blind people report being able to see during NDEs. This has been studied, for example, by Kenneth Ring at the University of Connecticut. Ring found that 15 out of 21 blind participants reported some kind of sight during NDEs.

Hallucinations?

Bethany noted that some scientists consider NDEs to be hallucinations produced by neurophysiological processes.

"The findings reported in this paper and cases of terminal lucidity and mindsight, however, appear to suggest otherwise in that they indicate the presence of complex and structured conscious experience during decline, breakdown, or absence of the neurobiological correlates commonly held to be causative factors of NDEs—and of conscious experience in general," he said.

He concluded that consciousness—including a sense of selfhood, complex visual imagery, and mental clarity—can sometimes outlive altered brain functioning, including even a flatline of electrical activity in the brain.

Terminal lucidity and mindsight are very rare phenomena, but NDEs are more numerous and "our results suggest that the continuity of visual imagery, mentation, and sense of selfhood is the rule rather than the exception during NDEs."

Bethany wrote: "It remains for future researchers to confirm or disconfirm our informal observation through formal analysis."

Source: By Tara MacIsaac & His study, "Complex Visual Imagery and Cognition During Near-Death Experiences," can be found in Volume 34, No. 2, of the Journal of Near-Death Studies.

Joy in the face of suffering: -

Images of dying nun with radiant smile awaiting her meeting with Jesus Christ go viral

Sister Cecilia smiles radiantly as she is surrounded by relatives and friends while awaiting her ‹encounter with The One, Jesus Christ,› on her hospital bed.

Enduring the pain and suffering from a *losing battle with cancer*, a nun from Argentina still showed a radiant, smiling face for days *until she breathed her last on June 22. She was 43.*

Images showing Sister Cecilia's *wondrously joyful face* with nary a hint of pain circulated on social media over the weekend, filling readers with awe and wonder as they shared the images and their heartfelt prayers.

Even Pope Francis was moved by her images and story and assured her of his prayers. In a voice message, the pope told her that he knew of her offering and that he loved her very much.

Behind the images of Sister Cecilia is an even gripping and inspiring story about this young Carmelite nun as originally published in the Spanish-language edition of the Aleteia news site. Her images and the accounts about her life can also be viewed from the Facebook page Curia General de los Carmelitas Descalzos.

Translating the accounts on Sister Cecilia into English, Aleteia says those who knew her and witnessed her suffering attest that the nun's testimony of joy and peace in her life was just as radiant as her face.

Sister Cecilia Maria lived at a monastery in Argentina, dedicated to a life of contemplative prayer. At the monastery, she played the violin and was known for her sweetness and constant smile.

She took up nursing and earned her degree at the age of 26. She then decided to be a nun, making her final profession of faith in 2003.

Last January, she was diagnosed with cancer of the tongue. The disease quickly metastasized into her lungs.

Despite her illness, she remained joyful and at peace in appearance as she lay in bed, surrounded by numerous family members who showered her with love and affection. For instance, her nieces and nephews gathered at the hospital garden sent her messages and helium balloons and entertained her from the window of her hospital room.

Despite her condition, she put on her habit and participated at Mass in the hospital chapel.

"Those who saw her spoke of her face as showing peace and joy — as someone awaiting the encounter with the One to whom she had given her life, Our Lord Jesus Christ," Aleteia says.

Last May, Sister Cecilia, unable to speak because of her condition, wrote these words, originally in Spanish, on a piece of paper: "I am very content, astonished by the work of God through suffering, and by so many people who pray for me."

Hours before she died, the Carmelite was still able to receive Communion. She also wrote her last request: "I was thinking about how I would like my funeral to be. First, some intense prayer and then a great celebration for everyone.

Don't forget to pray but don't forget to celebrate either!"

According to the Catholic News Agency, the discalced Carmelites announced her death as follows:

"Jesus! Just two lines to let you know that our dearly beloved sister gently fell asleep in the Lord, after such a painful illness, always borne with joy and her surrender to her Divine Spouse.

We send you all our love, grateful for your support and prayer during this entire time, *so painful yet so wonderful at the same time. We believe she flew directly to heaven,* but we also ask you to not cease commending her to your prayers, so from heaven she may repay you. A big hug from her Sisters in Santa Fe."

What a wonderful testimony that this nun was being *totally victorious in spirit,* in the midst of *great adversity* and pain.

She died praising Jesus, (almost like the martyrs of old, who died praising God, even in the jaws of the lions, or burning at the stake, in the days of Rome- a recorded fact!), *knowing that Jesus would come for her.*

What a beautiful soul!

Following are a few appropriate Bible verses for the occasion: -

1PE.1:6 Wherein ye greatly rejoice, though now for a season, if need be, ye are in heaviness through manifold temptations:

1PE.1:7 That the trial of your faith, being much more precious than of gold that perisheth, though it be tried with fire, might be found unto praise and honour and glory at the appearing of Jesus Christ:

1PE.1:8 Whom having not seen, ye love; in whom, though now ye see him not, yet believing, *ye rejoice with joy unspeakable and full of glory:*

1PE.1:9 Receiving the end of your faith, even the *salvation* of your souls.

See chapter 45 from my book "**Out of the Bottomless Pit I**" called "**Life After Death**"

If you have not yet received the Joy of salvation, please go to this link on this website: http://www.outofthebottomlesspit.co.uk/418605189

See how a top scientist tells how *there must be a God*, as there is so much evidence.

the video on the above link is followed by a simple message on Salvation. God bless You.

CHAPTER 60

'LIGHT' AT BIRTH

THE FOLLOWING IS an amazing discovery which everyone should know about. We are told by science that there is no soul and that we are but a bag of chemicals living on a piece of chance rock, and that we are of no consequence in their bigger picture of things. However, most of us know that as in most things we have been lied to by the 'Powers that be' and their media as well as their science and in almost all areas of society. Fortunately, there are honest scientists and those who want the public to know the truth and that there is a god of the universe and that our planet is unique and beautiful and each one of God's creations are very important to Him. God is the Spirit of Love itself. Finally, scientists can detect the moment the soul of a human or other creature receives the 'spirit of life 'From the hand of God.

Genesis 2.7"And the LORD God formed man *of* the dust of the ground, and breathed into his nostrils the breath of life; and man became a living soul."

For me, images released recently by North-western University scientists of tiny light flashes signalling the moment of human conception are evocative of a larger, cosmic-sized truth espoused by both science and the Bible. Namely, the creation of the universe itself – the mother of all moments of conception – was likewise marked by an explosion of light.

According to their article in Scientific Reports, the North Western researchers collected immature human eggs from willing female patients at the Fertility Centre of Illinois – eggs that would have been discarded in the normal course of the patients' fertility treatments. The researchers used special chemicals to mimic the moments of conception – the law forbidding them to use actual sperm. In each case, they discovered, the decisive moment was accompanied by a small burst of zinc atoms. The eruptions appeared as flashes of light because of fluorescing agents used by the scientists.

According to science – at precisely a moment of conception known as recombination & decoupling – an incomprehensible outburst of light accompanied the creation of hydrogen and helium, the first atoms of the embryonic cosmos. To this day, the dim afterglow of that seminal light – the so-called cosmic microwave background – is visible to certain kinds of powerful telescopes.

According to inflation and big bang theories, it didn't end there. Hydrogen atoms eventually began to fuse, the way they do in a hydrogen bomb, and – voila! – once again, in a flash of light, the first stars came into being. They, in turn – like colossal stoves – cooked up the heavier elements known to us today. Including the zinc atoms that explode, like fireworks, every time a human being is conceived.

I find it notable that the Bible agrees with science that the universe was conceived in a paroxysm of illumination – I imagine, unlike anything we've ever seen. According to Genesis 1:3, that event happened at exactly the moment God uttered the immortal words, "Let there be light."

The Bible's explanation of things goes even further, by actually assigning a sacred status to light. In 1 John 1:5, light is identified with the Creator himself: "God is light; in him there is no darkness at all."

Scientists don't use that sort of language, of course, but amazingly, they do agree that light very definitely has a transcendent status. It wasn't always the case, though: scientists made that discovery only relatively recently.

The momentous change of heart began in 1905, when an unknown outsider named Albert Einstein published his heretical theory of special relativity. According to Einstein, contrary to what scientists had always believed, light experiences a reality wholly unlike the one you and I do – inhabits an other-worldly realm where, among other things, the commonplace laws of space and time are not obeyed. Like God, if you will, light transcends the restrictions of the ordinary, physical world.

Scientists were slow in coming around to believe Einstein's heterodoxy. But today, it is a key component of the modern scientific catechism. – source Michael Guillen Ph.D. May 01, 2016

Like the Bible, therefore, science now agrees that whenever we interact with light, we interact with something that is at once in this world, but not of this world. Chief among these divine-like encounters are those instances when light makes abrupt, attention-getting appearances. Like a moment of creation when something truly special suddenly comes into existence that wasn't there before – be it a human embryo, a star, or an entire universe. And Booz took Ruth, and she became his wife, and he went into her; and the Lord gave her conception, and she bore a son."

(Ruth 4:13)

The following video below is absolutely incredible. It shows the **moment life begins**. We believe this should definitely help convince everyone of the absolute miraculous supernatural power behind conception.

We are also reminded of the verse from Revelation, chapter eleven: "...the spirit of life from God entered into them, and they stood upon their feet", and of course Genesis 2:7, "And God formed the man of dust of the earth, and breathed upon his face the breath of life, and the man became a living soul."

Stunning Video: Bright Flash Of Light When Life Begins: https://youtu.be/ovzGmRrtVys?t=35
Scientists capture 'fireworks' during moment of conception

Formerly with the Washington Time Scientists have captured the moment a human sperm meets an egg on film, and found the union is "fireworks" show that produces a blast of white light.

The phenomenon was discovered about five years ago in a mouse, but it's never before been seen in humans.

Specifically, scientists noted that at the exact moment of conception, an explosion of fiery sparks is emitted. And what's more, researchers found different sizes of light and said the size can actually reveal the quality of the egg that's being fertilized, the Telegraph reported.

In short, researchers from North-western University in Chicago said the brighter the fireworks, the healthier the egg. And the practical benefit of that finding is that it enables medical officials to identify the best fertilized eggs for in-vitro fertilization procedures.

Scientists attribute the flash to a trigger release of calcium that occurs when the sperm enters the egg, and that deposit causes an expulsion of zinc. As the zinc pours forth, it carries with it small molecules that give off a fluorescent light.

Eggs flash as they meet sperm, capturing the moment life begins/Image: North-western University

"It was remarkable," said Teresa Woodruff, one of the researchers who wrote up their findings, the Telegraph reported. "We discovered the zinc spark just five years ago in the mouse, and to see the zinc radiate out in a burst from each human egg was breath-taking. This means if you can look at the zinc spark at the time of fertilization, you will know immediately which eggs the good ones are to transfer in in-vitro fertilization."

Roughly 50 percent of fertilized eggs don't develop properly, due it's believed to faulty genetic coding, the Telegraph reported. Clinics currently can check for genetic mutations via some invasive procedures, but the procedures alone could damage the egg.

Now, the new findings could help with such determinations, minus the risky invasiveness.

A fluorescent flash captures the moment that sperm enzyme enters the egg/Image: North Western University

"This is an important discovery because it may give us a non-invasive and easily visible way to assess the health of an egg and eventually an embryo before implantation," said Eve Feinberg, another doctor involved in the study, the Telegraph reported. There are no tools currently available that tell us if it's a good quality egg. Often, we don't know ... until we see if a pregnancy ensues. That's the reason this is so transformative. If we have the ability up front to see what a good egg is and what's not, it will help us know which embryo to transfer, avoid a lot of heartache and achieve pregnancy much more quickly."

The findings could also go toward underscoring what the pro-life movement has insisted for years – that life starts at conception, rather than birth.

"It's a way of sorting egg quality in a way that we've never been able to assess before," said Woodruff. "All of biology starts at the time of fertilization, yet we know next to nothing about the events that occur in the human."

APPENDIX: EXTRAS: '110 OTHER IMPORTANT RELATED TOPICS':

LIFE AFTER DEATH: LIFE AFTER DEATH – www.outofthebottomlesspit.co.uk

USA GOVERNMENT ASSASSINATED 5-STAR GENERAL PATTON?

STRANGE DEATHS? – www.outofthebottomlesspit.co.uk

THE TOWERING INFERNO 19/06/17 STRANGE DEATHS? – www.outofthebottomlesspit.co.uk

It Turns Out That As Many As 457 Deaths Might Have Tragically Occured At The Grenfell Tower! All Being Covered Up By The Authorities:

'Hollow Earth' Blog: Pact Made To Rule The Outer Earth?: Hollow Earth – Blog – www.outofthebottomlesspit.co.uk

BOOK OF ENOCH CHAPTER 18 & STRANGE THINGS IN THE ANTARCTIC: BOOK OF ENOCH – www.outofthebottomlesspit.co.uk

UFO'S & X-FILES: UFO'S & X FILES – www.outofthebottomlesspit.co.uk

EVIDENCE OF UFO SIGHTINGS THROUGH TIME: UFO SIGHTINGS – www.outofthebottomlesspit.co.uk

NIBIRU & 7 PLANETS: Planet X NIBIRU – www.outofthebottomlesspit.co.uk

Transhumanist Candidate Wants "Brain Implants to **Manage Violent Actions of Prisoners"... And Society**: TRANSHUMANISM – www.outofthebottomlesspit.co.uk

TERMINATORS: TRANSHUMANISM II – www.outofthebottomlesspit.co.uk

ZOMBIE: German wings pilot behaved like a 'mass spree-killer': Psychologist says Lubitz acted like a 'US school shooter' who commits atrocity then kills himself: CRASHED PLANE TERROR – www.outofthebottomlesspit.co.uk

UNDERGROUND TUNNELS: Archaeologist: 12,000-Year-Old Underground Tunnels Are Real and Stretch from Scotland to Turkey: ANCIENT TECH II – www.outofthebottomlesspit.co.uk

HALLOWEEN HELL?: HALLOWEEN HELL – www.outofthebottomlesspit.co.uk

'OUT OF THE BOTTOMLESS PIT' I – by S.N.Strutt -2014: CHAOS & THE NWO – www.outofthebottomlesspit.co.uk

Why is it important to read my books? What makes them special?
WGO? Comments – www.outofthebottomlesspit.co.uk

WHAT IS GOING ON? Comments – www.outofthebottomlesspit.co.uk

WHAT WAS GOING ON 2?: WHAT'S GOING ON? – www.outofthebottomlesspit.co.uk

Of all the endangered species, Truth is the most endangered. I am watching it go out: -

INTERNET CONTROL: http://www.outofthebottomlesspit.co.uk/412590101

'BIG BROTHER' IS HERE: http://www.outofthebottomlesspit.co.uk/412684080

NEW WORLD ORDER: http://www.outofthebottomlesspit.co.uk/412194674

MARK OF THE BEAST: http://www.outofthebottomlesspit.co.uk/412733219

FAKE NEWS & THE MASTER OF PROPOGANDA: FAKE NEWS – www.outofthebottomlesspit.co.uk

AMERICA THE 'GREAT WHORE' IS DUE FOR JUDGEMENT – REVELATION 17-18. What If God's Judgments Are Soon Coming Upon America? AMERICA DESTROYED? – www.outofthebottomlesspit.co.uk

WHAT PEOPLE SAY ABOUT MY WEBSITE? PUBLIC REACTIONS – www.outofthebottomlesspit.co.uk

THEY STAGED THE WHOLE THING! LATEST NEWS – www.outofthebottomlesspit.co.uk

BEGINNINGS OF THE PLAGUE: LATEST NEWS! ARCHIVE – www.outofthebottomlesspit.co.uk

ARCHIVE 10/10/14 – 21/06/18: LATE NEWS ARCHIVE 2 – www.outofthebottomlesspit.co.uk

NEWS ARCHIVE 3 – www.outofthebottomlesspit.co.uk

THE DANGERS OF 5-G 5-G DANGERS – www.outofthebottomlesspit.co.uk

CHINA GETS A WITNESS ABOUT JESUS CHRIST IN THE STARS 2000 YEARS AGO: SIGNS OF THE MESSIAH – www.outofthebottomlesspit.co.uk

CYCLOPIAN DISCOVERY – www.outofthebottomlesspit.co.uk

PLAGUE OF LOCUSTS: LOCUST PLAGUE – www.

outofthebottomlesspit.co.uk

WUHAN CRISIS -BEGINNINGS: KILLER VIRUS I – www.outofthebottomlesspit.co.uk

THE TIDALWAVE OF THE CORONAVIRUS: KILLER VIRUS II – www.outofthebottomlesspit.co.uk

EARLY DAYS OF WUHAN: EXTREME VIDEOS – www.outofthebottomlesspit.co.uk

HOW TO PROTECT FROM THE PLAGUE? HOW TO PROTECT – www.outofthebottomlesspit.co.uk

QUARANTEEN: 'LOCKDOWN' – www.outofthebottomlesspit.co.uk

MANY LINKS TO THE DISASTER OF THE PLAGUE: 'LOCKDOWN' – www.outofthebottomlesspit.co.uk

HAARP & WEATHER CONTROL: CHEMTRAILS II – www.outofthebottomlesspit.co.uk

Biological Weapons And Genetically Modified Foods Designed To Kill Not Feed The Populations: GMS – www.outofthebottomlesspit.co.uk

Horrific Nuclear Tests By The USA On The Islands Of The Pacific: Nuclear Testing – www.outofthebottomlesspit.co.uk

RECORD TEMPERATURES RECORD TEMPERATURES – www.outofthebottomlesspit.co.uk

THE BIG LIE THE LIE OF EVOLUTION – www.outofthebottomlesspit.co.uk

The Geo-Centric Earth Or The Earth Is The Centre Of The Universe: SCIENCE II – www.outofthebottomlesspit.co.uk

Weather Machines -H.A.A.R.P. & Chemtrails, Along With Geo-Engineering.: CHEMTRAILS – www.outofthebottomlesspit.co.uk

ICE-AGE: ICE AGE? – www.outofthebottomlesspit.co.uk

ICE-AGE: ICE-AGE II – www.outofthebottomlesspit.co.uk

Ice-Age & Haarp Dangers

The Dangers Of Both Weather Modification & An Ice-Age: GEO ENGINEERING – www.outofthebottomlesspit.co.uk

GLOBAL WARMING? CLIMATE CH LIES 1 – www.outofthebottomlesspit.co.uk

MORE LIES: CLIMATE CH LIES 1 – www.outofthebottomlesspit.co.uk

GEO ENGINEERING: CLIMATE CHA LIES 3 – www.outofthebottomlesspit.co.uk

Signs Your Body Is Too Acidic and Ways to Quickly Alkalize It:
HEALTH TIPS – www.outofthebottomlesspit.co.uk

PROPHECIES ABOUT: 1) THE SON OF MAN: 2) THE SON OF GOD: 3) THE ELECT ONE: 4) LION OF JUDAH: 5) THE MESSIAH: NEWSLETTERS – www.outofthebottomlesspit.co.uk

POPULATION CONTROL: EUGENICS: SEXES CONTROL – www.outofthebottomlesspit.co.uk

HOW TO STAY WARM IN THE COLD: SURVIVAL – www. outofthebottomlesspit.co.uk

DECEPTION & HOW IT USED TO CONTROL THE MIND OF THE MASSES: THE CONTROLLERS – www.outofthebottomlesspit. co.uk

PRE-TRIB OR POST-TRIB?: END-TIME RAPTURE – www. outofthebottomlesspit.co.uk

WORMWOOD: WORMWOOD – www.outofthebottomlesspit.co.uk

JESUS 'THE WORD OF GOD' – CREATOR: 'THE WORD OF GOD' – www.outofthebottomlesspit.co.uk

REVIEWS TO OUT OF THE BOTTOMLESS PIT BOOK 1: REVIEWS for BOOK 1 – www.outofthebottomlesspit.co.uk

THE GODS OF EGYPT: CH 7 FALLEN ANGELS – www.outofthebottomlesspit.co.uk

INTRODUCTION TO MY 1ST BOOK ON YOUTUBE: OUT THE BOTTOMLESS PIT BOOK 1: BOTTOMLESS PIT BK 1 – www. outofthebottomlesspit.co.uk

MY 7 INSIGHTS BOOKS: EZDRAS INSIGHTS: EZDRAS INSIGHTS – www.outofthebottomlesspit.co.uk

ENOCH INSIGHTS: ENOCH INSIGHTS BOOK – www.outofthebottomlesspit.co.uk

THE DWARF-SIZED PHARAOH: JASHER INS. ARTICLES – www.outofthebottomlesspit.co.uk

PUBLIC COMMENTS ON MY BOOKS: COMMENTS JASHER INS – www.outofthebottomlesspit.co.uk

'JASHER INSIGHTS' I & II: JASHER INSIGHTS – www.outofthebottomlesspit.co.uk

JUBILEE YEAR – WHAT IS ITS SIGNIFICANCE?: JUBILEES INSIGHTS 2 – www.outofthebottomlesspit.co.uk

A GLIMPSE AT MY 6TH BOOK 'JUBILEES INSIGHTS': JUBILEES INSIGHTS – www.outofthebottomlesspit.co.uk

ALL MY VIDEOS: 'INSIGHT BOOK VIDEOS – www.outofthebottomlesspit.co.uk

LONGEVITY CHART FROM ADAM TO JOSEPH: LONGEVITY CHART – www.outofthebottomlesspit.co.uk

EDEN INSIGHTS: 'EDEN INSIGHTS' – www.outofthebottomlesspit.co.uk

EDEN INSIGHTS & REACTIONS: ' INSIGHTS' BOOKS' – www.outofthebottomlesspit.co.uk

MY 8TH BOOK 'THE TESTAMENTS OF THE 12 PATRIARCHS INSIGHTS': WHAT IS GOING ON ?! – www.outofthebottomlesspit.co.uk

ECONOMIC CRASH: FINANCIAL CRASH SEPT – www.outofthebottomlesspit.co.uk

MY VIDEOS ON ECONOMICS:

FOOD AS A WEAPON: EUGENICS – www.outofthebottomlesspit.co.uk

Population Control: The Eugenics Connection: EUGENICS II – www.outofthebottomlesspit.co.uk

EUGENICS: EUGENICS II – www.outofthebottomlesspit.co.uk

RED FLAG EVENTS: RED FLAG EVENTS – www.outofthebottomlesspit.co.uk

"Brain Scanners": BIG BROTHER – www.outofthebottomlesspit.co.uk

'SHADOW GOVERNMENT THAT RULES THE WORLD': NEW WORLD ORDER 3 – www.outofthebottomlesspit.co.uk

TOTAL CORRUPTION: N.W.O 1 – www.outofthebottomlesspit.co.uk

THE DEATH TRIANGLE: WAR-BOOM-BUST!: WAR BOOM BUST – WW3 – www.outofthebottomlesspit.co.uk

INTERNET KILL SWITCH: INTERNET CONTROL – www.outofthebottomlesspit.co.uk

MENE, MENE, TEKEL, UPHARSIN: THE CERN DECEPTION – www.outofthebottomlesspit.co.uk

Hidden History Reveals Future Plans of The New World Order: HIDDEN NWO 2 – www.outofthebottomlesspit.co.uk

INTERNATIONAL WARS AND VIOLENCE. WHO IS BEHIND IT ALL? CORRUPTION – www.outofthebottomlesspit.co.uk

9/11 DISASTER 2001: 9/11 2001 – www.outofthebottomlesspit.co.uk

THE WEST IS IN DANGER: WAR WITH RUSSIA? – www.outofthebottomlesspit.co.uk

THE FIRES IN NORTHERN CALIFORNIA HAVE BEEN STARTED DELIBERATELY: LASERS DESTROY CALIF – www.outofthebottomlesspit.co.uk

SURVIVAL: BE PREPARED: SURVIVAL BE PREPARED – www.outofthebottomlesspit.co.uk

ANTARCTICA: HIDDEN UNDERGROUND BASES: NAZIS & the SWASTIKA – www.outofthebottomlesspit.co.uk

OUR COMPLETELY MAD WORLD: CRAZY LAWS – www.outofthebottomlesspit.co.uk

VOLCANOES OUT OF CONTROL: VOLCANOES – www.outofthebottomlesspit.co.uk

EARTHQUAKES ARE ON THE INCREASE: EARTHQUAKES – www.outofthebottomlesspit.co.uk

(Pg 169) IMPROVING ON THE IMAGE OF GOD! TRANSHUMANISM – www.outofthebottomlesspit.co.uk

GARDEN OF EDEN INSIDE A HOLLOW EARTH?: GARDEN OF EDEN – www.outofthebottomlesspit.co.uk

CANOPY OF WATER OR ICE AROUND THE EARTH IN PRE-FLOOD TIMES?: BEFORE THE GR. FLOOD – www.outofthebottomlesspit.co.uk

WHAT'S GOING ON 3: WHAT IS GOING? III – www.outofthebottomlesspit.co.uk

HYPERBARIC OXYGEN: HYPERBARIC OXYGEN – www.outofthebottomlesspit.co.uk

MORE ABOUT THE V.: RADIO SHOWS & PUB C – www.outofthebottomlesspit.co.uk

NUCLEAR WAR? WORLD WAR III – www.outofthebottomlesspit.co.uk

DEADLY 5-G CELL TOWERS: DEADLY CELL TOWERS – www.outofthebottomlesspit.co.uk

PUTIN KNOWS A 3RD WAY?: What If Vladimir Putin Does Know a "Third Way" for Society?: PUTIN'S 3RD WAY? – www.outofthebottomlesspit.co.uk

CASH ELIMINATION: CASH ELIMINATION – www.outofthebottomlesspit.co.uk

GEO-CENTRIC EARTH: BIBLICAL CREATION – www.

outofthebottomlesspit.co.uk

SIGNS SIGNS 2018-2019 II – www.outofthebottomlesspit.co.uk

**Highly Advanced Nanotechnology Is At 'The Tip Of The Needle!'
– Fully Programmable And Self-Assembling Tech Used In Vaxxes As
Globalists Move Towards Completing The Gilgamesh Project: Highly
Advanced Nanotechnology Is At The Tip Of The Needle (allnewspipe-
line.com)**

(https://www.youtube.com/watch?feature=player_
embedded&v=VIGLqFI2W7s#t=299)

COVID ATTACK 13/06 – www.outofthebottomlesspit.co.uk

WARRIORS AGAINST EVIL: WARRIORS OF THE WORD –
www.outofthebottomlesspit.co.uk

**5-G Towers: Microwave Dangers To Our Brains: http://www.
outofthebottomlesspit.co.uk/412195486**

ALIENS ELONGATED SKULLS – www.outofthebottomlesspit.co.uk

I am a true believer of ancient aliens. I believe aliens are the fallen angels
and their offspring the giants as brought out in the Book of Enoch chapter 6,
and the Bible Genesis chapter 6, and the Book of Jubilees, chapter 5, book of
Jasher chapter 4 –

You Can Find Out More Information About The Origin Of Giants &
Demons In My Book "Out Of The Bottomless Pit' Book I" In Chapter 8, &
Also Many Other Chapters In The Book.

**My Dream Where I Visited The Devil's Dark Castle In The Dark
Kingdom**

It is good not to be shallow in our desires. Don't desire the wrong things
or you might end up very sorry. Don't go peering into the Dark Kingdom or
you might fall therein and end up being sorry!

Ghost Ship: GHOST SHIPS – www.outofthebottomlesspit.co.uk

**SEE MORE ABOUT LIFE & DEATH IN MY BOOK:- "OUT OF
THE BOTTOMLESS PIT"**

(http://www.outofthebottomlesspit.co.uk/411713687)

**LINK to ALL 8 of my books at AMAZON: www.amazon.com/
author/777.7**

**YOU CAN FIND MY BOOKS AND VIDEOS AT AMAZON:
www.amazon.com/author/777.7 or https://www.amazon.
com/S-N-Strutt/e/B00P7WYMQO**

9 781782 229759